W9-ACY-525

SEP - - 2008

WI

grzimek's
Student Animal Life Resource

• • • •

grzimek's
Student Animal Life Resource

• • • •

Corals, Jellyfishes, Sponges, and Other Simple Animals

Catherine Judge Allen, MA, ELS, author

Madeline S. Harris, project editor
Neil Schlager and Jayne Weisblatt, editors

THOMSON

GALE

Detroit • New York • San Francisco • San Diego • New Haven, Conn. • Waterville, Maine • London • Munich

THOMSON
GALE

Grzimek's Student Animal Life Resource: Corals, Jellyfishes, Sponges, and Other Simple Animals

Catherine Judge Allen, MA, ELS

Project Editor
Madeline S. Harris

Editorial
Stephanie Cook, Melissa Hill

Indexing Services
Synapse, the Knowledge Link Corporation

Rights and Acquisitions
Margaret Abendroth, Timothy Sisler

Imaging and Multimedia
Randy Bassett, Michael Logusz, Dan Newell, Chris O'Bryan, Robyn Young

Product Design
Tracey Rowens, Jennifer Wahi

Composition
Evi Seoud, Mary Beth Trimper

Manufacturing
Wendy Blurton, Dorothy Maki

LIBRARY OF CONGRESS CATALOGING-IN-PUBLICATION DATA

Allen, Catherine Judge.
Grzimek's student animal life resource. Corals, jellyfishes, sponges, and other simple animals / Catherine Judge Allen, author ; Neil Schlager and Jayne Weisblatt, editors.
        p. cm.
    Includes bibliographical references and index.
    ISBN 0-7876-9412-6 (hardcover : alk. paper)
    1. Corals—Juvenile literature. 2. Jellyfishes—Juvenile literature. 3. Sponges—Juvenile literature. 4. Invertebrates—Juvenile literature. I. Harris, Madeline S. II. Schlager, Neil, 1966- III. Weisblatt, Jayne. IV. Grzimek, Bernhard. V. Title.
    QL377.C5A45 2005
    593.6—dc22

ISBN 0-7876-9402-9 (21-vol set), ISBN 0-7876-9412-6

This title is also available as an e-book
Contact your Thomson Gale sales representative for ordering information.

Printed in Canada
10 9 8 7 6 5 4 3 2 1

Contents

Reader's Guide

Grzimek's Student Animal Life Resource: Corals, Jellyfishes, Sponges, and Other Simple Animals offers readers comprehensive and easy-to-use information on Earth's simple animals. Phylum entries provide an overview of a group of classes, and class entries provide an overview of a particular class. Entries are arranged by taxonomy, the science through which living things are classified into related groups. Each entry includes sections on physical characteristics; geographic range; habitat; diet; behavior and reproduction; animals and people; and conservation status. All entries are followed by one or more species accounts with the same information as well as a range map and photo or illustration for each species. Entries conclude with a list of books, periodicals, and Web sites that may be used for further research.

ADDITIONAL FEATURES

Grzimek's Student Animal Life Resource: Corals, Jellyfishes, Sponges, and Other Simple Animals includes a pronunciation guide for scientific names, a glossary, an overview of Simple Animals, a list of species in the volume by biome, a list of species by geographic range, and an index. The volume has 162 full-color maps, photos, and illustrations to enliven the text, and sidebars provide additional facts and related information.

NOTE

Grzimek's Student Animal Life Resource: Corals, Jellyfishes, Sponges, and Other Simple Animals has standardized information in the Conservation Status section. The World Conservation

Union (IUCN) Red List provides the world's most comprehensive inventory of the global conservation status of plants and animals. Using a set of criteria to evaluate extinction risk, the IUCN recognizes the following categories: Extinct, Extinct in the Wild, Critically Endangered, Endangered, Vulnerable, Conservation Dependent, Near Threatened, Least Concern, and Data Deficient. These terms are defined where they are used in the text, but for a complete explanation of each category, visit the IUCN web page at http://www.iucn.org/themes/ssc/redlists/RLcats2001booklet.html.

ACKNOWLEDGEMENTS

Gale would like to thank several individuals for their assistance with this volume. Catherine Judge Allen wrote the text. At Schlager Group Inc., Neil Schlager and Jayne Weisblatt coordinated the writing and editing of the volume.

Special thanks are also due for the invaluable comments and suggestions provided by the *Grzimek's Student Animal Life Resource: Corals, Jellyfishes, Sponges, and Other Simple Animals* advisors:

- Mary Alice Anderson, Media Specialist, Winona Middle School, Winona, Minnesota
- Thane Johnson, Librarian, Oklahoma City Zoo, Oklahoma City, Oklahoma
- Debra Kachel, Media Specialist, Ephrata Senior High School, Ephrata, Pennsylvania
- Nina Levine, Media Specialist, Blue Mountain Middle School, Courtlandt Manor, New York
- Ruth Mormon, Media Specialist, The Meadows School, Las Vegas, Nevada

COMMENTS AND SUGGESTIONS

We welcome your comments on *Grzimek's Student Animal Life Resource: Corals, Jellyfishes, Sponges, and Other Simple Animals* and suggestions for future editions of this work. Please write: Editors, *Grzimek's Student Animal Life Resource: Corals, Jellyfishes, Sponges, and Other Simple Animals*, U•X•L, 27500 Drake Rd., Farmington Hills, Michigan 48331-3535; call toll free: 1-800-877-4253; fax: 248-699-8097; or send e-mail via www.gale.com.

Pronunciation Guide for Scientific Names

Acanthaster planci ah-KAN-thuh-ster PLANK-eye

Acanthocephala ah-KAN-thoh-sef-fal-ay

Acoela ah-KOHL-ay

Adenophorea ah-den-oh-FOR-ee-ay

Aequorea victoria ee-KWOR-ee-ay vik-TOR-ee-ay

Aglantha digitale ah-GLAN-thay dih-jih-TAL-ee

Amphipholis squamata am-fee-FOH-lihs SKWAH-mah-tay

Angiostrongylus cantonensis an-jee-oh-STRON-jih-lus kanton-EN-sis

Anthozoa an-tho-ZOH-ay

Antipathella fiordensis an-tih-PATH-ell-ay fee-or-DEN-sis

Appendicularia ah-pen-dik-u-LAR-ee-ay

Ascidiacea

Asplanchna priodonta az-PLANK-nay pree-oh-DON-tay

Asterias amurensis as-TEH-ree-as ah-myur-EN-sis

Asteroidea as-teh-ROY-dee-ay

Astropecten irregularis as-troh-PE-ten ir-reg-u-LAR-iss

Authopleura xanthogrammica ah-thoh-PLUR-ay zan-thoh-GRAM-ee-kay

Barentsia discreta bah-RENT-see-ay dis-KREH-tay

Botryllus schlosseri boh-TRIL-us sh-LOSS-er-eye

Branchiostoma floridae bran-chee-oh-STOH-may FLOR-ih-day

Cephalochordata sef-ah-loh-kor-DAH-tay

Cestoda SES-toh-day

Cestum veneris SES-tum VEN-eh-rihs

Chaetognatha chee-tog-NATH-ay

Chironex fleckeri CHIH-roh-necks FLEK-er-eye

Chrysaora quinquecirrha chrih-SAH-or-ay kwin-KAY-sir-hay

Concentricycloidea kon-sen-trih-sy-kloh-IH-dee-ay

Convolutriloba longifissura kon-voh-LOO-trih-loh-bay lawn-jih-FIS-yur-ay

Corallium rubrum kor-ALL-ee-um ROO-brum

Crinoidea krih-noh-IH-dee-ay

Ctenophora teh-noh-FOR-ay

Cubozoa kyu-bo-ZOH-ay

Cycliophora sy-klee-oh-FOR-ay

Dactylogyrus vastator dak-til-oh-JIE-rus vah-STAY-tor

Dendraster excentricus den-DRAS-ter eck-SEN-trih-kus

Desmoscolex squamosus dez-moh-SKOH-lecks skwah-MOH-sus

Diadema savignyi die-ah-DEM-ay sav-IG-nee-eye

Dicrocoelium dendriticum dih-kroh-SEE-lee-um den-DRIH-tih-kum

Dicyemodeca deca dih-sy-moh-DEH-kay DEH-kay

Didemnum studeri dih-DEM-num STOO-dih-rye

Diphyllobothrium latum die-fy-loh-BOH-three-um LAT-um

Dirofilaria immitis dih-roh-FIL-air-ee-ay IM-mih-tihs

Distaplia cylindrica dis-TAP-lee-ay sih-LIN-drih-kay

Distichopora violacea dis-tih-CHOP-or-ay vie-oh-LAY-see-ay

Dugesia tigrina duh-JEH-see-ay tie-GRIN-ay

Echinococcus granulosus eh-kin-oh-KOH-kus gran-u-LOH-sus

Echinocyamus pusillus eh-kin-oh-sy-AM-us puh-SILL-us

Echinoderes sensibilis eh-kin-oh-DEH-res sen-SIH-bih-lis

Echinoidea eh-kin-oh-IH-dee-ay

Endoxocrinus parrae en-dock-so-KRIN-us PAR-ree

Entoprocta en-toh-PROK-tay

Eukrohnia fowleri yu-kroh-NEE-ay FOW-ler-eye

Fasciola hepatica fas-see-OH-lay he-PAT-ih-kay

Gastrotricha gas-troh-TRIH-kay

Gnathostomulida nath-oh-stoh-MULE-ee-day

Haplognathia ruberrima hap-lohg-NATH-ee-ay roo-BEH-ree-may

Hemichordata heh-mee-kor-DAH-tay

Holothuroidea hah-loh-thuh-ROY-dee-ay

Hydrozoa hie-droh-ZOH-ay

Kinorhyncha kee-noh-RINE-kay

Leodia sexiesperforata lee-OH-dee-ay sex-ee-es-per-FOR-ah-tay

Lepidodermella squamata leh-pih-doe-DER-mel-lay skwah-MAH-tay

Limnognathia maerski lim-nohg-NATH-ee-ay mee-ERSK-eye

Linckia laevigata LINK-ee-ay lee-VIH-gah-tay

Linuche unguiculata lin-YU-kee un-gwee-kyu-LAH-tay

Lophelia pertusa loh-FEE-lee-ay per-TUH-say

Loricifera lor-ih-SEE-feh-ray

Macracanthorhynchus hirudinaceus mack-rah-kan-thoh-RIN-kus hih-roo-dih-NAY-see-us

Mermis nigrescens MER-mis nih-GREH-senz

Mespilia globulus meh-SPIL-ee-ay GLOH-byu-lus

Metridium senile meh-TRIH-dee-um SEN-il-ee

Micrognathozoa my-kroh-NATH-oh-zoh-ay

Millepora alcicornis mil-leh-POR-ay al-see-KOR-nis

Mnemiopsis leidyi nee-mee-OP-sis LEE-dee-eye

Moniliformis moniliformis mon-il-ih-FOR-mis mon-il-ih-FOR-mis

Monoblastozoa mon-oh-blas-toh-ZOH-ay

Monogenea mon-oh-jen-EE-ay

Nemaster rubiginosa nee-MAS-ter roo-bih-jin-OH-say

Nematomorpha nee-mah-toh-MOR-fay

Nemertea ne-MER-tee-ay

Notoplana acticola noh-toh-PLAN-ay ak-tee-KOH-lay

Novodinia antillensis noh-voh-DIN-ee-ay an-til-EN-sis

Oerstedia dorsalis eer-STED-ee-ay dor-SAL-is

Oikopleura labradoriensis eye-koh-PLUR-ay lab-rah-dor-ee-EN-sis

Oligotrema sandersi oh-lee-go-TREE-may SAN-derz-eye

Ophiactis savignyi oh-fee-AK-tis sav-IG-nee-eye

Ophiuroidea oh-fee-yu-ROY-dee-ay

Orthonectida or-thoh-NEK-tih-day

Paragordius varius pah-rah-GOR-dee-us VAR-ee-us

Pelagia noctiluca pel-AH-jee-ay nok-tih-LOO-kay

Pheronema carpenteri feh-ROH-nee-may kar-PEN-teh-rye

Physalia physalis fih-SAH-lee-ay fih-SAH-lis

Placozoa plak-oh-ZOH-ay

Polystoma integerrimum pol-ee-STOH-may in-teh-jer-ree-mum

Porifera por-IH-feh-ray

Priapulida pree-ap-PUL-ih-day

Priapulus caudatus pree-AP-pul-us kaw-DAY-tus

Proteocephalus longicollis pro-tee-oh-SEF-fal-us lon-jee-KOHL-lis

Pseudocolochirus violaceus soo-doh-koh-loh-KIH-rus vie-oh-LAH-see-us

Pterosagitta draco teh-roh-SAJ-ih-tay DRAY-koh

Ptychodera flava tie-ko-DEH-ray FLAH-vay

Pyrosoma atlanticum pie-roh-SOH-may at-LAN-tih-kum

Rhombozoa rom-boh-ZOH-ay

Rhopalura ophiocomae roh-pah-LUR-ay oh-fee-oh-KOH-mee

Rotifera roh-TEE-feh-ray

Rugiloricus cauliculus roo-jih-LOH-ree-kus kaw-LEE-kyu-lus

Salinella salve sah-leh-NEH-lay SAL-vee

Saxipendium coronatum sack-sih-PEN-dee-um kor-oh-NAH-tum

Schistosoma mansoni skih-stoh-SOH-may MAN-son-eye

Scotoplanes globosa skoh-toh-PLAN-ez gloh-BOH-say

Scyphozoa skih-foh-ZOH-ay

Secernentea sek-ker-NEN-tee-ay

Seison nebaliae SAY-ee-son nee-BAH-lee-ee/def>

Soleneiscus radovani soh-len-ee-IHS-kus rad-oh-VAN-eye

Sorberacea sor-ber-AK-see-ay

Spongilla lacustris SPON-jil-lay lah-KUS-tris

Stylochus inimicus STIH-loh-kus in-IM-ih-kus

Symbion pandora SIM-by-on pan-DOR-ay

Thaliacea thal-ee-ah-SEE-ay

Thalia democratica THAL-ee-ay dem-oh-KRAT-ik-ay

Thelenota rubralineata theh-leh-NOH-tay roo-bra-LIN-ee-at-tay

Trematoda tree-MAH-toe-day

Trichoplax adhaerens TRI-koh-placks ad-HEE-renz

Turbellaria ter-bell-EH-ree-ay

Xyloplax medusiformis ZY-lo-placks meh-doo-sih-FOR-mis

Words to Know

A

Algae Plantlike growths that live in water and have no true roots, stems, or leaves.

Asexual Without the uniting of egg and sperm for the transfer of DNA from two parents.

B

Bilateral symmetry The body form in which the right and left halves of the body match each other.

Budding A method of asexual reproduction by which a bump develops on an animal, grows to full size, and then breaks off to live as a new individual.

C

Carnivorous Meat eating.

Crustaceans Water-dwelling animals that have jointed legs and a hard shell but no backbone.

D

Diatom A type of algae with a shell.

E

Estuary The area where a river meets the sea.

F

Fertilization The joining of egg and sperm to start development.

Filter feeder An animal that eats tiny particles of food floating in the water that flows through it.

H

Host An animal or plant in or on which a parasite lives.

I

Invertebrate An animal without a backbone.

L

Larva An early stage some animals go through before changing form to become an adult. The plural is larvae.

M

Medusa A tentacled, jellylike, freely swimming, umbrella-shaped body form.

Metamorphosis The changes in form that some animals make to become adults.

Mollusk An animal with a soft, unsegmented body that may or may not have a shell.

N

Notochord A flexible rod of cells that supports the body in some simple animals.

Nucleus The control center of a cell.

P

Parasite An animal or plant that lives on or in another animal or plant without helping it and usually harming it.

Plankton Microscopic plants and animals drifting in water.

Polyp A body type that consists of a tubular sac with a mouth and tentacles on the top.

Predator An animal that attacks and kills other animals for food.

Protist A one-celled living thing without a nucleus.

Protozoan A one-celled living thing that resembles an animal in that it gets its food from its surroundings rather than making food itself as plants do.

S

Sexual With the uniting of egg and sperm and the transfer of DNA from two parents.

Suspension feeder An animal that takes in and eats small particles floating in the water.

T

Tissue A group of cells with the same function.

V

Vertebrate An animal with a backbone.

Getting to Know Corals, Jellyfishes, Sponges, and Other Simple Animals

PHYSICAL CHARACTERISTICS

An animal is a living thing made up of many cells and it is not a plant. Simple animals are those without a fluid-filled body cavity between the outer body wall and the digestive tract. Examples of simple animals are sponges, corals, jellyfishes, sea stars, sea urchins, roundworms, and flatworms such as tapeworms. All simple animals are invertebrates (in-VER-teh-brehts), meaning they do not have a spinal column made up of a series of bones. The simplest animals, sponges, have many cells but do not have true tissues, or groups of cells with the same function. More complex simple animals, such as corals and jellyfishes, do have tissues but no organs. The most complex of the simple animals, sea squirts and lancelets, have a flexible rod that is a simple form of the spinal column of vertebrates (VER-teh-brehts).

HABITAT

Almost all simple animals live in water or in other animals. Most simple animals that live in water live in the sea, but some live in the fresh water of ponds and rivers. Some simple sea animals live on surfaces such as rock, shell, sand, and mud. Other simple sea animals, such as jellyfishes, float freely in open water.

Green anemones, California mussels, and ochre sea stars are all examples of simple animals, animals without backbones. (© Stuart Westmorland/CORBIS.)

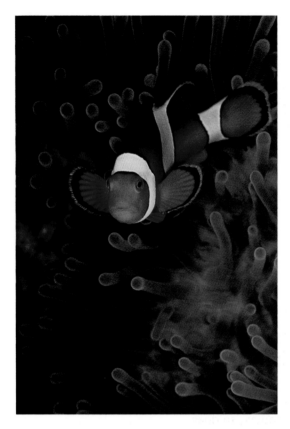

Some animals that live in other animals do not harm them; often one or both animals benefit. For example, pearlfish live in the anuses of sea cucumbers without hurting them. Other animals, called parasites (PAIR-uh-sites), harm the animals in which they live, called the hosts. For example, tapeworms are parasites that cause disease in their human hosts.

DIET

Some simple sea animals, such as sponges, eat tiny particles of food floating in the water that flows through them. These animals are filter feeders. Some simple animals take in and eat small particles floating, or suspended, in the water. These animals are suspension feeders. Other simple animals, such as jellyfishes, which use their tentacles for this purpose, attack and kill other animals and eat them. These animals are predators (PREH-duh-ters). Animals that live inside or on the surface of another animal and eat its cells, body fluids, food, and waste are parasites.

This anemonefish is protected from many of its predators by living among the stinging tentacles of the anemone. In turn, it keeps the anemone clean, and aggressively keeps other creatures away. (© Tony Wu/ www.silent-symphony.com.)

BEHAVIOR

Behavior is the actions animals take to adjust to and interact with their environment. The animals use behavior to find

Some simple animals, such as this octopus, attack and kill other animals and eat them. (JLM Visuals.)

The sea urchin can move to a new location by walking on its tube-feet, which are extended here. (Jane Burton. Bruce Coleman, Inc.)

food and a place to live, to defend themselves, and to reproduce. As the bodies of animals become more complex, so does their behavior. Sponges, which have the simplest bodies, have the least coordinated behavior. Corals and jellyfishes can contract, or withdraw, to protect their most vulnerable body parts. Animals such sea stars and sea urchins can crawl away to hide under a rock or change direction and swim away to escape predators.

REPRODUCTION

An animal species is a group of individuals that shares a common pool of genes. The genes determine all of the animal's characteristics and are made of DNA. Reproduction is the copying of an individual animal's DNA and the transfer of the copy into a newly formed individual. Reproduction can be asexual (ay-SEK-shuh-wuhl) or sexual (SEK-shuh-wuhl).

In asexual reproduction the offspring develop from a single parent, and the copy of the DNA is nearly identical to the original. No new combinations of genes result from mixing genes from two parents. For example, an animal simply splits in half

and grows into two full-sized individuals. Or a body part breaks off and develops into a whole new animal. In a third method a bud develops on an animal, grows to full size, and then breaks off to live as a new individual. Asexual reproduction has the advantage of allowing a very fast rate of reproduction with a resulting rapid increase in the population of a species. The primary disadvantage of asexual reproduction is that it does not allow much genetic variation. As a result, the population as a whole becomes unable to adapt to changing environmental conditions.

In sexual reproduction, the DNA copy is not exact, and the genetic makeup of the offspring differs from that of its parents. Each parent's DNA is reduced by half before being joined with the half set of DNA supplied by the other mating partner. Before the DNA is reduced by half, however, gene segments reorganize to form unique combinations of genes. This process is known as crossing over and is the event that distinguishes sexual from asexual reproduction. Crossing over combined with the uniting of DNA from two unique individuals when egg and sperm join during fertilization (FUR-teh-lih-zay-shun) results in the varied offspring that characterize most animal species.

Many animals, particularly simple animals, use both asexual and sexual reproduction at various times. It is rare for both asexual and sexual reproduction to occur at the same time, however. In many simple animals, the asexual and sexual processes occur in different seasons or in different generations. In other groups of simple animals, such as parasite flatworms, asexual and sexual processes are used in two different stages of life.

In most animals, males produce sperm, and females produce eggs. In some animals, however, the same individual produces both sperm and eggs. Some animals produce both sperm and eggs at the same time, and some do so at different stages of life.

Sperm and egg come together in a variety of ways among simple animals. Some animals release their sperm or eggs directly into the surrounding water. In groups such as sponges, corals, and jellyfishes, this method is the only way eggs and sperm come together. In some animals males release their sperm, females release their eggs, and fertilization takes place outside the body. In other animals, the male releases sperm, the female takes up the sperm, and fertilization takes place inside her body. In still other animals, the males transfer sperm directly into the female for fertilization inside her body.

During development cells multiply and organize into layers called germ layers. Each layer then gives rise to certain tissues. A few simple animals do not have specific germ layers. Some scientists place sponges in this group, but other scientists say sponges have two germ layers. Animals in the jellyfishes and corals group and comb jellies have two germ layers. All other animals, simple and complex, have three germ layers. The inner layer typically develops into the digestive system. The outer layer develops into the skin and nervous system. The middle layer develops into the waste disposal system, muscle, and bone.

CLASSIFICATION

Living things are classified into the following groups: kingdom, phylum (FYE-luhm), class, order, family, genus (JEE-nuhs), and species (SPEE-ceez). Species is the narrowest group. Living things in the same species have the most in common and can reproduce with one another. Kingdom is the broadest group. The kingdoms are animal, plant, fungus, protist (PROH-tist), and moneran (moh-NEER-uhn). Protists are one-celled living things that have a nucleus (NOO-klee-uhs). Examples are amoebas (uh-MEE-buhs) and algae (AL-jee). Monerans are one-celled living things that do not have a nucleus. Bacteria are monerans.

*Mating flatworms (*Pseudoceros bilurcus*) with insemination marks. (© A. Flowers & L. Newman/Photo Researchers, Inc.)*

After hatching or being born, the young of complex animals look like adults but do not have a mature reproductive system. Most simple animals, however, go through a stage called a larva (LAR-vuh)—the plural is larvae(LAR-vee)—before they become adults. The transition from larva to adult, known as metamor-

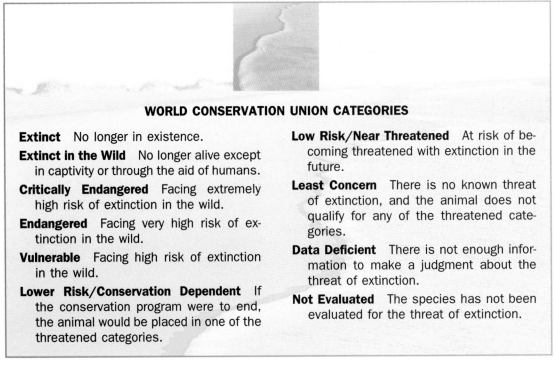

WORLD CONSERVATION UNION CATEGORIES

Extinct   No longer in existence.

Extinct in the Wild   No longer alive except in captivity or through the aid of humans.

Critically Endangered   Facing extremely high risk of extinction in the wild.

Endangered   Facing very high risk of extinction in the wild.

Vulnerable   Facing high risk of extinction in the wild.

Lower Risk/Conservation Dependent   If the conservation program were to end, the animal would be placed in one of the threatened categories.

Low Risk/Near Threatened   At risk of becoming threatened with extinction in the future.

Least Concern   There is no known threat of extinction, and the animal does not qualify for any of the threatened categories.

Data Deficient   There is not enough information to make a judgment about the threat of extinction.

Not Evaluated   The species has not been evaluated for the threat of extinction.

phosis (meh-tuh-MOR-fo-sus), requires changes in the form, behavior, and functions of the animal. A larva is a fully functional animal that can feed and move about independently. The most common task of larvae is traveling to colonize new environments for the species. This process is especially important for animals such as corals and sponges, which are fixed in one spot as adults.

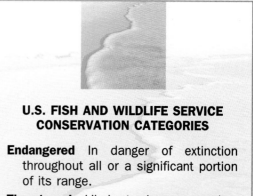

U.S. FISH AND WILDLIFE SERVICE CONSERVATION CATEGORIES

Endangered In danger of extinction throughout all or a significant portion of its range.

Threatened Likely to become endangered in the near future.

SIMPLE ANIMALS AND PEOPLE

Simple animals can be harmful or helpful to people. A huge number of simple animals, such as tapeworms, flukes, roundworms, and heartworms, are parasites that cause disease in humans and domesticated animals throughout the world. And animals such as jellyfish and sea urchins can cause great pain when touched. On the other hand, substances from simple animals such as sponges and sea squirts can be used to make drugs for treating viral diseases and cancer. People also like to visit the seashore and the aquarium to observe the beauty of animals such as corals and sea stars.

CONSERVATION

Simple animals are often taken for granted, but these animals are important in the mechanics of nutrient and energy

Aquariums are popular places for people to see and learn about the animals that live underwater. (© Paul A. Souders/CORBIS.)

transfer, decomposition, and carbon and nitrogen cycling on which life depends. Each year thousands of species cease to exist. Gone with those species may be life-saving medicines, models for research, and contributions to the balance of the environment. Conservation is the effort to protect species at risk because of harm done by humans. The World Conservation Union (IUCN) is an organization that collects information on the health and status of animals worldwide. The U.S. Fish and Wildlife Service does the same thing in the United States.

FOR MORE INFORMATION

Books:

Aaseng, Nathan. *Invertebrates*. New York: Venture, 1993.

Carson, Rachel. *The Edge of the Sea*. 1955. Reprint, Boston: Mariner, 1998.

Layman, Dale. *Biology Demystified*. New York: McGraw-Hill, 2003.

Niesen, Thomas M. *The Marine Biology Coloring Book*. 2nd ed. New York: HarperResource, 2000.

Silverstein, Alvin, Virginia Silverstein, and Robert Silverstein. *Invertebrates*. New York: Twenty-First Century, 1996.

Stalcup, Brenda, ed. *Endangered Species: Opposing Viewpoints*. San Diego, CA: Greenhaven, 1996.

Wells, Sue, and Nick Hanna. *The Greenpeace Book of Coral Reefs*. New York: Sterling, 1992.

Zimmer, Carl. *Parasite Rex*. New York: Free Press, 2000.

Web sites:

"Animal." All Science Fair Projects. http://www.all-science-fair -projects.com/science_fair_projects_encyclopedia/Animal (accessed on January 13, 2005).

"World's Largest Conservation Gathering Opens to Escalating Global Species Extinction Crisis." World Conservation Union. http://www.iucn.org/themes/ssc/red_list_2004/main_ EN.htm (accessed on January 13, 2005).

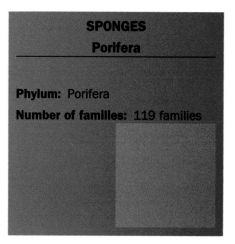

phylum

CHAPTER

PHYSICAL CHARACTERISTICS

Sponges are clumps of cells arranged around masses of tubes. The surface is covered with small holes. The movement of whip-like cells in the center of the sponge draws water through the holes and into the sponge. A pumping action moves the water through the sponge and out through a large hole at the end of each tube. The body of many sponges is supported by tiny rods or star-shaped structures called spicules (SPIH-kyoolz). In some sponges the spicules cover the outside of the body. In others they are interlocked to make a delicate framework. Sponges that do not have spicules are supported by strong, flexible fibers made of a protein called spongin. Some sponges have skeletons made of both spicules and spongin.

Sponges have a variety of shapes. Some form a crust on their rocky habitat. Some form a single straight tube. Others are vase shaped or cup shaped. Some sponges are massive clumps. Others are fan shaped. Some sponges have mitten-shaped or finger-like bulges on the body wall. Others are treelike or bushy. The height and width of sponges ranges from less than one inch (a few millimeters) to about 5 feet (1.5 meters). Sponges can be soft or hard, flexible or brittle. Some sponges are an almost colorless white or beige, and some are camouflage greenish brown. Some are brightly colored yellow or fluorescent reddish orange. Others are delicate shades of purple, lavender, light brown, or blue.

GEOGRAPHIC RANGE

Sponges live all over the world.

■ **phylum**

class

subclass

order

monotypic order

suborder

family

IS BOB REALLY A SPONGE?

One of the most famous cartoon characters of the early twenty-first century is the square-pants-wearing SpongeBob, who looks like the brightly colored, rectangular objects many people use to clean their kitchen sinks. These cleaning tools, however, are not sponges. Most are made from cellulose, which is the main component of the cell walls of plants and also is used to make paper. Other kitchen "sponges" are made of plastic. The tan, irregularly shaped clumps that some people use for taking baths, for applying makeup, and for painting are the skeletons of dead sea sponges.

HABITAT

Most sponges live in the sea, but a few species live in freshwater. Many sponges live on reefs. Most sponges need a firm surface on which to attach, such as rocks or the skeletons of dead sponges and coral. Other sponges live on sand or mud at the bottom of the deep sea. Freshwater sponges live in lakes and streams.

DIET

Sponges eat tiny particles such as bacterial plankton that they filter from the water that flows through them. A few sponges, however, are carnivorous (kar-NIH-vuh-rus), or meat eating. They engulf and digest small crustaceans (krus-TAY-shuns), or water-dwelling animals that have jointed legs and a hard shell but no backbone.

BEHAVIOR AND REPRODUCTION

Most sponges attach themselves to the material on which they live. Some can penetrate deep inside rocks, coral, and shells. The main activity of sponges is pumping water through themselves to get food and oxygen, eliminate waste, and, for some sponges, process enough sand to make spicules. Sponges can control the amount of flow through their bodies by narrowing or partly closing off their intake and exit holes. Some sponges compete for space with corals and other sponges by releasing toxic chemicals.

Some sponges are either male or female, but others produce both eggs and sperm. Sponges use either sexual (SEK-shuh-wuhl) or asexual (ay-SEK-shuh-wuhl) reproduction. They are perhaps the most efficient animal at asexual reproduction, which happens without the uniting of egg and sperm or the transfer of DNA from two parents. Sponges can reproduce asexually when a piece of the adult's body breaks off and grows into a separate adult. In another method buds develop on the parent and then break off when they are large enough to live on their own.

Sexual reproduction is done by the uniting of egg and sperm and the transfer of DNA from two parents. Male sponges release sperm, which is taken inside females for fertilization (FUR-teh-lih-ZAY-shun), or the joining of egg and sperm. In some species of sponges the fertilized (FUR-teh-lyzed) eggs are released and then hatch outside the female's body. In most sponges, however, larvae (LAR-vee) develop inside the female's body and are born alive through the sponge's water-exit hole. Larvae are animals in an early stage that change form before becoming adults. Sponge larvae swim or crawl around for a few hours or days and then settle at the bottom of the water before transforming into adult sponges and attaching themselves to their permanent home.

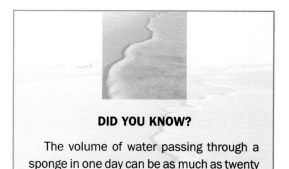

DID YOU KNOW?

The volume of water passing through a sponge in one day can be as much as twenty thousand times the volume of the sponge.

SPONGES AND PEOPLE

Some sponges produce compounds that can be used to make drugs for fighting diseases caused by viruses and bacteria. Other sponges are harvested and sold as bath sponges.

CONSERVATION STATUS

Sponges are not threatened or endangered.

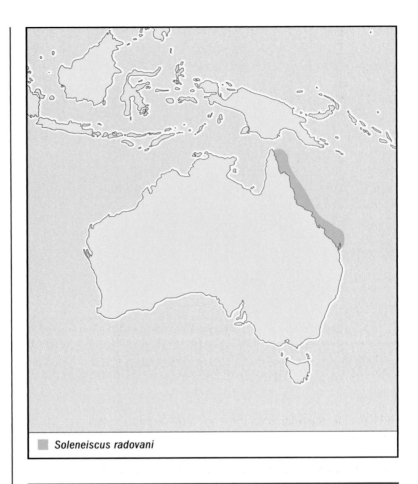

Soleneiscus radovani

NO COMMON NAME
Soleneiscus radovani

Physical characteristics: Sponges of the species *Soleneiscus radovani* (abbreviated as *S. radovani*) are bushy looking and bright yellow. They have single, delicate tubes branching from a large tube in the center of the sponge. The outer tubes are about one-sixteenth of an inch (2 millimeters) in diameter. The entire sponge is less than 4 inches (10 centimeters) in diameter. *S. radovani* sponges are soft and delicate and easily torn.

Geographic range: *S. radovani* sponges live on the Great Barrier Reef, Australia.

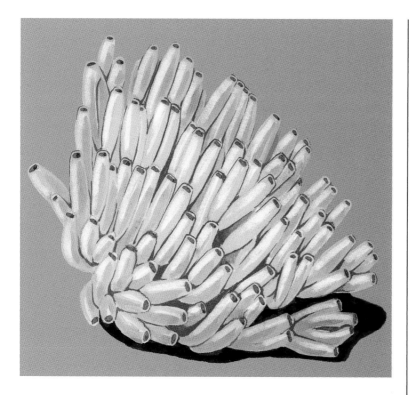

Habitat: *S. radovani* sponges live in small patches of coral under overhangs.

Diet: *S. radovani* sponges are filter feeders that eat whatever is in the water that flows through them.

Behavior and reproduction: *S. radovani* sponges give birth to live young. Other than that, scientists do not know how these sponges behave or reproduce.

***Soleneiscus radovani* and people:** *S. radovani* sponges have no known importance to people.

Conservation status: *S. radovani* sponges are not threatened or endangered. ∎

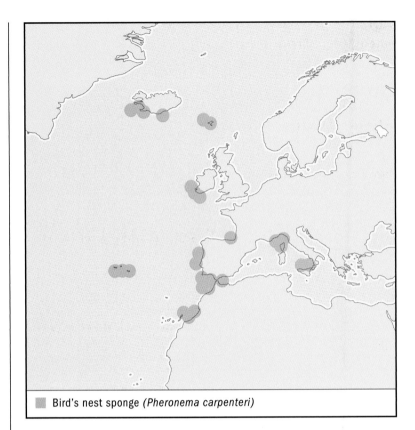

Bird's nest sponge (*Pheronema carpenteri*)

BIRD'S NEST SPONGE
Pheronema carpenteri

Physical characteristics: The shape of bird's nest sponges ranges from tall and narrow, like a barrel, to short and wide, like a cake. These sponges grow to a height of about 10 inches (25 centimeters) and a width of about 8 inches (20 centimeters). The thick, hollow body tapers to a single sharp-edged upper opening. Short thin, hair-like silica spicules surround the opening and stick out of the upper third of body. Longer spicules cover the lower third of the body and anchor the sponge in soft mud. The spicules on the middle third of the body are arranged in a pattern that looks like the interlocking twigs of a bird's nest. Bird's nest sponges are white.

Geographic range: Bird's nest sponges live in the northeastern part of the Atlantic Ocean from Iceland to northern Africa, including the Mediterranean Sea.

Habitat: Bird's nest sponges live on soft, muddy bottoms in the very deep ocean.

Diet: Bird's nest sponges are probably filter feeders.

Behavior and reproduction: Scientists do not know how bird's nest sponges behave or reproduce.

Bird's nest sponges and people: Scientists are trying to find out why there are so many bird's nest sponges in the deep ocean, where there are usually very few of any animal.

Conservation status: Bird's nest sponges are not threatened or endangered. ■

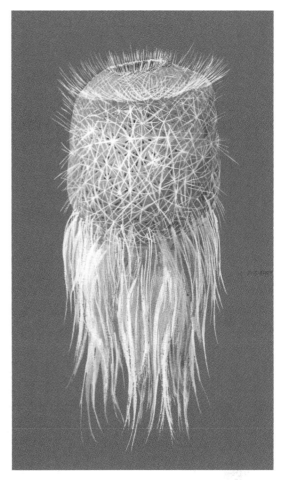

Scientists are trying to find out why there are so many bird's nest sponges in the deep ocean, where there are usually very few of any animal. (Illustration by Emily Damstra. Reproduced by permission.)

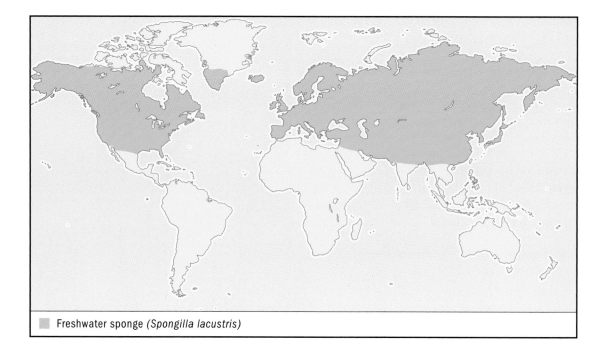

Freshwater sponge (*Spongilla lacustris*)

FRESHWATER SPONGE
Spongilla lacustris

Physical characteristics: Freshwater sponges are crustlike, branched, or clumped. The texture is fragile and soft, and the color is whitish or green. Freshwater sponges have irregularly scattered and barely visible water-exit holes. The surface is uneven and roughened by spicules.

Geographic range: Freshwater sponges live in North America, Europe, and Asia.

Habitat: Freshwater sponges live in standing and running fresh water.

Diet: Freshwater sponges are filter feeders.

Behavior and reproduction: Scientists know little about how freshwater sponges behave. These sponges reproduce asexually by forming buds in late summer that spend the winter in a dormant state and emerge from the adult in the spring. Freshwater sponges reproduce sexually during the summer, giving birth to live larvae.

Freshwater sponges have irregularly scattered and barely visible water-exit holes. The surface is uneven and roughened by spicules. (Illustration by Michelle Meneghini. Reproduced by permission.)

Freshwater sponges and people: Freshwater sponges have no known importance to people. Some scientists believe they may be helpful as indicators of water pollution.

Conservation status: Freshwater sponges are not threatened or endangered. ∎

FOR MORE INFORMATION

Books:

Aaseng, Nathan. *Invertebrates.* New York: Venture, 1993.

Carson, Rachel. *The Edge of the Sea.* 1955. Reprint, Boston: Mariner, 1998.

Layman, Dale. *Biology Demystified.* New York: McGraw-Hill, 2003.

Niesen, Thomas M. *The Marine Biology Coloring Book.* 2nd ed. New York: HarperResource, 2000.

Wells, Sue, and Nick Hanna. *The Greenpeace Book of Coral Reefs.* New York: Sterling, 1992.

Web sites:

Hartman, Holly. "The Science of SpongeBob." Pearson Education Fact Monster. http://www.factmonster.com/spot/spongebobscience.html (accessed on January 20, 2005).

Hill, Malcolm S., and April L. Hill. "Freshwater Sponges as Indicators of Water Pollution: An Investigative Undergraduate Lab." *Labstracts.* http://www.zoo.utoronto.ca/able/news/fall2000/page2-f00.htm (accessed on January 21, 2005).

"Porifera Questions." OceanLink: Ask a Scientist, Answer Archive. http://oceanlink.island.net/ask/porifera.html#anchor92351 (accessed on January 21, 2005).

"Sponges." Sponge Reef Project. http://www.pgc.nrcan.gc.ca/marine/sponge/index_e.htm (accessed on January 21, 2005).

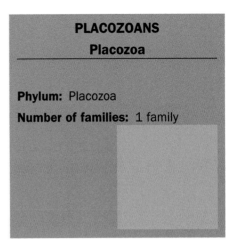

PLACOZOANS

Placozoa

Phylum: Placozoa

Number of families: 1 family

phylum

C H A P T E R

PHYSICAL CHARACTERISTICS

Placozoans (PLACK-uh-zoh-uhns) are shape-shifting blobs up to one-sixteenth of an inch (2 millimeters) in diameter. There is only one species, *Trichoplax adhaerens*. The grayish white body is covered with tiny structures that look like hairs. Placozoans consist of several thousand cells that form two thin layers of tissue but not organs. There is only one known species of placozoan, and it is a tiny, flattened bag of cells that has a top and a bottom but no front or rear. A narrow space between the two layers of cells is filled with a gel-like substance.

Some scientists believe that placozoans may be the earliest form of animal life. Results of molecular studies suggest that placozoans are closely related to the group that includes corals and jellyfish. If confirmed, this finding would imply that placozoans are a simple form of more complex ancestors that had tissues and organs, including muscles and nerves.

Although the bodies of placozoans are made up of several thousand cells, there are only a few cell types. The top layer is thin and loosely constructed of cover cells that bear a single whiplike structure and contain droplets of fatty material. The bottom layer is made up of a thicker, denser layer of gland cells without a whip as well as other cells with a whip. The fluid-filled space between the top and bottom layers contains a network of loosely organized cells known as fiber cells. The fiber cells are connected to one another and to the top and bottom layers by branched extensions. The fiber cells are thought to function as both muscle and nerve cells. The fiber cells contain bacteria that live in placozoans.

phylum

class

subclass

order

monotypic order

suborder

family

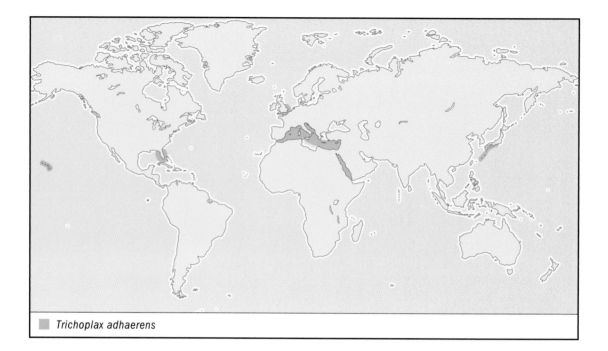

Trichoplax adhaerens

GEOGRAPHIC RANGE

Scientists do not know whether placozoans are widely distributed around the world. These animals are so hidden that their diversity may be much greater than scientists realize. The placozoans that have been studied are samples cultured in laboratory aquariums near warm seas.

HABITAT

Scientists do not know where placozoans live under natural conditions. They may live on the surface of underwater rocks and on the shells of bottom-dwelling sea animals.

DIET

Placozoans eat waste material, protozoans (proh-tuh-ZOH-uhns), and algae (AL-jee). Protozoans are one-celled living things that resemble animals in that they get their food from their surroundings rather than making it themselves as plants do. Algae are plantlike growths that live in water and have no true roots, stems, or leaves.

BEHAVIOR AND REPRODUCTION

In aquariums and laboratories, placozoans have been observed to creep along by beating the hairlike structures on their

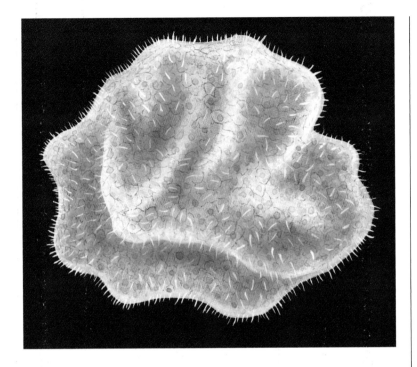

bottom surface. They often lift themselves, forming a bag in which they digest their food. The feeding behavior of placozoans depends on the amount of available food. When there is little food, placozoans move rapidly with frequent, random changes in shape. When there is much food, however, placozoans flatten themselves and move around less.

Placozoans appear to use asexual (ay-SEK-shuh-wuhl) reproduction, or reproduction without the uniting of egg and sperm for the transfer of DNA from two parents, in three ways. In the first method, the body divides in half to make two new individuals. In the second method, small parts separate from the body and grow into new individuals. In the third method, buds develop on the parent, grow to full size, and then break off to live as new individuals. A few scientists have observed sexual reproduction in laboratory vessels containing two different clones of placozoans.

PLACOZOANS AND PEOPLE

Placozoans have no known importance to humans.

CONSERVATION STATUS

Placozoans are not threatened or endangered.

FOR MORE INFORMATION

Books:

Grel, Karl G., and A. Ruthmann. "Placozoa." In *Microscopic Anatomy of Invertebrates: Placozoa, Porifera, Cnidaria, and Ctenophora.* Edited by Frederick W. Harrison and J. A. Westfall. New York: Wiley, 1991.

Web sites:

Howey, Richard L. "A Weird Wee Beastie: *Trichoplax adhaerens.*" Microscopy-UK. http://www.microscopy-uk.org.uk/mag/indexmag.html? http://www.microscopy-uk.org.uk/mag/artoct98/tricho.html (accessed on December 13, 2004).

"Introduction to Placozoa: The Most Simple of All Known Animals." University of California, Berkeley, Museum of Paleontology. http://www.ucmp.berkeley.edu/images/WebLiftComb.gif (accessed on December 13, 2004).

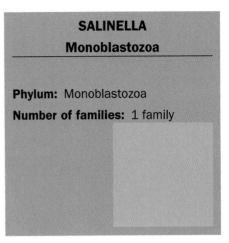

phylum
CHAPTER

PHYSICAL CHARACTERISTICS

Monoblastozoa (MAHN-uh-blast-uh-zoh-uh) has only one species, *Salinella salve*. This animal was found in 1892 in a culture of material from salt beds in Argentina. Because *Salinella* has not been observed since its discovery, some scientists doubt that it exists. According to the scientist who wrote the only published record of *Salinella*, the body consists of a single cell layer and lacks tissues and organs.

Salinella differs from other simple animals because it lacks internal cells. In this regard, *Salinella* appears to be more closely related to one-celled living things than to animals. If researchers are able to find new specimens of *Salinella* and study them in detail, they may find that this species represents an intermediate stage between one-celled living things and animals.

The body of *Salinella* consists of about one hundred cells in a single cell layer enclosing a digestive cavity. The digestive cavity is open at both ends. The opening at one end functions as a mouth and that at the other end as an anus (AY-nuhs). There are bristles around the mouth and anus. The top surface of the animal is covered with a sparse collection of bristles. The bottom surface is somewhat flattened but is covered with tiny hairlike fibers. The cell walls facing the inner cavity also are heavily covered with these hairlike fibers.

GEOGRAPHIC RANGE

Salinella has been found only in Argentina.

phylum

class

subclass

order

monotypic order

suborder

family

Salinella salve

HABITAT

Scientists do not know where *Salinella* lives under natural conditions.

DIET

Salinella eats by ingesting small particles into its internal cavity. Undigested particles are carried to the anus by the movement of hairlike fibers.

BEHAVIOR AND REPRODUCTION

Salinella moves by gliding on its hairlike fibers. It uses asexual (ay-SEK-shuh-wuhl) reproduction, or reproduction without the uniting of egg and sperm for the transfer of DNA from two parents, by splitting in half and growing into two full-sized individuals. However, another mode of reproduction was seen

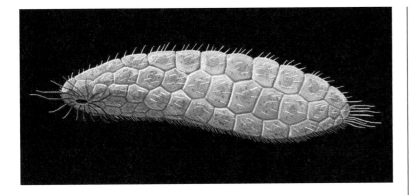

Salinella salve *was found in 1892 in a culture of material from salt beds in Argentina. Because* Salinella *has not been observed since its discovery, some scientists doubt that it exists. (Illustration by Dan Erickson. Reproduced by permission.)*

in culture. *Salinella* appeared to form a cyst by the coupling of two individuals. Although the details of the process are unknown, a one-celled individual that possibly came from the cyst was found in the culture. It is not known whether sexual (SEK-shuh-wuhl) reproduction, or reproduction by the uniting of egg and sperm and the transfer of DNA from two parents, takes place within the cyst.

SALINELLA AND PEOPLE

Salinella has no known importance to people.

CONSERVATION STATUS

Salinella is not threatened or endangered.

FOR MORE INFORMATION

Books:

Barnes, R. S. K., Peter Calow, and Peter Olive. *The Invertebrates: A Synthesis.* 3rd ed. Malden, MA: Blackwell, 2001.

Brusca, Richard C., Gary J. Brusca, and Nancy Haver. *Invertebrates.* 2nd ed. Sunderland, MA: Sinauer, 2002.

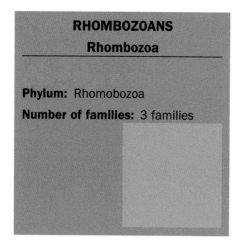

RHOMBOZOANS
Rhombozoa

Phylum: Rhomobozoa
Number of families: 3 families

phylum

PHYSICAL CHARACTERISTICS

Rhombozoans (RAHM-boh-ZOH-uhns) are parasites (PAIR-uh-sites) that live in the kidneys of bottom-dwelling octopuses, cuttlefish, and sometimes squid. Parasites are animals or plants that live on or in another animal or plant, called a host, without helping it and usually harming it. The body of rhombozoans is made up of only eight to forty cells in a simple arrangement. They have the fewest cells of any animal.

Rhombozoans have two types of organization. One type is wormlike embryos and adults. This form consists of a central cell shaped like a cylinder and a layer of eight to thirty outer cells that have hairlike fibers. At the front of the animal, four to ten of the outer cells form a cap, the hairlike fibers of which are shorter and denser than on the outer cells toward the rear of the animal. The shape of the cap varies among species of rhombozoans. The second type of organization is an embryo that consists of thirty-seven or thirty-nine cells that are more specialized than the cells of wormlike rhombozoans. Inside these embryos are four large cells, each containing another cell that may give rise to the next generation. It is these specialized embryos that invade the host animal.

GEOGRAPHIC RANGE

Rhombozoans live in the northern, eastern, and western parts of the Pacific Ocean; in the waters around New Zealand and Australia; in the Mediterranean Sea; in the northern, eastern, and western parts of the Atlantic Ocean; in the Gulf of Mexico; and in the Antarctic Ocean.

HABITAT

In the wormlike form, rhombozoans live only in the kidneys of octopuses, cuttlefish, and sometimes squid.

DIET

Rhombozoans absorb nutrients from the urine of their hosts.

BEHAVIOR AND REPRODUCTION

In both the wormlike phase and as specialized embryos, rhombozoans swim by movement of the hairlike fibers on their bodies. Scientists do not know how the specialized embryos infect a new host and develop into wormlike rhombozoans. Wormlike embryos develop asexually from a cell of a parent and grow into adults. Asexual (ay-SEK-shuh-wuhl) reproduction is that which takes place without the uniting of egg and sperm for the transfer of DNA from two parents. Crowding of rhombozoans in a host's kidney can cause a shift from asexual to sexual reproduction. When crowding occurs, rhombozoans develop a sex organ that contains both eggs and sperm. The mature sperm unite with eggs, and the fertilized (FUR-teh-lyzed) eggs develop into the specialized form of embryos.

RHOMBOZOANS AND PEOPLE

Rhombozoans have no known importance to people.

CONSERVATION STATUS

Rhombozoans are not threatened or endangered.

Dicyemodeca deca

NO COMMON NAME
Dicyemodeca deca

Physical characteristics: The body length of an adult *Dicyemodeca deca* (abbreviated as *D. deca*) does not exceed one–thirty-second of an inch (1 millimeter). There are twenty-three or twenty-four outer cells. The cap is disk shaped. The specialized embryos consist of thirty-five cells and are approximately 0.001 inch (33 micrometers) long.

Geographic range: *D. deca* lives in the northeastern part of the Pacific Ocean.

Habitat: *D. deca* lives in the kidneys of the giant Pacific octopus.

Diet: *D. deca* absorbs nutrients from the urine of its host.

Behavior and reproduction: The wormlike and specialized embryo forms of *D. deca* swim by movement of their hairlike fibers. Adults have two sex organs that contain about sixteen egg-related cells and fifteen sperm-related cells.

Dicyemodeca deca and people: *D. deca* has no known importance to people.

Conservation status: *D. deca* is not threatened or endangered.   ■

FOR MORE INFORMATION

Books:

Barnes, R. S. K., Peter Calow, and Peter Olive. *The Invertebrates: A Synthesis.* 3rd ed. Malden, MA: Blackwell, 2001.

Brusca, Richard C., Gary J. Brusca, and Nancy Haver. *Invertebrates.* 2nd ed. Sunderland, MA: Sinauer, 2002.

Web sites:

Furuya, Hidetaka, and Kazuhiko Tsuneki. "Biology of Dicyemid Mesozoans." *Zoological Science.* http://www.cephbase.utmb.edu/refdb/pdf/7851.pdf (accessed on January 23, 2005).

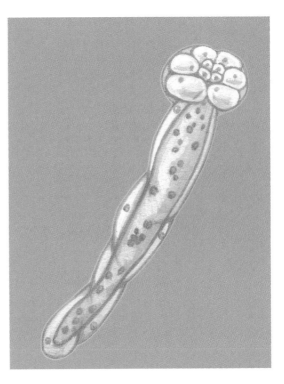

Dicyemodeca deca *lives in the kidneys of the giant Pacific octopus. (Illustration by Marguette Dongvillo. Reproduced by permission.)*

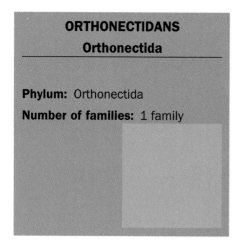

ORTHONECTIDANS

Orthonectida

Phylum: Orthonectida
Number of families: 1 family

phylum

CHAPTER

■ **phylum**

class

subclass

order

monotypic order

suborder

family

PHYSICAL CHARACTERISTICS

Orthonectidans (or-thuh-NEK-tih-duhns) are parasites (PAIR-uh-sites) that live in the tissues of sea-dwelling invertebrates (in-VER-teh-brehts). A parasite is an animal or plant that lives in or on another animal or plant, called a host, without helping it and usually harming it. Invertebrates are animals without a backbone. Depending on the species of orthonectidan, either the sexes are separate or both male and female reproductive organs are present in the same animal. Adult orthonectidans are 0.002 to 0.031 inch (50 to 800 micrometers) long. The body of an adult orthonectidan consists of a jacket of body cells arranged in rings around an internal mass. Some of these body cells have hairlike fibers and some do not. Contracting muscle cells in the sex organ run in the lengthwise, circular, and oblique directions.

GEOGRAPHIC RANGE

Orthonectidans live in the coastal regions of the northwestern part of the Atlantic Ocean and the Mediterranean Sea, the northwestern part of the Pacific Ocean near Japan, and the northeastern part of the Pacific Ocean along the coast of the United States.

HABITAT

Orthonectidans live in the tissues of sea-dwelling invertebrates, such as flatworms; segmented worms; mollusks (MAH-lusks), or animals with soft, unsegmented bodies that may or may not have a shell; sea stars, sea urchins, sea cucumbers, and their relatives; and sea squirts.

22   **Grzimek's Student Animal Life Resource**

DIET

Orthonectidans absorb nutrients within the host's cells.

BEHAVIOR AND REPRODUCTION

Orthonectidans are parasites that alternate between asexual (ay-SEK-shuh-wuhl) and sexual stages within the host animal. Asexually produced masses of young orthonectidans may develop into sexual forms. Asexual reproduction takes place without and sexual reproduction takes place with the uniting of egg and sperm for the transfer of DNA from two parents. During mating male orthonectidans make brief contact with females and release sperm. Fertilization (FUR-teh-lih-zay-shun), the joining of egg and sperm to start development, takes place inside the female. Embryos form about twenty-two hours later. When the embryos are fully developed, the female ruptures and dies, releasing larvae (LAR-vee) that disperse and enter a new host. Larvae are animals in an early stage that change form before becoming adults.

ORTHONECTIDANS AND PEOPLE

Orthonectidans have no known importance to people.

CONSERVATION STATUS

Orthonectidans are not threatened or endangered.

What's in a Name?

The name orthonectidan means "straight swimming," but these animals usually swim in a spiral motion.

Rhopalura ophiocomae

NO COMMON NAME
Rhopalura ophiocomae

Physical characteristics: Females of *Rhopalura ophiocomae* (abbreviated as *R. ophiocomae*) reach a length of 0.01 inch (260 micrometers), males a length of 0.005 inch (130 micrometers). The division of the body is much sharper in males than in females. In females numerous eggs form a compact mass that occupies most of the body. In males the sperm mass is in the middle third of the body.

Geographic range: *R. ophiocomae* lives off the coasts of France, Great Britain, Italy, and Washington and California in the United States.

Habitat: *R. ophiocomae* lives in the reproductive and digestive tracts of dwarf brittle stars.

Diet: *R. ophiocomae* absorbs nutrients in the host's cells.

Behavior and reproduction: *R. ophiocomae* usually swims with a spiraling motion. To mate, males and females bring their reproductive openings together long enough for the transfer of sperm from the male

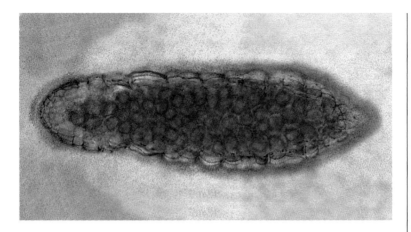

In Rhopalura ophiocomae, *the female's numerous eggs form a compact mass that occupies most of the body. (Specimens in Nouvel collection, Santa Barbara Museum of Natural History, photograph by Hidetaka Furuya. Reproduced by permission.)*

to the female. Fertilization takes place inside the female. When the embryos are fully developed, the female ruptures and dies, releasing larvae that disperse and enter a new host.

R. ophiocomae and people: *R. ophiocomae* has no known importance to people.

Conservation status: *R. ophiocomae* is not threatened or endangered. ◼

FOR MORE INFORMATION

Books:

Barnes, R. S. K., Peter Calow, and Peter Olive. *The Invertebrates: A Synthesis.* 3rd ed. Malden, MA: Blackwell, 2001.

Brusca, Richard C., Gary J. Brusca, and Nancy Haver. *Invertebrates.* 2nd ed. Sunderland, MA: Sinauer, 2002.

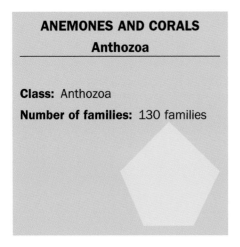

ANEMONES AND CORALS

Anthozoa

Class: Anthozoa

Number of families: 130 families

class

PHYSICAL CHARACTERISTICS

Anemones (uh-NEH-muh-nees) and corals are polyps (PAH-luhps), which are tubular sacs with a mouth and tentacles on a flattened upper surface called the oral disk. Most of these animals have stingers in their tentacles. The mouth and tentacles face up, and the base of the polyp is attached to the material on which the animal lives. The mouth opening leads into a digestive cavity. Hair-like fibers lining the digestive tract funnel water into the body. Anemones and corals live alone or in colonies. Solitary animals are commonly 0.5 to 2 inches (1.3 to 5 centimeters) in diameter at the oral disk, but the largest species grows to 3 feet (1 meter) across. The polyps of colonial species are typically smaller than those of anemones and corals that live alone, but the colonies themselves can be quite large. Anemones and corals look like flowers, bushes, feathers, fans, and even a brain.

Many species of anemones and corals make skeletons. In some of these species the living tissue lies above an outer skeleton made of calcium carbonate secreted by the outer layer of tissue. It is these skeletons that form the framework of tropical coral reefs. Other species secrete a flexible black inner skeleton that has thorns on its surface. Still other species secrete an inner skeleton made of calcium carbonate, a protein called gorgonin, or a combination of the two. Soft corals lack a supporting inner skeleton and can inflate or deflate by funneling water into or out of themselves.

GEOGRAPHIC RANGE

Anemones and corals live in oceans all over the world.

HABITAT

Anemones and corals live in the sea in areas that are exposed at low tide all the way to the deepest ocean. Solitary forms may be attached to a hard material or may burrow into soft bottom mud or sand. Colonies build a crust on hard surfaces or build massive skeletons. Reef-building corals usually live in clear, shallow, warm water, although a few species live in the cold, dark, deep sea.

DIET

Most anemones and corals eat plankton, or microscopic plants and animals drifting in water. Drifting prey are captured when they come in contact with the extended tentacles. Prey capture also may involve the firing of stingers. Many corals make slimy mucus that traps floating and sinking food particles. Large sea anemones may feed on crabs, clams and mussels, and fish. Many anemones and corals also receive nutrition from algae (AL-jee) living inside them. Algae are plantlike growths that live in water and have no true roots, stems, or leaves.

BEHAVIOR AND REPRODUCTION

Anemones and corals aggressively defend their space from neighboring animals of the same and different species. The tentacles used for defense are modified feeding tentacles. Some corals develop sweeper tentacles after prolonged contact with foreign species. These tentacles are five to ten times longer than feeding tentacles and have more stingers. The sweeper tentacles search an area around the coral polyp and cause tissue death in neighboring species on contact. Similar structures in sea anemones are called catch tentacles.

Several species of anemones and corals produce light when an intruder makes contact with the colony. This light may be a bright green flash from a tube or a wave of light across the colony as polyps flash in sequence from the point of contact. The light probably is used to startle predators.

Anemones and corals use asexual (ay-SEK-shuh-wuhl) or sexual reproduction. Sexual reproduction takes place with, and asexual reproduction takes place without, the uniting of egg and sperm and the transfer of DNA from two parents. For asexual reproduction anemone and coral polyps split either lengthwise or crosswise and form two new individuals. In many sea

CORAL REEFS

Coral polyps excrete, or discharge, a calcium carbonate shell around their bodies. As the animals die, the shells harden, and new polyps grow over them. After many years of this process, coral reefs form. Coral reefs are important to the environment because they support thousands of species of animals and plants and they protect the shore from the ocean. During the tsunami of December 2004 in the Indian Ocean, communities that were protected by coral reefs suffered much less damage than other communities. Human activities such as fishing, hotel construction, and pollution have damaged coral reefs.

anemones pieces of the base tear off or break free and develop into new individuals. After a free-living larva (LAR-vuh) settles, it transforms into a polyp that repeatedly divides to give rise to additional polyps, all of which remain connected by living tissue. A larva is an animal in an early stage that changes form before becoming an adult. In some species, buds may be released from the polyps of the parent colony, and these then settle and develop a new colony. For many hard corals, damage caused by storms or strong wave action produces fragments that grow into new colonies.

Depending on the species, anemones and corals have separate sexes or have both sexes in the same animal. Anemones and corals lack well-defined sex organs. Rather, the eggs and sperm accumulate in a layer of tissue. The eggs and sperm are shed into the body cavity and are either released through the mouth for fertilization (FUR-teh-lih-zay-shun), the joining of egg and sperm to start development, outside the body, or stay inside the animal for fertilization inside the body with release of the embryos through the mouth at a later time. Embryos of anemones and corals develop into larvae (LAR-vee) that may or may not feed and that can stay in open water for days to weeks.

One of the most spectacular behaviors of anemones and corals is the simultaneous release of sperm and eggs by many colonies over a wide area of coral reef. During these mass spawning events, huge slicks of eggs and sperm and developing larvae can be seen on the water surface, attracting a variety of predators that feed on the spawned eggs.

ANEMONES, CORALS, AND PEOPLE

Coral reefs are a major tourist destination and source of recreation. Corals provide a habitat for a variety of animals that humans use for food, such as fish, clams, and crabs. Anemones and corals are sold for home aquariums, and coral skeletons are used to make jewelry. Coral skeletons are used as building material and in bone grafts, because the structure of the coral skeleton is similar to that of human bone. Some corals produce compounds that have been harvested to make drugs for treating cancer.

CONSERVATION STATUS

The World Conservation Union (IUCN) lists two species of anemones and corals as Vulnerable, or facing high risk of extinction in the wild.

ANEMONES AND CLOWNFISH

Clownfish live with giant sea anemones in coral reefs. The anemone eats prey it paralyzes with poisonous stingers discharged from its tentacles. Clownfish are immune to the stingers and can nestle among the tentacles without harm. The bright colors and markings of the clownfish attract larger fish to the anemone. If they come too close, the larger fish are stung by the tentacles and eaten by the anemone. The clownfish shares in the meal.

Giant green anemone *(Anthopleura xanthogrammica)*

GIANT GREEN ANEMONE
Anthopleura xanthogrammica

Physical characteristics: Giant green anemones have a large, flat oral disk almost 10 inches (25 centimeters) in diameter. The body column is densely covered with hollow, sticky, wartlike bumps. The tentacles and disk are emerald green. The column is olive or brownish.

Geographic range: Giant green anemones live off the western coast of North America from Alaska to Baja California.

Habitat: Giant green anemones live in areas exposed at low tide where they are subject to strong wave action.

Diet: Giant green anemones feed on sea urchins, crabs, and mussels. These anemones benefit when urchins fleeing from predatory sea stars fall into their tentacles. They also obtain nutrients from algae that live in them.

Behavior and reproduction: Scientists do not know how giant green anemones behave. These animals have separate sexes and can reproduce when they are five to ten years old. The larvae eat algae. These anemones do not use asexual reproduction.

Giant green anemones and people: Giant green anemones produce toxins that stimulate human heart muscle and have been considered for medical use.

Conservation status: Giant green anemones are not threatened or endangered. ■

Giant green anemome benefit when urchins fleeing from predatory sea stars fall into their tentacles. (Jim Zipp/Photo Researchers, Inc.)

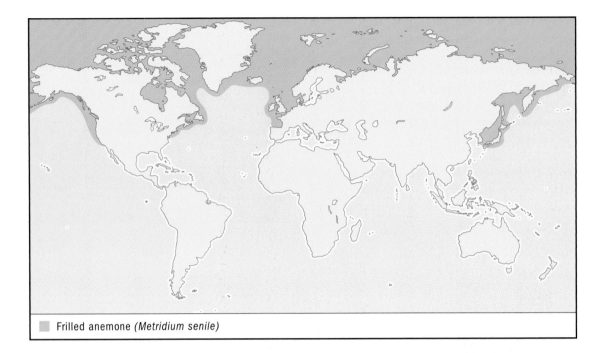

Frilled anemone *(Metridium senile)*

FRILLED ANEMONE
Metridium senile

Physical characteristics: Frilled anemones have hundreds to thousands of small, slender tentacles on a lobed crown, giving them a feathery appearance. They are about 12 inches (30 centimeters) tall. The body column is smooth with a distinct collar below the tentacles. The color varies from white to brownish orange.

Geographic range: Frilled anemones live in the Arctic region, and their range extends south to New Jersey, United States, in the western part of the Atlantic Ocean; Spain in the eastern part of the Atlantic; southern California, United States, in the eastern part of the Pacific Ocean; and South Korea in the western part of the Pacific.

Habitat: Frilled anemones attach themselves to rocks, shells, wood, and other hard materials in areas exposed at low tide to water as deep as 540 feet (165 meters).

Diet: Frilled anemones trap prey in mucus-coated tentacles. Prey include tiny crustaceans and the larvae of mollusks. Crustaceans

(krus-TAY-shuns) are water-dwelling animals that have jointed legs and a hard shell but no backbone. Mollusks (MAH-lusks) are animals with a soft, unsegmented body that may or may not have a shell.

Behavior and reproduction: Frilled anemones adjust the length of their body column to the flow of the current. They use catch tentacles equipped with stingers to attack other species in competition for their space. The tips of the catch tentacles remain attached to the victim. Frilled anemones have separate sexes. The males release sperm into the water, and fertilization takes place inside the female's body.

These anemones reproduce asexually by splitting in two or when a piece of the base breaks off and grows into a new individual.

Frilled anemones and people: Frilled anemones have no known importance to people.

Conservation status: Frilled anemones are not threatened or endangered. ■

■ Red coral (*Corallium rubrum*)

RED CORAL
Corallium rubrum

Physical characteristics: Red coral forms tree-shaped colonies. This coral has a red calcium carbonate skeleton almost 20 inches (50 centimeters) tall. Tiny hard rods are embedded in the outer part of the animal's body. Feeding tubes with eight tentacles can be completely withdrawn into the animal's tissue. Red coral also has tiny nonfeeding tubes that lack tentacles and contain the sex organs.

Geographic range: Red coral lives in the central and western parts of the Mediterranean Sea and in the Atlantic Ocean off the coast of southern Portugal and northern Africa.

Habitat: Red coral lives on cave walls, vertical cliffs, and overhangs in water 33 to 820 feet (10 to 250 meters) deep.

Diet: Red coral uses its tentacles to capture animal plankton. It also may directly absorb dissolved nutrients from the water through its outer layer of tissue.

Behavior and reproduction: Scientists do not know how red coral behaves. This coral has separate sexes. Male colonies release sperm that swim and are carried by currents to female colonies. Eggs are fertilized inside the females and develop inside for about thirty days. Nonfeeding larvae are released and swim for as long as fifteen days before settling. Red coral sometimes but rarely reproduces asexually.

Red coral and people: The skeleton of red coral is highly valued for jewelry. The ancient Phoenicians, Egyptians, and Romans used coral for trade. According to Greek legend, red coral confers magical powers such as defending ships against lightning and eliminating hatred from the home. Powdered coral skeleton is sold as an herbal medicine to treat digestive and other disorders.

Conservation status: Red coral is not threatened or endangered.   ■

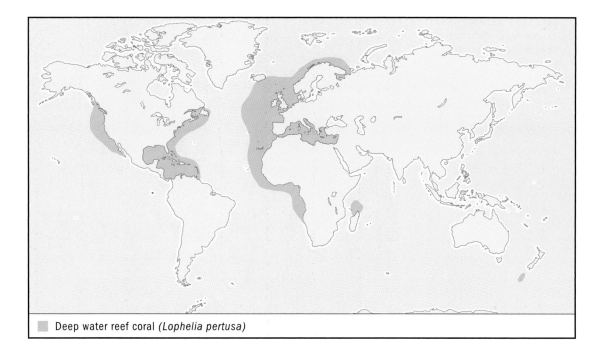

Deep water reef coral (*Lophelia pertusa*)

DEEP WATER REEF CORAL
Lophelia pertusa

Physical characteristics: Deep water reef coral is white or pink and forms irregularly branched bushy or treelike colonies up to 6 feet, 6 inches (2 meters) tall. The brittle tubular branches are about three-eighths to five-eighths inch (1 to 1.5 centimeters) thick.

Geographic range: Deep water reef coral lives in the Atlantic Ocean, the northwestern part of the Pacific Ocean, the Indian Ocean, and in the waters south of New Zealand.

Habitat: Deep water reef coral lives in cold, deep water on hard material. Colonies combine to build reefs and mounds as large as 660 feet (200 meters) high, 0.6 mile (1 kilometer) wide, and 3 miles (5 kilometers) long.

Diet: Deep water reef coral feeds on animal plankton.

Behavior and reproduction: Scientists do not know how deep water reef coral behaves or whether it uses sexual reproduction. Asexual

Deep water reef coral lives in cold, deep water on hard material. Colonies combine to build reefs and mounds as large as 660 feet (200 meters) high, 0.6 mile (1 kilometer) wide, and 3 miles (5 kilometers) long. (Illustration by Emily Damstra. Reproduced by permission.)

reproduction of new colonies occurs when the fragile branches break and fragments continue to grow.

Deep water reef coral and people: Deep water reef coral has no known importance to people.

Conservation status: Deep water reef coral is not threatened or endangered. ■

Black coral (*Antipathella fiordensis*)

BLACK CORAL
Antipathella fiordensis

Physical characteristics: Black coral grows in densely branched treelike colonies that reach a height of more than 16 feet (5 meters). The tiny white polyps are arranged in rows. Six tentacles surround a raised mouth. The skeleton is made of a black protein and is covered with spines.

Geographic range: Black coral lives only in waters near southwestern New Zealand.

Habitat: Black coral attaches itself to the walls of narrow inlets from the sea that are 13 to 328 feet (4 to 100 meters) deep.

Diet: Black coral eats animal plankton, which it captures by direct contact with its tentacles.

Behavior and reproduction: Black coral has sweeper tentacles that are up to eight times longer and more densely covered with stingers than other tentacles. The coral uses these tentacles in aggressive competition for space. Black coral has separate sexes. The male releases sperm into the water. After development inside the female, the larvae are born freely swimming.

Black coral and people: The skeleton of black coral is used to make jewelry.

Conservation status: Black coral is not threatened or endangered. ■

FOR MORE INFORMATION

Books:

Carson, Rachel. *The Edge of the Sea.* 1955. Reprint, Boston: Mariner, 1998.

Cousteau Society. *Corals: The Sea's Great Builders.* New York: Simon & Schuster, 1992.

Niesen, Thomas M. *The Marine Biology Coloring Book.* 2nd ed. New York: HarperResource, 2000.

Wells, Sue, and Nick Hanna. *The Greenpeace Book of Coral Reefs.* New York: Sterling, 1992.

Web sites:

"About Coral and Coral Reefs." Coral Reef Adventure. http://www.coralfilm.com/about.html (accessed on January 24, 2005).

"Conservationists Fear Worst over Tsunami Damage, Urge Lessons to be Learned." *Terradaily.* http://www.terradaily.com/2005/050109021602.j5xmgg5g.html (accessed on January 31, 2005).

"Corals and Anemones." Sea and Sky. http://www.seasky.org/reeflife/sea2b.html (accessed on January 25, 2005).

"Welcome to Corals." National Oceanic and Atmospheric Administration. http://www.nos.noaa.gov/education/kits/corals/welcome.html (accessed on January 25, 2005).

Class: Hydrozoa

Number of families: 114 families

class

phylum

◆ **class**

subclass

order

monotypic order

suborder

family

PHYSICAL CHARACTERISTICS

Hydroids (HIGH-droyds) have two body forms. One is the medusa (mi-DOO-suh), a jelly-like, umbrella-shaped, freely swimming form with a mouth and tentacles that face down. The other is a colony of polyps (PAH-luhps), or tube-shaped sacs that have a mouth and tentacles that face up. The polyp form is fixed to the material on which it lives. Most hydroids have both a medusa and a polyp stage.

Medusae (mi-DOO-see, the plural of medusa) have a typical and easily recognizable body shape. The shape of polyps ranges from giant coral-like colonies through feathers and flowers to microscopic balls of tissue. The umbrella of medusae can be one–sixty-fourth of an inch to more than 6 feet (500 microm-eters to 2 meters) in diameter. The medusae and polyps of most hydroids are clear and filmy. Among colored species, the color often comes from the food the hydroids eat. The most common color is red from crustaceans (krus-TAY-shuns), which are water-dwelling animals, such as shrimp, that have jointed legs and a hard shell but no backbone. Other colors are green, white, orange, yellow, blue, and purple.

Hydroid colonies are made up of different types of polyps that work together to serve the entire colony. One type catches prey and defends the colony's territory. Another type takes the prey from the catcher-defenders and swallows and digests it. A third type of polyp is in charge of reproduction.

GEOGRAPHIC RANGE

Hydroids live all over the world.

HABITAT

Hydroids live in all water habitats, from sea caves to deep-sea trenches, from lakes and ponds to rocky coasts and between grains of sand.

DIET

Hydroid polyps and medusae feed on almost all animals, from plankton, or microscopic plants and animals drifting in water, to fish.

BEHAVIOR AND REPRODUCTION

Some medusae remain immobile in the water, their tentacles outstretched, ambushing their prey. Others cruise across the water to catch their prey. Polyps simply extend their tentacles to catch passing prey. They also form currents by moving their tentacles to direct food particles toward their mouths.

Polyps compete for space and defend their territory. Medusae are sharply individual but can be gathered by winds and currents to form large swarms. When hungry, both polyps and medusae are always in search of food. When the body cavity is full of food, the tentacles usually are contracted, showing that these animals probably can control their stinger discharge.

Most polyps have separate sexes. Males release sperm in the water, and the sperm swim toward eggs that are on the female's body. Fertilization (FUR-teh-lih-ZAY-shun), the joining of egg and sperm to start development, usually takes place inside the female's body, and she releases the larvae (LAR-vee) into the water, where they fall to the bottom and settle near the parent colony. Larvae are animals in an early stage that change form before becoming adults.

Among medusae, males release sperm and females release eggs in the water, where fertilization occurs and larvae develop. The larvae reproduce asexually by budding, or producing bumps that develop to full size and then break off to live as new individuals. Asexual (ay-SEK-shuh-wuhl) means without, and sexual means with, the uniting of egg and sperm for the transfer of DNA from two parents. Therefore, a single larva that develops from a bud produces a polyp colony that in its turn produces many adult medusae.

WHAT'S IN A NAME?

The words hydroid and medusa come from Greek myth. The hydra was the many-headed monster that fought Hercules, who would cut off a head only to see two heads replace it. Medusa was one of the gorgons, three snake-haired sisters who would turn anyone who looked at them to stone.

HYDROIDS AND PEOPLE

The medusae of hydroids prey on the eggs and larvae of fish that people need for food. Some hydroids are used for scientific research. Others inhibit the functioning of power plants by clogging their pipes and reduce the speed of ships by attaching themselves to their hulls. Some medusae and polyp colonies inflict severe stings on humans.

CONSERVATION STATUS

Hydroids are not threatened or endangered.

FIRE CORAL
Millepora alcicornis

Physical characteristics: The polyps of fire coral colonies form massive, horn-shaped, upright branches. Large feeding polyps are surrounded by smaller catching-defending polyps. The feeding polyps are short and stout, with four to six short tentacles around the mouth. The catching-defending polyps are long, slender, and mouthless. The reproductive polyps are embedded in the surface of the coral. Fire coral is usually yellow or brown with white tips. The medusae of fire coral do not have tentacles and live for only a short time.

Geographic range: Fire coral lives in the Pacific and Indian oceans and in the Red and Caribbean seas. Specific distribution map not available.

Habitat: Fire coral lives on ledges and reefs in water less than 98 feet (30 meters) deep.

Diet: Fire coral feeds on animal plankton, mostly crustaceans.

Behavior and reproduction: Scientists do not know how fire coral behaves. It reproduces by the budding of tiny medusae from the polyp colony. These medusae live only a few hours, but before dying, they

The polyps of fire coral colonies form massive, horn-shaped, upright branches. Large feeding polyps are surrounded by smaller catching-defending polyps. (David Hall/Photo Researchers, Inc.)

release eggs and sperm. Fertilization occurs in the water, and larvae develop, settle, and form new colonies.

Fire coral and people: The stings of fire coral cause severe burns.

Conservation status: Fire coral is not threatened or endangered. ∎

NO COMMON NAME
Distichopora violacea

Physical characteristics: *Distichopora violacea* (abbreviated as *D. violacea*) lives as a polyp colony that looks like coral. It is purple with white tips. There are an equal number of catching-defending polyps on both sides of a row of irregularly shaped holes on the surface of the colony.

Geographic range: *D. violacea* lives in the Indian and Pacific oceans and in the Red Sea. Specific distribution map not available.

Habitat: *D. violacea* lives in shallow seawater.

Diet: Scientists do not know what *D. violacea* eats.

Behavior and reproduction: Scientists do not know how *D. violacea* behaves or reproduces.

***Distichopora violacea* and people:** *D. violacea* has no known importance to people.

Conservation status: *D. violacea* is not threatened or endangered. ■

Distichopora violacea *is a vivid purple, growing here under a ledge near Lizard Island, North Great Barrier Reef, Australia. (Photograph by Leslie Newman and Andrew Flowers. Reproduced by permission.)*

NO COMMON NAME
Aglantha digitale

Physical characteristics: *Aglantha digitale* (abbrviated as *A. digitale*) is a medusa with a cylindrical umbrella that is about three-eighths of an inch to 1.5 inches (10 to 40 millimeters) high. The umbrella is about twice as tall as it is wide and has a small cone at the top. The mouth has four simple lips. Eight long, sausage-shaped sex glands hang freely inside the hydroid just under the top of the umbrella. *A. digitale* has eighty or more very short tentacles at the base of its umbrella.

Geographic range: *A. digitale* lives in the Arctic Ocean and in the northern parts of the Atlantic and Pacific oceans. Specific distribution map not available.

Habitat: *A. digitale* lives in the open ocean from the surface down to about 2000 feet (600 meters).

Diet: *A. digitale* eats animal plankton.

Aglangha digitale *lives in the Arctic Ocean and in the northern parts of the Atlantic and Pacific oceans. (Illustration by Emily Damstra. Reproduced by permission.)*

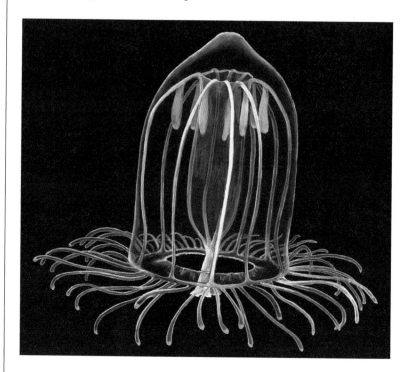

Behavior and reproduction: *A. digitale* uses its entire umbrella for jet propulsion. Males release sperm and females release eggs into the water. When fertilization occurs, a free-floating larva develops.

***Aglantha digitale* and people:**   *A. digitale* has no known importance to people.

Conservation status: *A. digitale* is not threatened or endangered.   ■

NO COMMON NAME
Aequorea victoria

Physical characteristics: The polyp colonies of *Aequorea victoria* (abbreviated as *A. victoria*) are small and unbranched and have creeping stems. The outer covering is thin and has a cap made of many flaps. The colony of *A. victoria* has twenty tentacles connected by a membrane at the base. The medusae of *A. victoria* are small when they leave the polyp colony, having only two tentacles and four canals. They can grow up to almost 5 inches (13 centimeters) wide and 1.5 inches (4 centimeters) high with as many as 150 tentacles. The umbrella is saucer to half-dome shaped, and the mouth is fringed.

Geographic range: *A. victoria* lives in the northeastern part of the Pacific Ocean. Specific distribution map not available.

Habitat: The polyp colonies of *A. victoria* grow on mussel shells. The medusae are plankton in the coastal and open parts of the sea.

Diet: Scientists do not know what the polyp colonies of *A. victoria* eat. The medusae feed on fish larvae and on jellylike plankton.

Behavior and reproduction: *A. victoria* secretes, or gives off, a protein that produces a blue light when it reacts with the calcium in seawater. The polyp form and newly released medusae are tiny and rarely seen. Medusa production is very intense, because the species is found in swarms. The eggs and sperm released by these swarms of medusae produce great quantities of larvae.

Aequorea victoria secretes a protein that produces a blue light when it reacts with the calcium in seawater. The polyp form and newly released medusae are tiny and rarely seen. (© Mick McMurray/SeaPics.com)

***Aequorea victoria* and people:** The light-producing protein secreted by *A. victoria* is used to measure cellular levels of calcium.

Conservation status: *A. victoria* is not threatened or endangered. ∎

PORTUGUESE MAN OF WAR
Physalia physalis

Physical characteristics: A Portuguese man of war colony consists of a large, purplish blue gas-filled balloon that floats on the sea surface carrying the polyps. The balloon can reach a length of almost 12 inches (30 centimeters). A sail running lengthwise along the top of the balloon allows the man of war to move with the wind. The polyps form clusters at the mouth end of the balloon. Each cluster has a reproductive polyp and a feeding-defending polyp. Each feeding-defending polyp

A Portuguese man of war colony consists of a large, purplish blue gas-filled balloon that floats on the sea surface carrying the polyps. The balloon can reach a length of almost 12 inches (30 centimeters). A sail running lengthwise along the top of the balloon allows the man of war to move with the wind. (© Peter Scoones/Photo Researchers, Inc.)

has a tentacle covered with extremely poisonous stingers. The tentacles can be several yards (meters) long.

Geographic range: Portuguese men of war live in the warm waters of the Pacific, Indian, and Atlantic oceans and in the Mediterranean Sea. Specific distribution map not available.

Habitat: Portuguese men of war live at the surface of the ocean. They frequently are blown ashore by strong winds.

Diet: Portuguese men of war eat plankton and small fish that they kill with their tentacles.

Behavior and reproduction: Portuguese men of war gather in large groups called navies. The sail on a man of war is either right-oriented or left-oriented, much as people are right-handed or left-handed. The wind moves "left-handed" men of war to the right and right-handed men of war to the left. Portuguese men of war have separate sexes and release their eggs and sperm into the sea, where fertilization occurs and larvae develop. The larvae bud and grow into adults that reproduce sexually.

Portuguese men of war and people: Portuguese men of war inflict very painful stings on swimmers who become tangled in their tentacles and on waders who step on them.

Conservation status: Portuguese men of war are not threatened or endangered. ■

FOR MORE INFORMATION

Books:

Carson, Rachel. *The Edge of the Sea.* 1955. Reprint, Boston: Mariner, 1998.

Niesen, Thomas M. *The Marine Biology Coloring Book.* 2nd ed. New York: HarperResource, 2000.

Web sites:

Borneman, Eric. "Venomous Corals: The Fire Corals." *Reefkeeping.* http://www.reefkeeping.com/issues/2002-11/eb/ (accessed on January 26, 2005).

"Introduction to Hydrozoa." University of California, Berkeley, Museum of Paleontology. http://www.ucentimetersp.berkeley.edu/cnidaria/hydrozoa.html (accessed on December 17, 2004).

"Portuguese Man-of-War (Bluebottle—*Physalia spp*—Hydroid)." Hawaiian Lifeguard Association. http://www.aloha.com/ lifeguards/portugue.html (accessed on January 27, 2005).

phylum
◆ **class**
subclass
order
monotypic order
suborder
family

PHYSICAL CHARACTERISTICS

Box jellies have a cube-shaped body, or bell, also called an umbrella. The mouth is inside the bell. Tentacles are attached to each of the four lower corners of the bell. Some box jellies have several tentacles attached to each corner, and others have only one tentacle at each corner. A structure near the base of the bell contains one balance organ and six eyes.

GEOGRAPHIC RANGE

Box jellies live in warm coastal waters worldwide.

HABITAT

Box jellies live over sand just above the sea bottom during the day and move toward the surface at night.

DIET

Box jellies eat fish and crustaceans (krus-TAY-shuns), which are water-dwelling animals that have jointed legs and a hard shell but no backbone.

BEHAVIOR AND REPRODUCTION

Because box jellies can see, they are difficult to study because they react to the presence of their human observers by swimming away. Box jellies are active swimmers capable of moving 10 to 20 feet (3 to 6 meters) per minute. They move toward light and are active during the day and night, although they may feed only during the night or predawn hours.

The life history of box jellies has two stages: bottom-dwelling polyp and freely swimming medusa. A polyp (PAH-luhp) is a body type that consists of a tubular sac with a mouth and tentacles on the top. The medusa (mi-DOO-suh) is the tentacled, jelly-like, umbrella-shaped body form. The eggs and sperm from male and female medusae (mi-DOO-see, the plural of medusa) are released into the water and combine outside the body to form a larva (LAR-vuh), or early stage of the animal that changes form before becoming an adult. The larva settles on the bottom and becomes a polyp. The entire polyp of a box jelly becomes the young medusa.

BOX JELLIES AND PEOPLE

Box jellies are often known as "killer box jellies," although only one type, the sea wasp, is lethal to humans.

CONSERVATION STATUS

Box jellies are not threatened or endangered.

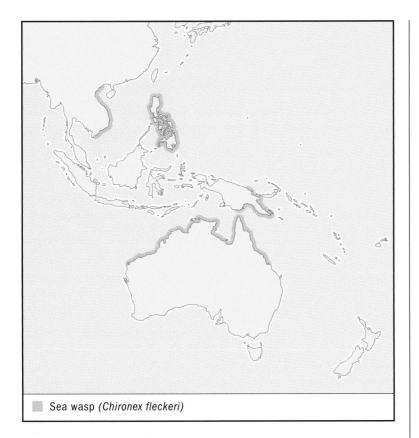

Sea wasp (*Chironex fleckeri*)

SEA WASP
Chironex fleckeri

Physical characteristics: Sea wasps reach a diameter of about 12 inches (30 centimeters) but because they are transparent, they are difficult to see despite their large size. There are as many as fifteen tentacles in each corner of a sea wasp, and the tentacles can be as long as 98 feet (30 meters).

Geographic range: Sea wasps live in waters on the northern shore of Australia, on the coast of Papua New Guinea, around the Philippines, and on the coast of Vietnam.

Habitat: Sea wasps live in shallow seawater near the coast.

Diet: Sea wasps eat fish and shrimp.

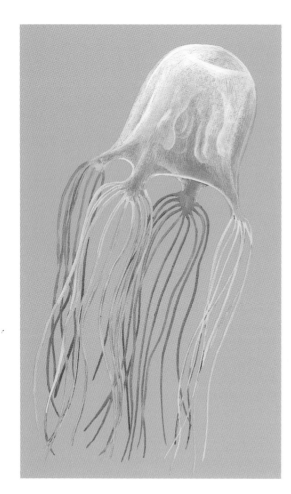

Sea wasps reach a diameter of about 12 inches (30 centimeters) but because they are transparent, they are difficult to see despite their large size. (Illustration by John Megahan. Reproduced by permission.)

Behavior and reproduction: Sea wasps swim around pier pilings. Polyps have been found in mangrove swamps and river outlets, but scientists do not know how the larvae (LAR-vee, the plural of larva) find their way to these locations. Polyps start to transform into medusae in the spring and continue until the rainy season, when they are flushed out into the ocean.

Sea wasps and people: The venom of sea wasps causes nerve, heart, and skin damage. Death occurs very quickly. Antivenin is available but must be administered rapidly. Vinegar can be used to remove undischarged stingers.

Conservation status: Sea wasps are not threatened or endangered. ■

FOR MORE INFORMATION

Books:

Aaseng, Nathan. *Invertebrates.* New York: Venture, 1993.

Periodicals:

Seymour, Jamie. "One Touch of Venom: A Box Jellyfish Is a Killer." *Natural History* (September 2002): 72–75.

Web sites:

"Sea Wasp." Extreme Science. http://www.extremescience.com/ DeadliestCreature.htm (accessed on January 28, 2005).

Class: Scyphozoa

Number of families: 20 families

class

CHAPTER

PHYSICAL CHARACTERISTICS

Jellyfish have one or both of two body forms: bottom-dwelling polyp and freely swimming medusa. The medusa (mi-DOO-suh) is the jelly-like, usually bell- or umbrella-shaped, usually tentacled form. The polyp (PAH-luhp) consists of a tubular sac with a mouth and tentacles on top. Polyps are less than one-eighth inch (4 millimeters) long. Medusae (mi-DOO-see, the plural of medusa) can be as large as 80 inches (2 meters) in diameter. Near the edge of the bell most jellyfish have tentacles used for feeding. The tentacles have millions of stingers that inject toxin into or entangle their prey. Some jellyfish have hundreds of these tentacles. Rather than tentacles, some jellyfish have mouth arms on the underside of the bell. These arms also have stingers for feeding. Other jellyfish have one thick tentacle on the upper surface of the bell. Some jellyfish have a stalk that they attach to seaweed or sea grasses. Stalked jellyfish have eight arms, each bearing a cluster of as many as one hundred short, clubbed tentacles.

GEOGRAPHIC RANGE

Jellyfish live in all the oceans of the world.

HABITAT

Jellyfish medusae live in seawater from shore areas exposed at low tide to the very deep ocean. The polyps are attached to hard surfaces, such as rocks, shells, and plants, at various depths.

phylum

● **class**

subclass

order

monotypic order

suborder

family

DIET

Jellyfish eat plankton, which is microscopic plants and animals drifting in water; fish eggs and larvae (LAR-vee), or young animals that must change form before becoming adults; other jellies; and small crustaceans (krus-TAY-shuns), which are water-dwelling animals that have jointed legs and a hard shell but no backbone.

BEHAVIOR AND REPRODUCTION

The most noticeable behavior of jellyfish is rhythmic pulsing of the swimming bell, which moves them through the water. The swimming pulsations are coordinated by nerve centers around the edge of the bell. Medusae can sense light and dark and can determine their orientation in the water. Some jellyfish swim continuously. This feature is important for oxygen exchange, which occurs over the entire body surface, and for feeding. Several species swim against the current. The result is that they all swim in the same direction and may become concentrated in large masses. Some species move up in the water at night and down in the day. The polyps can move using a "foot" and its extensions.

Most jellyfish catch prey by the tentacles and fold the arm inward to bring the prey to the mouth. Many jellyfish do not swim actively while feeding but remain nearly motionless with their tentacles extended above the bell. For some medusae, the pulsations of the swimming bell force water through the tentacles and create whirlpools that bring prey into contact with the tentacles and oral arms.

Jellyfish use both asexual and sexual reproduction. Asexual (ay-SEK-shuh-wuhl) means without, while sexual means with the uniting of egg and sperm for the transfer of DNA from two parents. The bottom-dwelling forms of some jellyfish reproduce asexually by budding new polyps from the body or foot. Polyps also produce medusae by another asexual budding process that takes place at a certain time of year and is triggered by environmental factors, such as changes in temperature or light level. During this process the polyp splits in two and forms one to several small medusae. The fully formed medusae break free by swimming pulsations and grow to adults over the course of a month or longer.

The medusae of most species have separate sexes, but in a few species the same animal makes both eggs and sperm. No mating occurs. Sperm strands are released into the water by males and are taken up by females during feeding. In most species the fertilized (FUR-teh-lyzed) eggs, those that have united with sperm, develop into small larvae that swim to a suitable bottom material, attach, and develop into polyps. Some species lack a polyp stage.

JELLYFISH AND PEOPLE

All jellyfish sting, but the stings of small animals and those with short tentacles often are not painful to humans. Jellyfish can be a nuisance to people who catch or farm fish and sell it for food. Besides damaging the fish caught in nets, large masses of jellyfish tear the nets. Jellyfish break up on the enclosures of fish farms and sting and kill the fish. Jellyfish are also an important food in Japan and China, and fishing for cannonball jellyfish has started in the Gulf of Mexico.

CONSERVATION STATUS

Jellyfish are not threatened or endangered.

HOLD THE PEANUT BUTTER

In some parts of the world the swimming bell of jellyfish is processed in a mixture of salt and a preservative and packaged. The semidried jellyfish is rehydrated, desalted, boiled briefly, and served in a variety of dishes. The prepared jellyfish has a special crunchy texture.

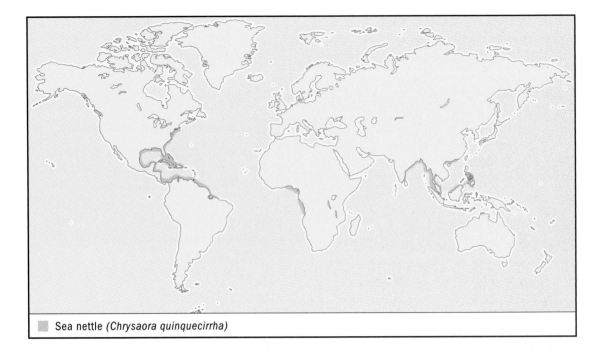

Sea nettle (*Chrysaora quinquecirrha*)

SPECIES ACCOUNTS

SEA NETTLE
Chrysaora quinquecirrha

Physical characteristics: The swimming bell of sea nettles can reach 10 inches (25 centimeters) in diameter, but most sea nettles are much smaller. The edges of the swimming bell are petal shaped. One large tentacle emerges from between the petals, and twice as many small tentacles arise from beneath the petals. Eight sense structures are present in alternate spaces between the petals. The narrow oral arms are long and filmy. The colors of medusae range from milky white to white with radiating purplish red stripes on the bell.

Geographic range: Sea nettles live on both sides of the Atlantic Ocean, in the Indian Ocean, and in the eastern part of the Pacific Ocean.

Habitat: Sea nettle medusae live in estuaries (EHS-chew-AIR-eez), the areas where rivers meet the sea.

Diet: Sea nettle medusae eat small crustaceans, comb jellies, and fish eggs and larvae. The polyps eat oyster larvae.

Behavior and reproduction: Sea nettle medusae swim constantly in slow circles. They feed continuously. The life cycle of sea nettles has both a polyp and a medusa stage. The release of eggs and sperm takes place around dawn.

Sea nettles and people: Sea nettles have an irritating sting.

Conservation status: Sea nettles are not threatened or endangered. ■

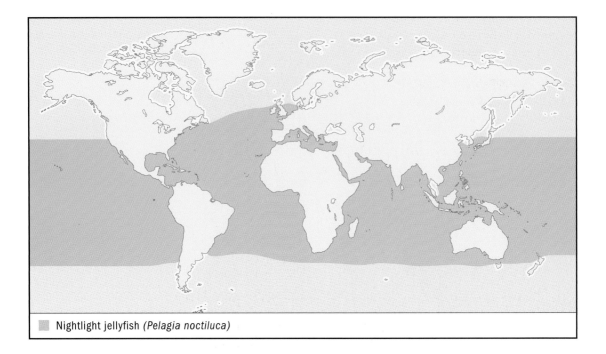

Nightlight jellyfish *(Pelagia noctiluca)*

NIGHTLIGHT JELLYFISH
Pelagia noctiluca

Physical characteristics: The swimming bell of a nightlight jellyfish usually is less than 3.5 inches (9 centimeters) in diameter. It has a bumpy surface caused by clusters of stinging cells, which give a purple or yellowish color to the bell. Four long oral arms and eight long tentacles alternate with eight sense structures in the spaces between folds on the bell. There is no polyp stage.

Geographic range: Nightlight jellyfish live in the Atlantic and Pacific oceans and in the Mediterranean Sea.

Habitat: Nightlight jellyfish live in surface waters of the open ocean but sometimes are carried on the current into shallow coastal waters.

Diet: Nightlight jellyfish eat animal plankton.

Behavior and reproduction: The medusae of nightlight jellyfish emit a blue-green light when they are touched or injured. Mucus released from the damaged area continues to glow, so that at night the jellyfish look like glowing balls in a boat's wake. Nightlight jellyfish do not have a polyp stage. The larvae develop without ever settling on the bottom.

Nightlight jellyfish and people: Nightlight jellyfish have a painful sting, which can cause a severe reaction.

Conservation status: Nightlight jellyfish are not threatened or endangered. ■

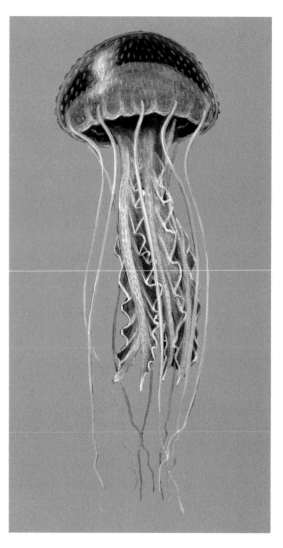

The medusae of nightlight jellyfish emit a blue-green light when they are touched or injured. Mucus released from the damaged area continues to glow, so that at night the jellyfish look like glowing balls. (Illustration by Joseph E. Trumpey. Reproduced by permission.)

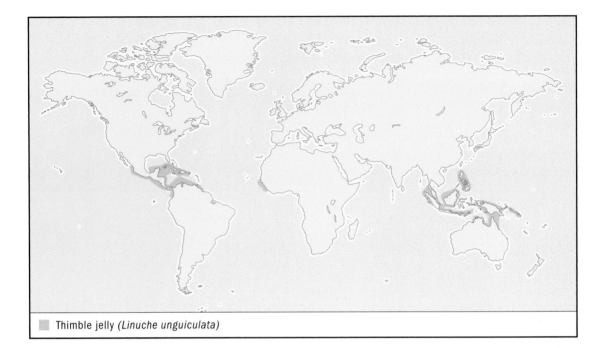

Thimble jelly (*Linuche unguiculata*)

THIMBLE JELLY
Linuche unguiculata

Physical characteristics: The medusae of thimble jellies are only 1 inch (2.5 centimeters) high. These jellies are shaped like a thimble, which is a hard cap some people put on a fingertip while sewing. There is a shallow groove near the top of the bell. Thimble jellies have eight very short tentacles and eight sense structures alternating between sixteen folds at the bell margin. The outside of the bell is transparent and has numerous warts of stinging cells. The inner part of the bell is white with greenish brown spots. The polyps form colonies and are covered by a thin, hard sheath.

Geographic range: Thimble jellies live in oceans all over the world.

Habitat: The medusae of thimble jellies live near the surface in warm near-shore waters. The polyps live on coral rubble.

Diet: The medusae of thimble jellies catch a variety of animal plankton on their folds. The colored spots in the bell are filled with algae that transfer nutrients to the medusa. Algae (AL-jee) are plantlike growths that live in water and have no true roots, stems, or leaves.

Behavior and reproduction: Thimble jellies usually live in large groups just beneath the surface. They are very active swimmers, moving in circles. The fertilized eggs of thimble jellies form large larvae that live as plankton for three to four weeks. They settle and form an unbranched colony of polyps. Each polyp can produce as many as forty medusae.

Thimble jellies and people: Stings from the larvae or new medusae of thimble jellies cause a disorder called seabather's eruption. This disorder is characterized by a prickling sensation and red bumps that last for seven to twelve days. It is irritating but not dangerous and becomes worse when the jellies become trapped under a swimsuit.

Conservation status: Thimble jellies are not threatened or endangered.   ■

FOR MORE INFORMATION

Books:

Byatt, Andrew, Alastair Fothergill, and Martha Holmes. *The Blue Planet.* New York: DK, 2001.

Garcia, Eulalia. *Jellyfish: Animals with a Deadly Touch.* Milwaukee, WI: Gareth Stevens, 1997.

Niesen, Thomas M. *The Marine Biology Coloring Book.* 2nd ed. New York: HarperResource, 2000.

Web sites:

"Frequently Asked Questions about Stinging Marine Organisms." Safesea.net. http://www.safesea.net/faq.cfm?cfid=4949282&cftoken=87834841 (accessed on December 17, 2004).

"Things You May Have Been Wondering about Jellies." The Jellies Zone. http://jellieszone.com/jelliesfaq.htm (accessed on January 28, 2005).

phylum
CHAPTER

PHYSICAL CHARACTERISTICS

The body of a comb jelly consists of two clear tissue layers that enclose a jellylike layer. Comb jellies can be as small as a berry or long and ribbon shaped. The outside of the body is covered with eight rows of short fibers that look like the teeth of a comb. The combs are used for swimming and emit flashes of light. Comb jellies have tentacles that do not have stingers but are covered with sticky structures used to capture prey. These animals have a balancing organ that consists of a hard center covered with hairlike fibers. This organ is attached to the comb rows. The digestive system has two openings, but elimination of waste out the anus (AY-nuhs) is rare. Defecation of undigested material occurs primarily through the mouth.

GEOGRAPHIC RANGE

Comb jellies live in all of the oceans of the world.

HABITAT

Most comb jellies live in open ocean. Some live at the bottom.

DIET

Comb jellies eat animal plankton or microscopic animals drifting in water, other jellies, crustaceans, mollusks, and fish larvae. Crustaceans (krus-TAY-shuns) are water-dwelling animals that have jointed legs and a hard shell but no backbone. Mollusks (MAH-lusks) are animals with a soft, unsegmented body that may or may not have a shell. Larvae (LAR-vee) are animals in an early stage that must change form before becoming adults.

■ **phylum**
class
subclass
order
monotypic order
suborder
family

BEHAVIOR AND REPRODUCTION

Comb jellies control water flow around themselves for movement by jet propulsion and "flying," for the capture and eating of prey, and for escaping from predators. Comb jellies either actively seek their prey or wait in ambush for it. Their long tentacles have muscular cores and a covering that contains sticky cells. The tentacles trail through the water or are twirled about by various circular movements of the body. When the tentacles touch prey, the sticky cells burst and discharge a strong, sticky material. Comb jellies that have very short tentacles trap plankton in mucus on their body surface, and the particles are carried to the jelly's mouth by currents produced by hairlike fibers.

Most comb jellies make both eggs and sperm. Only a few species have separate sexes. Most comb jellies release their eggs and sperm into the water. Fertilization (FUR-teh-lih-ZAY-shun), or the joining of egg and sperm to start development, takes place outside the body. In some species, however, fertilization takes place inside the body. Almost all comb jellies fertilize (FUR-teh-lyze) themselves. The larvae swim freely during their transformation into adults.

COMB JELLIES AND PEOPLE

Some comb jellies are harmful to fish that are caught and sold for food.

CONSERVATION STATUS

Comb jellies are not threatened or endangered.

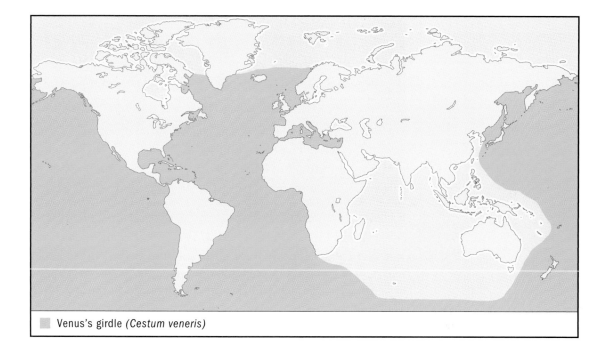

Venus's girdle (*Cestum veneris*)

VENUS'S GIRDLE
Cestum veneris

Physical characteristics: Venus's girdles are ribbon shaped, reaching a length of almost 5 feet (1.5 meters) but a width of only about 3 inches (8 centimeters). The comb rows are all on one side of the ribbon, and the mouth is on the other side.

Geographic range: Venus's girdles live in the Atlantic and Pacific oceans, Antarctic waters, and the Mediterranean Sea.

Habitat: Venus's girdles live in the surface waters of the sea.

Diet: Venus's girdles eat small crustaceans and mollusks.

Behavior and reproduction: Venus's girdles swim across the water 3 to 6 feet (1 to 2 meters) before moving up or down 2 to 4 inches (5 to 10 centimeters) and reversing direction. Using this behavior, the Venus's girdle retraces its original path but 2 to 4 inches (5 to 10 centimeters) above or below it. A Venus's girdle captures prey on tentacles lying over its body, and the combs generate small whirlpools

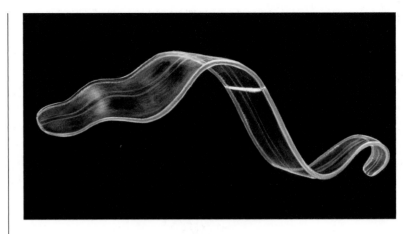

that may increase prey movement and capture as the Venus's girdle moves back and forth through the water. Venus's girdles have an escape behavior that consists of snakelike movements of the long body that allow the animal to move several body lengths in seconds. Venus's girdles make both eggs and sperm, which they release into the water for fertilization and development of larvae outside the body.

Venus's girdles and people: Venus's girdles have no known importance to people.

Conservation status: Venus's girdles are not threatened or endangered. ∎

SEA WALNUT
Mnemiopsis leidyi

Physical characteristics: Sea walnuts reach a length of about 4 inches (10 centimeters). Four deep furrows run from the top to bottom of the animal.

Geographic range: Sea walnuts live off the eastern shores of North and South America and have been introduced into the Black Sea.

Habitat: Sea walnuts live in shallow waters near shore and in bays and estuaries (EHS-chew-AIR-eez), the areas where rivers meet the sea.

Diet: Sea walnuts eat barnacle larvae, tiny crustaceans, fish eggs and larvae, and other animal plankton.

Behavior and reproduction: Sea walnuts spend most of their time actively swimming. Scientists do not know how sea walnuts reproduce.

Sea walnuts and people: Accidental introduction of sea walnuts into the Black Sea during the 1970s caused the collapse of fishing in

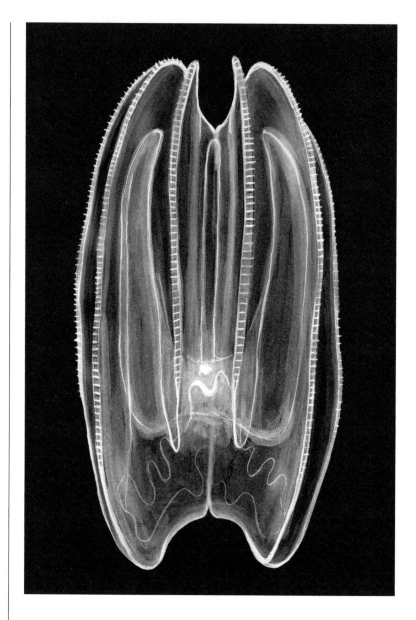

that area, and many people lost their jobs. The fish could not survive because the sea walnuts had eaten their food. To control the invader, scientists brought in another species of comb jelly—one that feeds on sea walnuts. By 2004 sea walnuts had invaded the Caspian Sea, and scientists were considering the same means of control.

Conservation status: Sea walnuts are not threatened or endangered. ▪

FOR MORE INFORMATION

Books:

Carson, Rachel. *The Edge of the Sea.* 1955. Reprint, Boston: Mariner, 1998.

Niesen, Thomas M. *The Marine Biology Coloring Book.* 2nd ed. New York: HarperResource, 2000.

Silverstein, Alvin, Virginia Silverstein, and Robert Silverstein. *Invertebrates.* New York: Twenty-First Century, 1996.

Web sites:

"'Alien' Jellyfish Threatening Caspian Sea." U.N. Wire. http://www.unwire .org/UNWire/20040310/449_13861.asp (accessed on January 29, 2005).

Amos, William H. "Venus's Girdle." Microscopy-UK. http://www.microscopy-uk.org.uk/mag/indexmag.html?http://www.microscopy-uk.org.uk/mag/artmay04/wavenus.html (accessed on January 29, 2005).

Mills, C. E. "Ctenophores." University of Washington. http://faculty .washington.edu/cemills/Ctenophores.html (accessed on January 29, 2005).

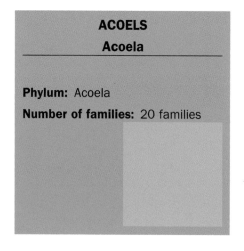

ACOELS

Acoela

Phylum: Acoela
Number of families: 20 families

phylum

CHAPTER

■ **phylum**

class

subclass

order

monotypic order

suborder

family

PHYSICAL CHARACTERISTICS

Acoels (AY-seels) are tiny wormlike sea animals. They are the simplest animals with bilateral symmetry (bye-LAT-er-uhl SIH-muh-tree), meaning the right and left halves of the body match each other. Most acoels are no longer than about one-sixteenth of an inch (2 millimeters), although one species can reach a length of about five-eighths inch (15 millimeters). The bodies of acoels are flat ovals.

Acoels have either a simple mouth or none at all. The mouth is on the bottom of the animal. Acoels have no digestive tract, no system for eliminating waste or balancing salt content in their cells, and no reproductive organs. The nervous system is a loose net of fibers strung throughout the body. Most acoels have simple eyes. Almost all acoels have an organ for balance and for adjusting themselves to their surroundings.

GEOGRAPHIC RANGE

Acoels live in all the oceans of the world.

HABITAT

Acoels live in shallow coastal seawater. Some drift or swim in open water, and others live among sand grains on the sea bottom. A few species live on other invertebrates (in-VER-teh-brehts), or animals without a backbone. Some acoels live on Antarctic ice floes.

DIET

Acoels eat algae, plankton, and waste material. Algae (AL-jee) are plantlike growths that live in water and have no true roots, stems, or leaves. Plankton is microscopic plants and animals drifting in water.

BEHAVIOR AND REPRODUCTION

Acoels move by using tiny hairlike fibers that cover the entire outside of their bodies. Acoels use sexual reproduction, although some species also use asexual reproduction by splitting in two, by breaking off part of the female's body, or by budding. Asexual (ay-SEK-shuh-wuhl) means without and sexual means with the uniting of egg and sperm for the transfer of DNA from two parents. In budding a bump develops on the animal, grows to full size, and then breaks off to live as a new individual. Acoels have no distinct reproductive organs. Eggs and sperm form directly in the middle tissue layer.

ACOELS AND PEOPLE

Acoels have no known importance to people.

CONSERVATION STATUS

Acoels are not threatened or endangered.

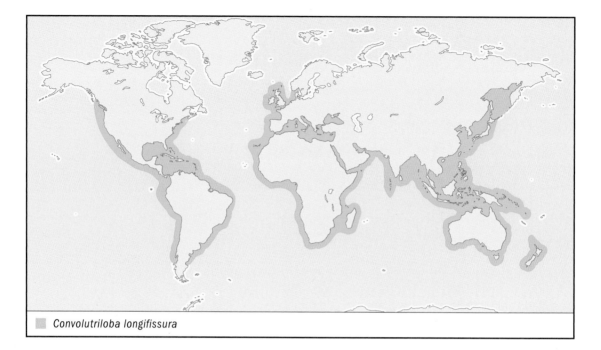

Convolutriloba longifissura

SPECIES ACCOUNT

NO COMMON NAME
Convolutriloba longifissura

Physical characteristics: *Convolutriloba longifissura* (abbreviated as *C. longifissura*) is a species of oval wormlike animals colored green by the presence of algae in their tissues. *C. longifissura* has hooks on its back that are used for defense and capturing prey.

Geographic range: *C. longifissura* lives all over the world.

Habitat: *C. longifissura* lives in sand beds in shallow seawater.

Diet: *C. longifissura* eats animals that are smaller than it is. It sometimes eats the algae that live in it.

Behavior and reproduction: Scientists do not know how *C. longifissura* behaves. It reproduces by mating between males and females. Eggs and sperm unite inside the female's body, and the fertilized (FUR-teh-lyzed) eggs are released. *C. longifissura* also reproduces asexually. The hindmost fourth of a female separates from the body and drops away. The fragment divides, and the new individuals form eyes and mouths over a period of two or three days. Meanwhile, the female regrows the lost section and repeats the breaking process, launching a new group of offspring every four days.

***Convolutriloba longifissura* and people:** *C. longifissura* has no known importance to people.

Conservation status: *C. longifissura* is not threatened or endangered. ■

FOR MORE INFORMATION

Books:

Brusca, Richard C., Gary J. Brusca, and Nancy Haver. *Invertebrates.* 2nd ed. Sunderland, MA: Sinauer, 2002.

Web sites:

Seifarth, Wolfgang. Marine Flatworms of the World. http://www.rzuser.uni-heidelberg.de/bu6/Introduction 11.html (accessed on January 29, 2005).

"When We Were Worms." BBC Online Network. http://news.bbc.co.uk/1/hi/sci/tech/299010.stm (accessed on January 29, 2005).

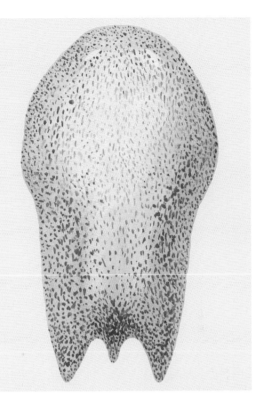

Convolutriloba longifissura *is species of oval wormlike animals that is green in color caused by the presence of algae in their tissues. (Illustration by Emily Damstra. Reproduced by permission.)*

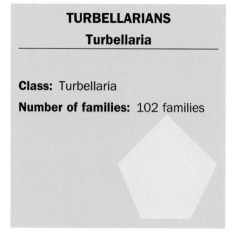

TURBELLARIANS

Turbellaria

Class: Turbellaria

Number of families: 102 families

class

phylum

● **class**

subclass

order

monotypic order

suborder

family

PHYSICAL CHARACTERISTICS

Turbellarians (ter-buh-LAIR-ee-uhns) are free-living flatworms. Free-living means they are not parasites (PAIR-uh-sites), which are animals or plants that live on or in other animals or plants without helping them and usually harming them. Turbellarians have three tissue layers and bilateral symmetry (bye-LAT-er-uhl SIH-muh-tree), meaning the right and left halves of the body match each other. These animals have a complex but incomplete digestive tract, meaning they have no anus (AY-nuhs) and all waste leaves the body through the mouth. Turbellarians have a brain and nerve cords that form a ladderlike nervous system. They have numerous sense organs at the front end of the body and touch receptors all over the body, especially around the mouth, and have organs for eliminating waste and controlling the salt balance in their cells. Turbellarians have no circulatory system, a factor that restricts the size and shape of the animals. Each turbellarian makes both eggs and sperm. The outer layer of turbellarians is covered with hairlike fibers and contains mucus-secreting cells and structures that can produce mass quantities of mucus to prevent the animal from drying out. Most turbellarians have eyelike structures for detecting light. Some species have a pair of these light-detecting structures on their front end, but larger species may have numerous pairs along the body.

GEOGRAPHIC RANGE

Turbellarians live all over the world.

HABITAT

Most turbellarians live in freshwater or seawater, but a few species live on land. Many of the tiny species of turbellarians live between grains of sand in watery habitats. Larger species live in open water or among submerged materials such as rocks, coral, and algae (AL-jee), the plantlike growths that live in water and have no true roots, stems, or leaves. Many species live in invertebrates (in-VER-teh-brehts), which are animals without a backbone, or fishes without harming them. Land-dwelling turbellarians live in damp leaf litter and soil.

DIET

Most turbellarians are predators or scavengers that feed on anything they can fit into their mouths, such as protozoans, crustaceans, worms, and mollusks. Protozoans (proh-tuh-ZOH-uhns) are one-celled living things that resemble animals in that they gets their food from their surroundings rather than making it themselves as plants do. Crustaceans (krus-TAY-shuns) are water-dwelling animals that have jointed legs and a hard shell but no backbone. Mollusks (MAH-lusks) are animals with soft, unsegmented bodies that may or may not have a shell.

Some turbellarians eat only certain foods, such as sponges, barnacles, or sea squirts. A few are close to being parasites because they graze on their live hosts. Land turbellarians feed on earthworms and snails. A few species of turbellarians have a relationship with the algae that live in them in which the algae supply the worm with carbohydrates and fats and the worm supplies the algae with nitrogen waste products and a safe haven.

BEHAVIOR AND REPRODUCTION

Some species of turbellarians secrete mucus that may contain poisonous or narcotic chemicals that slow or entangle prey. Turbellarians use a number of behaviors that prevent them from straying beyond their normal habitats and to keep themselves adjusted to their surroundings. For example, most turbellarians move toward something touching their belly and away from something touching their back. This ability allows bottom-dwelling forms to keep their bottom side down. Freely swimming turbellarians have special sense organs for adjusting themselves to gravity. Most species move away from light. This characteristic prevents the worms from coming out in the daylight, when water-dwelling species may be eaten and land-dwelling species may dry out.

All turbellarians have a strong sense of smell that can be used to find food and mates. Some of these worms swing their head back and forth to help determine the proper direction of the food source. Others use trial and error to determine the proper direction to find food. They move in one direction until the signal becomes weaker and then continue switching direction until the signal is strongest.

Turbellarians use both asexual and sexual reproduction. Asexual (ay-SEK-shuh-wuhl) means without and sexual means with the uniting of egg and sperm for the transfer of DNA from two parents. Many species divide asexually by splitting in two from side to side behind the mouth, and each part generates the rest of a body. The rear portion attaches to the material on which the worm lives, and the front portion crawls away. In some species the cells vary in their ability to regrow. The cells in the middle of the body have the strongest ability to regrow. If just the tail is cut off, it will not grow a new body, whereas the main portion of the body will grow a new tail. In some species several crosswise breaks develop that lead to a train of individuals that do not detach until they reach a certain stage. Other species detach fragments that form capsules and eventually develop into new individuals.

Individual turbellarians make both sperm and eggs, and their sexual reproductive systems are quite complicated. Fertilization (FUR-teh-lih-ZAY-shun), or the joining of egg and sperm to start development, usually occurs when worms align themselves with each other, and the penis of each worm is inserted into the female opening of the other worm and deposits sperm. The worms then go their separate ways with the sperm stored inside. Turbellarians either are born resembling adults and then grow to maturity or produce freely swimming larvae (LAR-vee), or animals in an early stage that change form before becoming adults.

TURBELLARIANS AND PEOPLE

The regrowth abilities of turbellarians have been studied extensively by scientists who want to understand healing and cell regrowth in humans. Several species of turbellarians kill food animals such as oysters, and a few species cause disease in ornamental fishes used in aquariums.

CONSERVATION STATUS

The World Conservation Union (IUCN) lists one species of turbellarians as Extinct, or no longer in existence.

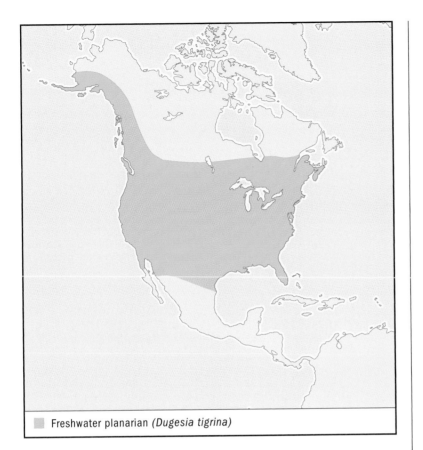

Freshwater planarian (*Dugesia tigrina*)

FRESHWATER PLANARIAN
Dugesia tigrina

Physical characteristics: The body of the freshwater planarian is lance shaped with ear-shaped structures on each side of the head. These worms are light to dark brown, and some forms have a stripe down the center of the back. This worm has midline, light spots on a dark background or dark spots on a light background. The large mouth is in the middle of the body.

Geographic range: Freshwater planarians live all over North America and are scattered in Europe, where they may have been introduced with water plants.

Habitat: Freshwater planarians live under rocks, plants, and debris in clear freshwater ponds, streams, and springs.

When hunting, freshwater planarians swing their heads from side to side better to sense sources of chemicals coming from food or prey. (Illustration by Marguette Dongvillo. Reproduced by permission.)

Diet: Freshwater planarians eat various invertebrates, including mosquito larvae.

Behavior and reproduction: Freshwater planarians hide under rocks during the day. When hunting they swing their head from side to side better to sense sources of chemicals coming from food or prey. Freshwater planarians use asexual reproduction by splitting from side to side. Freshwater planarians have a strong capacity for regrowing after splitting. Scientists have not found reproductive organs in some of these worms and believe splitting may be more common than sexual reproduction. When they do mate, each worm deposits several egg capsules. Freshwater planarians do not have larvae. Young worms hatch from eggs.

Freshwater planarians and people: Freshwater planarians are studied intensively as a model for cell regrowth in humans and other animals.

Conservation status: Freshwater planarians are not threatened or endangered. ■

Notoplana acticola

NO COMMON NAME
Notoplana acticola

Physical characteristics: Adults of the species *Notoplana acticola* (abbreviated as *N. acticola*) are 1 to 2 inches (2.5 to 6 centimeters) long. They are tan or pale gray with darker markings along the center. The body usually is widest toward the front but is tapered at both ends. There are tentacle-like eyelike structures in rounded clusters with scattered ones in front of, behind, and sometimes beside them. About twenty-five more complex eye structures are present in a lengthwise band.

Geographic range: *N. acticola* lives in the Pacific Ocean on the coast of North America.

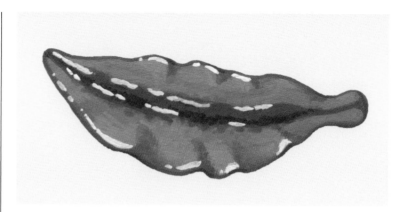

Habitat: *N. acticola* lives in shallow seawater on rocks.

Diet: *N. acticola* can eat prey up to half its size. It eats limpets, which are small, shelled mollusks; small barnacles; and worms.

Behavior and reproduction: *N. acticola* rapidly repairs its nerves if they are severed. Individuals of *N. acticola* make both eggs and sperm. They deposit their eggs in one another in late spring to early fall.

***Notoplana acticola* and people:** *N. acticola* has no known importance to people.

Conservation status: *N. acticola* is not threatened or endangered. ∎

Oyster leech (*Stylochus inimicus*)

OYSTER LEECH
Stylochus inimicus

Physical characteristics: The body of an oyster leech is oval or disk shaped with retractable tentacles. There are three types of eyes. The throat is long and in the middle of the body. Each oyster leech has both male and female reproductive organs close to each other in the rear of the body. Although they are called leeches, oyster leeches are not in the same group as the more familiar blood-sucking leeches, which are segmented worms, the same group that contains earthworms.

Geographic range: Oyster leeches live off both coasts of Florida, United States.

Habitat: Oyster leeches live under rocks and algae, in oyster shells, and in other invertebrates.

Diet: Oyster leeches feed on animal matter, including oyster tissue.

Behavior and reproduction: Oyster leeches tend to hide under debris or in shells of oysters and barnacles. After mating, which can last nine hours and involve more than four partners, an individual oyster leech can deposit seven thousand to twenty-one thousand eggs. Egg masses usually are attached to clean oyster shells. The worms cover their eggs to protect them. Larvae with six eyes hatch from the eggs. The larvae swim up and away from the bottom.

Oyster leeches and people: Oyster leeches enter, devour, and kill oysters, harming the livelihood of people who harvest and sell oysters.

Conservation status: Oyster leeches are not threatened or endangered. ■

FOR MORE INFORMATION

Books:

Aaseng, Nathan. *Invertebrates.* New York: Venture, 1993.

Niesen, Thomas M. *The Marine Biology Coloring Book.* 2nd ed. New York: HarperResource, 2000.

Silverstein, Alvin, Virginia Silverstein, and Robert Silverstein. *Invertebrates.* New York: Twenty-First Century, 1996.

Web sites:

"Oyster Leech." Smithsonian Marine Station at Fort Pierce. http://www.sms.si.edu/IRLFieldGuide/Stylochus_sp.htm (accessed on December 20, 2004).

Seifarth, Wolfgang. "Regeneration." Marine Flatworms of the World. http://www.rzuser.uni-heidelberg.de/ bu6/Introduction03.html (accessed on December 20, 2004).

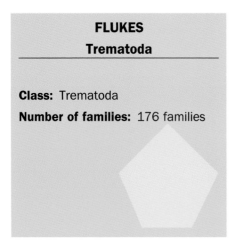

FLUKES

Trematoda

Class: Trematoda
Number of families: 176 families

class

PHYSICAL CHARACTERISTICS

Flukes (FLOOKS) are flatworms that are parasites (PAIR-uh-sites), which are animals or plants that live on or in other animals or plants, or hosts, without helping them and usually harming them. Flukes usually are leaf shaped and have suckers that they use for attaching to and feeding on their hosts. Flukes can be as small as one–thirty-second of an inch (1 millimeter) or as long as 23 feet (7 meters), but most are one-eighth to 2 inches (5 millimeters to 5 centimeters) long. Flukes have a hard covering that keeps them from being dissolved by the stomach juices of their hosts.

There are two types of flukes. One type has a direct life cycle, meaning there is only one host, often freshwater snails, in which development from egg to adult occurs. The other type of flukes has an indirect life cycle, meaning they infect different hosts during the various stages of life. Most of these flukes have two stages of development and at least two hosts.

GEOGRAPHIC RANGE

Flukes live all over the world.

HABITAT

The habitat of a fluke is the same as that of its host and can change as the fluke goes from host to host.

DIET

Flukes cannot live without nourishment from a host organism. In some species the larvae (LAR-vee), or animals in an early stage that change form before becoming adults, do not eat. Adult flukes eat blood cells, mucus, and body cells.

BEHAVIOR AND REPRODUCTION

Flukes with an indirect life cycle begin life as eggs in a primary host and then pass with the host's feces (FEE-seez) or waste into water or onto land. After the eggs hatch, the larvae move to another host, called the intermediate host, which is often a mollusk. Mollusks (MAH-lusks) are animals with a soft, unsegmented body that may or may not have a shell. The flukes change form, exit the host, and move to another intermediate host, which is frequently another mollusk, a fish, or an amphibian, and change form again. The life cycle continues when a new primary host eats the second intermediate host, at which point the fluke infects the primary host. Primary hosts often are mammals and birds.

In some species the first-stage larvae do not feed. For this reason, they must find a first intermediate host very quickly, usually within one or two days of hatching. In moving from the first to the second host, most flukes use environmental cues, such as light or water turbulence, to seek the new host. Some species also follow a chemical trail. In some species, however, the larvae seem to stumble upon rather than track their hosts. Some flukes with an indirect life cycle skip the second intermediate host and invade the primary host directly. Others live on plants rather than in a secondary host. The primary host then becomes infected by eating the fluke-infested vegetation.

Flukes with an indirect life cycle use asexual and sexual reproduction. Asexual (ay-SEK-shuh-wuhl) means without, and sexual means with, the uniting of egg and sperm and the transfer of DNA from two parents. When the first-stage larvae reach their destination within the first intermediate host, the asexual phase begins when the larvae lose their hairlike fibers and change into another form of larvae. The new larvae produce more of the same type of larvae or a transformed type. With asexual reproduction, the number of invading flukes can multiply very quickly inside the first intermediate host.

In the first intermediate host, the asexually produced larvae transform into free-living young flukes. The young flukes swim to the second intermediate host, which is typically prey for the primary host. Once on or in the second intermediate host, the young flukes transform again. It is only after the flukes finally

enter the primary host and become adults that they use sexual reproduction either by mating with other flukes or by fertilizing (FUR-teh-LYE-zing) themselves. Fertilization (FUR-teh-lih-ZAY-shun) is the joining of egg and sperm to start development. Almost all flukes make both eggs and sperm. Blood flukes have separate sexes, and the adult females and males mate with each other.

Flukes with a direct life cycle use only sexual reproduction. The entire life cycle occurs in one host, usually a mollusk. Although predators may eat the host species and temporarily harbor the worms, the worms can survive for only a short time in the predator's digestive tract and cannot reproduce or develop there.

FLUKES AND PEOPLE

Flukes pose a health threat to humans. Fluke diseases cause weakness, diarrhea, bleeding, fever, abdominal pain, and other severe symptoms.

CONSERVATION STATUS

Flukes are not threatened or endangered.

Lancet fluke *(Dicrocoelium dendriticum)*

LANCET FLUKE
Dicrocoelium dendriticum

Physical characteristics: Adult lancet flukes have pearly bodies shaped like long, thin leaves. The suckers are on the mouth and on the bottom of the worm toward the front of the body. The mouth sucker closest to the front is a bit smaller than the other suckers. Lancet flukes are about three-sixteenths to five-eighths of an inch (5 to 15 millimeters) long and one–thirty-second to a little more than one-sixteenth of an inch (2 millimeters) wide.

Geographic range: Lancet flukes live in the northeastern United States, Australia, northern and central Europe, Asia, and Africa.

Habitat: Lancet flukes live in dry habitats. The primary hosts are mammals such as sheep, cattle, pigs, rabbits, deer, and woodchucks. The first intermediate hosts are land-dwelling snails, and the second intermediate hosts are ants.

Diet: Lancet flukes feed on the cells of their hosts.

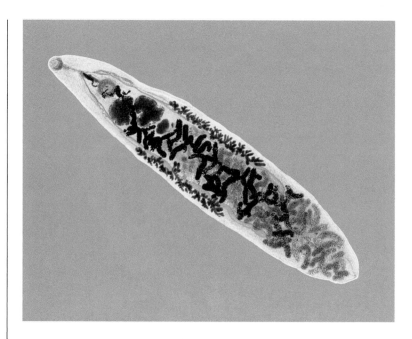

Behavior and reproduction: Lancet flukes begin life as eggs in the feces of their primary hosts. The eggs are picked up and carried by snails. The larvae form slime balls in the snail, which ejects them through its breathing pore. The larvae are picked up by ants and cause cramping in the ants' jaws. The cramping causes the ants to clamp down on blades of grass and become stuck. The larvae then are eaten by grazing animals, such as sheep and cattle, and develop to the adult stage in the animal's liver. The eggs leave the host in its feces, and the cycle starts over. Adult lancet flukes make both eggs and sperm and either mate with other flukes or fertilize themselves.

Lancet flukes and people: Lancet flukes cause liver disease in farm animals.

Conservation status: Lancet flukes are not threatened or endangered.   ■

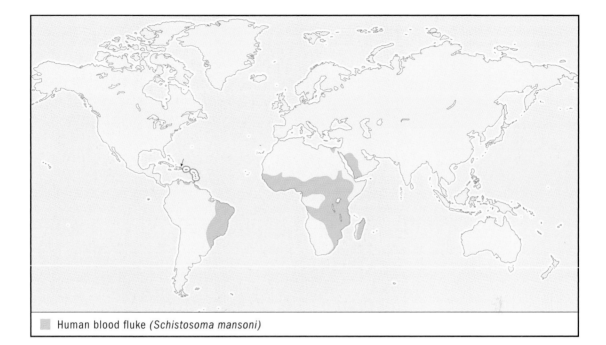

Human blood fluke *(Schistosoma mansoni)*

HUMAN BLOOD FLUKE
Schistosoma mansoni

Physical characteristics: Female human blood flukes are thin, cylindrical, and one-half to 1 inch (1.3 to 2.5 centimeters) long. Males are a little bit shorter and thicker. Males have small spiny suckers on the mouth and belly and a wrinkled back dotted with small bumps. Females usually spend their lives attached to males. Both males and females are white.

Geographic range: Human blood flukes live in the warm regions of the world, especially South America, Africa, the Caribbean, and the Middle East.

Habitat: The larvae of human blood flukes live in freshwater snails. The adults live in veins in the abdomens of mammals such as rodents, dogs, cattle, baboons, and humans.

Diet: Human blood flukes feed on blood in the abdominal veins of their hosts.

Behavior and reproduction: The eggs of human blood flukes hatch in freshwater areas and develop into larvae, which follow chemical, light, and gravitational cues to find and then penetrate the soft tissues of snails. The larvae transform into another type of larvae and swim out of the snails. The larvae actively seek out the next host by targeting fatty acids in the skin. They then penetrate the skin of a secondary host, which may be a person or other mammal. Once in the host, the larvae become immature flukes, travel to the circulatory system, and travel to veins near the large intestine. Once in the veins, the flukes mature, mate, and lay eggs, many of which leave the host's body with feces. The cycle begins again when the eggs make their way into the freshwater habitat of the snail. Adult male human blood flukes usually live joined with the females, the female remaining in the male's spine-covered reproductive canal, a groove that runs along the lower surface of the body.

Human blood flukes and people: Infection with human blood flukes causes disease in humans. The condition causes abdominal pain, diarrhea, intestinal bleeding, tiredness, and a decrease in red blood cells, leaving the victim weak and vulnerable to other diseases.

Conservation status: Human blood flukes are not threatened or endangered. ■

Fasciola hepatica

NO COMMON NAME
Fasciola hepatica

Physical characteristics: Adult *Fasciola hepatica* (abbreviated to *F. hepatica*) are a little more than 1 inch (3 centimeters) long and three-eighths of an inch (1 centimeter) wide. They have a spiny outer covering. The front end has a mouth sucker and a cone-shaped tip, and the rear end is tapered. The sucker on the fluke's lower surface is larger than the mouth sucker.

Geographic range: *F. hepatica* live all over the world but mainly in Europe, Mexico, and Central America.

Habitat: *F. hepatica* live in swampy freshwater areas inhabited by snails. Snails are their sole intermediate hosts. The primary hosts include grazing mammals such as sheep, cattle, and horses; farm animals such as hogs; pets such as dogs, cats, and rabbits; and humans.

Diet: *F. hepatica* feed on the lining of the ducts, or tubes, in the liver, causing hardening of the ducts.

Behavior and reproduction: The eggs of *Fasciola hepatica*, which are deposited in the environment in the primary host's feces, hatch in

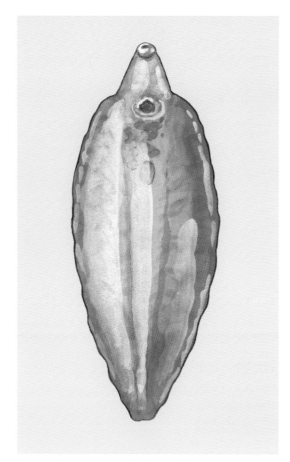

Fasciola hepatica *feed on the lining of the ducts, or tubes, in the liver, causing hardening of the ducts. (Illustration by Bruce Worden. Reproduced by permission.)*

freshwater areas, usually within about ten days, longer if temperatures are cool. These flukes have been known to survive in particularly cold water for several years. The embryos develop into larvae, which quickly swim to and penetrate the soft tissue of snails. The larvae produce more larvae, which transform. Larvae in their final stage live in the snails for four to eight weeks, then exit and swim to plants lying just below the water line. Passing plant-eating animals become infected when they eat the plants, often grass. Humans typically become infected by drinking water containing flukes or by eating greens such as watercress. The flukes travel to the abdominal cavity in the first twenty-four hours, then to the liver over the next few days. Within six to eight weeks, the flukes reach the liver ducts, where they mature and lay eggs. The eggs are then carried to the intestine and pass into the feces. The flukes sometimes spread to the lungs as well as the liver.

Fasciola hepatica and people: Humans infected with *F. hepatica* may have symptoms ranging from skin inflammation to pneumonia. Fluke infection can result in massive bleeding in horses, a reduction of milk production in dairy cattle, and death in sheep.

Conservation status: *Fasciola hepatica* are not threatened or endangered. ■

FOR MORE INFORMATION

Books:

Aaseng, Nathan. *Invertebrates.* New York: Venture, 1993.

Silverstein, Alvin, Virginia Silverstein, and Robert Silverstein. *Invertebrates.* New York: Twenty-First Century, 1996.

Zimmer, Carl. *Parasite Rex.* New York: Free Press, 2000.

Web sites:

Frey, Rebecca J. "Fluke Infections." AhealthyMe. http://www.ahealthyme .com/article/gale/100084581 (accessed on December 20, 2004).

Frisby, Holly. "*Dicrocoelium dendriticum* (Lancet Fluke)." PetEducation.com http://www.peteducation.com/article.cfm?cls=2&cat=1621&articleid=731 (accessed on December 20, 2004).

MONOGENEANS
Monogenea

Class: Monogenea
Number of families: 53 families

PHYSICAL CHARACTERISTICS

Monogeneans (mah-nuh-JEE-nee-uhns) are flatworm parasites that live mainly on fish skin and gills. Parasites (PAIR-uh-sites) are animals or plants that live on or in other animals or plants, or hosts, without helping them and usually harming them. Monogeneans have an organ at the rear of their bodies that holds hooks the worms use for attaching themselves to hosts. The organ holds large hooks, called anchors, and small hooks. Monogeneans live in only one host for their entire life cycle. Monogeneans are one–thirty-second to three-fourths of an inch (1 millimeter to 2 centimeters) long. Large monogeneans tend to be flat and leaf shaped, but the smaller worms are usually cylindrical. These flatworms are colorless and almost clear. When on fish skin some may be almost invisible to the human eye, either because they are clear or because they contain scattered coloring that matches the color of the host's skin. The digestive system of monogeneans consists of a muscular tube used to suck in food and a saclike or branched intestine with no anus (AY-nuhs). Monogeneans make both eggs and sperm.

GEOGRAPHIC RANGE

Monogeneans live all over the world.

HABITAT

Many monogeneans live on or in specific hosts, mainly the skin of freshwater and saltwater fishes. Some species live in the bladders of frogs and toads and the bladders or mouths of freshwater

phylum
◆ **class**
subclass
order
monotypic order
suborder
family

turtles. One species lives beneath the eyelids of a hippopotamus. Another lives on the skin of squids.

DIET

Most monogeneans feed on the skin of their hosts. Some eat blood.

BEHAVIOR AND REPRODUCTION

Many monogeneans move like leeches from their site of first attachment on the host to the site where they mate and lay their eggs. Many can change their location on the host throughout their lives. Some stay in one place. Some skin parasites breathe by wavy movements of their bodies. Some young and adult parasites can swim.

Monogeneans make both sperm and eggs. The male part of the reproductive system is usually first to mature. Fertilization (FUR-teh-lih-ZAY-shun), the joining of egg and sperm to start development, takes place in one of three ways: two worms mate and fertilize (FUR-teh-lyze) each other; one worm fertilizes another, but the favor is not returned; or one worm fertilizes itself. The fertilized eggs are released into the environment and produce infective larvae, which can swim freely by using hairlike fibers that cover their bodies. Larvae (LAR-vee) are animals in an early stage that change form before becoming adults.

The larvae of many monogeneans hatch at a particular time of day, which is often the same time the host is particularly vulnerable to invasion. Hatching may also be triggered by host cues such as chemicals, movement, or shadows. The larvae do not feed until they reach the host, which means that their survival as free-living animals and their chance of infecting a host are limited, usually to a period of several hours. Rather than depositing fertilized eggs in the environment, some monogeneans keep the eggs inside themselves for development and give birth to offspring that are usually full size at birth.

MONOGENEANS AND PEOPLE

In the wild, the number of monogeneans living on an individual host is low, and infestations of these parasites do not usually cause disease. In crowded fish farms, however, parasite populations often increase uncontrollably, and the hosts can be damaged or killed.

CONSERVATION STATUS

Monogeneans are not threatened or endangered.

Dactylogyrus vastator

NO COMMON NAME
Dactylogyrus vastator

Physical characteristics: Worms in the species *Dactylogyrus vastator* (abbreviated as *D. vastator*) are a little more than one–thirty-second of an inch (1.25 millimeters) long. They have two pairs of hooks. A set on the bottom surface of the worm is smaller than the set at the rear. These worms have three pairs of sticky sacs and four eyespots.

Geographic range: *D. vastator* lives in the northern parts of North America, Europe, and Asia.

Habitat: *D. vastator* lives in the gills of carp and goldfish, which live in freshwater.

Diet: *D. vastator* feeds on gill cells.

Behavior and reproduction: *D. vastator* worms attach themselves to their hosts with their hooks. The eggs are washed out of the host's gills and sink to the bottom of the water. Larvae emerge in three to five days, depending on water temperature. Larvae drawn into the gill cavity by the water current attach themselves to another host's gills. Some larvae may first attach to a host's skin and then migrate to the gills.

Dactylogyrus vastator and people: *D. vastator* kills young carp in fish-farming ponds. This problem is significant in areas where carp is bred for food.

Conservation status: *D. vastator* is not threatened or endangered. ■

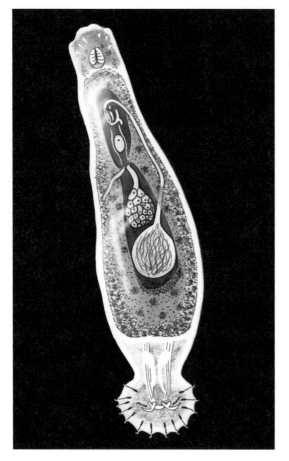

Dactylogyrus vastator *live in the gills of carp and goldfish. (Illustration by Barbara Duperron. Reproduced by permission.)*

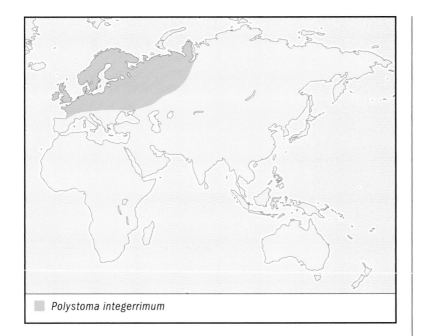

Polystoma integerrimum

NO COMMON NAME
Polystoma integerrimum

Physical characteristics: Adult *Polystoma integerrimum* (abbreviated to *P. integerrimum*) worms are about three-eighths of an inch (10 millimeters) long. The attachment organ has six muscular suckers, one pair of large hooks, and sixteen small hooks. There also are suckers around the mouth.

Geographic range: *P. integerrimum* lives in Europe.

Habitat: *P. integerrimum* lives in the bladders of common frogs.

Diet: *P. integerrimum* eats blood.

Behavior and reproduction: Adult *P. integerrimum* worms do not make eggs while their host frogs are living on land during most of year. When the frogs enter water to spawn in spring, the worms lay their eggs. The larvae that hatch invade the gills of frog tadpoles, or the frog's early water-dwelling stage. When the tadpoles change into frogs, the worms travel through the digestive tract and possibly the skin to the host's bladder, where they mature. A single egg that stays

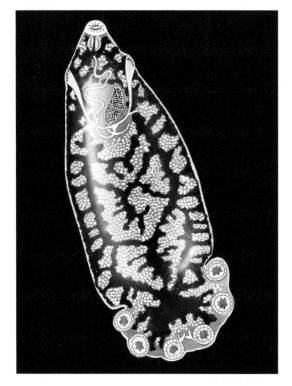

Polystoma integerrimum *lives in the bladders of common frogs. (Illustration by Barbara Duperron. Reproduced by permission.)*

in an adult worm develops and hatches, and the larva stays in the host of its parent, increasing the parasite infection in the host.

***Polystoma integerrimum* and people:** *P. integerrimum* has no known importance to people.

Conservation status: *P. integerrimum* is not threatened or endangered. ∎

FOR MORE INFORMATION

Books:

Zimmer, Carl. *Parasite Rex.* New York: Free Press, 2000.

Web sites:

"The Class: Monogenea." Kansas State University. http://www.ksu.edu/parasitology/classes/625monogene.html (accessed on January 31, 2005).

Reed, Peggy, Ruth Francis-Floyd, and RuthEllen Klinger. "Monogenean Parasites of Fish." University of Florida. http://edis.ifas.ufl.edu/FA033 (accessed on January 31, 2005).

class

CHAPTER

PHYSICAL CHARACTERISTICS

The body of most tapeworms is flat and much longer than it is wide, so that it looks like a tape or ribbon. The length varies from 0.02 inch (0.6 millimeter) to 98 feet (30 meters), the longest worms being found in sperm whales. Tapeworms are parasites that have no head, mouth, or digestive system. Parasites (PAIR-uh-sites) are animals or plants that live on or in other animals or plants, or hosts, without helping them and usually harming them. Tapeworms have a body covering through which they absorb nutrients from the host's intestine. This covering also protects the worms from the host's immune reactions and digestive acids. Tapeworms are whitish and as internal parasites they live in darkness.

The body of tapeworms has three regions: scolex (SKOH-leks), neck, and strobila (stroh-BYE-luh). The scolex is the head. It has spines, hooks, suckers, tentacles, glands releasing sticky secretions, or a combination of these structures that the worm uses to attach itself to the inner wall of the intestine of the final host, also called the primary host. Suckers are the most common attachment tool. Suckers are usually cup shaped and have powerful muscular walls. The neck is the region of the body just behind the scolex. It is usually short.

The strobila is behind the neck. It consists of a row of segments called proglottids (proh-GLAH-tuhds). The strobila is made up of anywhere from a few to more than one thousand proglottids but usually contains several dozen. Each proglottid starts development at the neck, and proglottids form one by one

throughout the life of the tapeworm in the final host. Just behind the neck, the proglottids are short and narrow. When a new proglottid forms at the neck, already formed proglottids are pushed toward the rear, grow, and eventually contain the reproductive organs.

Behind the new proglottids, each strobila contains the following types of proglottids, from front to back: premature proglottids, with the beginnings of reproductive organs; mature proglottids, which contain functioning male and female reproductive organs; postmature proglottids, which contain developing eggs; and gravid (GRA-vuhd) proglottids, which contain ripe eggs. The gravid proglottids at the end of the worm break off and pass into the environment with the host's feces (FEE-seez). A few species of tapeworms have no proglottids.

GEOGRAPHIC RANGE

Tapeworms live all over the world.

HABITAT

Tapeworms live in almost all land, sea, and freshwater habitats where vertebrates live. Vertebrates (VER-teh-brehts) are animals with a backbone. Most adult tapeworms live in the intestines of the final hosts, but a few species live in the body cavity. Tapeworm larvae, which live in a host called the intermediate host before moving to the final host, live in various types of tissue, such as liver, lung, muscle, body cavity, brain, and sometimes even the eyes. Larvae (LAR-vee) are animals in an early stage that change form before becoming adults.

DIET

Tapeworms eat by absorbing nutrients from their hosts' intestines.

BEHAVIOR AND REPRODUCTION

Scientists know little about the behavior of tapeworms in the intestines of their hosts. It seems that most tapeworms attach themselves at a certain site of the intestinal wall and stay there for their entire lives.

Tapeworms follow this general scheme as their life cycle. The eggs, each holding an embryo (EHM-bri-yo), pass into the environment with the final host's feces and are eaten by the intermediate host. In the intestine of the intermediate host, the embryos hatch and, using their hooks, bore through the intestinal wall and into the body cavity or an internal organ. In the new location the embryos transform into larvae. In most species the larvae have a fully developed scolex identical to that of adult tapeworms. The larvae enter the final host when it eats the intermediate host. In the final host the scolices (SKOH-luh-seez, the plural of scolex) of the larvae attach to the intestinal wall. The necks of the larvae start production of proglottids, and the strobila forms. With further development of proglottids, the worm starts producing eggs, which are released with feces into the environment. Some tapeworms have more than one intermediate host.

Most tapeworms make both eggs and sperm. Each proglottid contains one set of male reproductive organs and one set of female reproductive organs. In most species the male organs mature first, and proglottids first act as male organs. In species in which the female organs develop first, sperm develop in the male organs when the eggs develop in the female organs. Sperm from one tapeworm enter the female reproductive organs of another tapeworm during mating and are stored for a while before joining with eggs for the start of development of embryos.

TAPEWORMS AND PEOPLE

Fifty-seven species of tapeworms live in humans. Six of these species are considered a public health problem because they cause serious diseases. Tapeworms also are dangerous to animals kept by people, such as horses, sheep, cattle, dogs, cats, rabbits, and domestic birds. Tapeworms infect the fish that people eat and reduce production in fish farms.

CONSERVATION STATUS

Tapeworms are not considered threatened or endangered.

Tapeworms and More Tapeworms

Scientists are constantly finding new species of tapeworms. Thirty to forty species were discovered each year between 1992 and 2002.

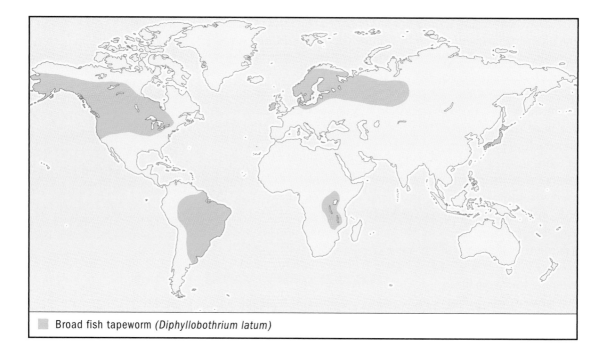

Broad fish tapeworm (*Diphyllobothrium latum*)

SPECIES ACCOUNTS

BROAD FISH TAPEWORM
Diphyllobothrium latum

Physical characteristics: The strobila of broad fish tapeworms is about 30 feet (9 meters) long and has three thousand to four thousand proglottids. The scolex is finger shaped.

Geographic range: Broad fish tapeworms live in Scandinavia, the Baltic states, Russia, the United States, Canada, Ireland, Japan, around some lakes and large rivers in Africa, and in South America.

Habitat: The final hosts of broad fish tapeworms are fish-eating mammals such as dogs, cats, bears, seals, and humans. The first intermediate hosts are crustaceans (krus-TAY-shuns), which are water-dwelling animals that have jointed legs and a hard shell but no backbone. The second intermediate hosts are fishes. All the hosts live in or near rivers and freshwater lakes.

Diet: Broad fish tapeworms absorb nutrients from their hosts.

Behavior and reproduction: Scientists do not know how broad fish tapeworms behave. These worms make both eggs and sperm. Eggs are released and pass into the environment with the final host's feces. The embryos hatch from the eggs in water. The embryos are covered by hairlike fibers and can swim several hours until being eaten by a small crustacean, the first intermediate host. In the intestine of the crustacean, the embryos lose the hairy covering, bore into the host's body cavity, and feed on nutrients in the host's body fluids. It takes 20 to 25 days for the embryos to develop into long larvae. The larvae make the host crustacean sick and slow, turning it into easy prey for fish. When the infected crustacean is eaten by a fish, which is the second intermediate host, the larvae travel from the fish's intestine into the muscles and turn into the next stage of larvae. People and animals, which are the final hosts, are infected with the larvae when they eat infected fish. After about two weeks in the host's intestine, the larvae transform into mature worms and start producing eggs.

Broad fish tapeworms and people: The disease caused by broad fish tapeworms is one of the most widespread diseases caused by tapeworms. The symptoms are diarrhea, abdominal discomfort, weakness, and in some cases, anemia (uh-NEE-mee-uh), which is a deficiency of red blood cells. The drug treatment is very efficient.

Conservation status: Broad fish tapeworms are not considered threatened or endangered. ■

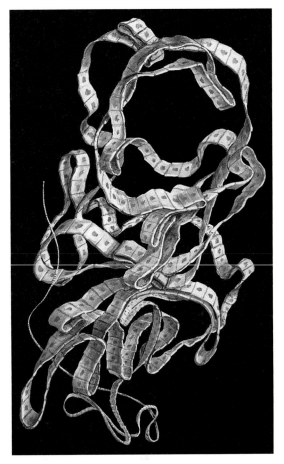

The final hosts of broad fish tapeworms are fish-eating mammals such as dogs, cats, bears, seals, and humans. (Illustration by Brian Cressman. Reproduced by permission.)

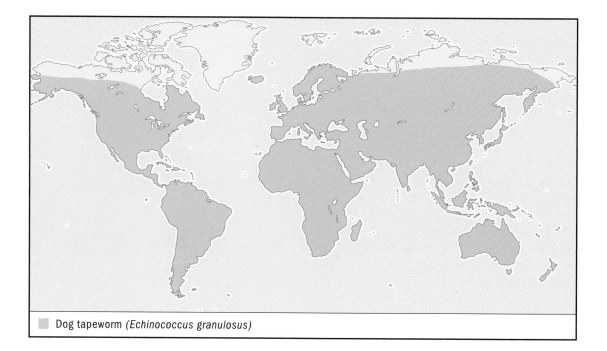

Dog tapeworm (*Echinococcus granulosus*)

DOG TAPEWORM
Echinococcus granulosus

Physical characteristics: Adult dog tapeworms are 0.1 to 0.2 inch (3 to 6 millimeters) long. The body consists of the scolex, a short neck, and 3 to 5 proglottids. The scolex has 30 to 36 hooks. The gravid proglottids are very long.

Geographic range: Dog tapeworms live all over the world.

Habitat: Adult dog tapeworms live in the intestines of meat-eating mammals, mainly dogs, wolves, and jackals. The larvae live in the liver, lungs, and muscles of plant-eating mammals such as sheep, cattle, camels, pigs, goats, and horses. The habitat includes areas where humans live and work, such as pastures, farms, and villages.

Diet: Dog tapeworms absorb nutrients from their hosts.

Behavior and reproduction: The released gravid proglottids of dog tapeworms can crawl, and the larvae probably climb up grasses. Some gravid proglottids may stay around the anus of the dog, contaminating

body that may or may not have a shell. Crustaceans (krus-TAY-shuns) are water-dwelling animals that have jointed legs and a hard shell but no backbone. Larvae (LAR-vee) are animals in an early stage that change form before becoming adults.

BEHAVIOR AND REPRODUCTION

Most anoplans and enoplans live alone. They glide with the help of hairlike fibers on their belly and mucus they produce. Some species swim with wavy movements, but only for a short time. Most anoplans and enoplans have separate sexes. They reproduce by releasing their eggs and sperm into the water. Fertilization (FUR-teh-lih-ZAY-shun), or the joining of egg and sperm to start development, takes place and larvae develop outside the body. In some species fertilized (FUR-teh-lyzed) eggs are deposited in a jelly-like cocoon in which the larvae develop. In a few species eggs are fertilized inside the female, and the young are born looking like small adults rather than as larvae.

ANOPLANS, ENOPLANS, AND PEOPLE

Some of the toxins made by anoplans and enoplans have been studied for use in drugs that help the memory of people with Alzheimer's disease.

CONSERVATION STATUS

The World Conservation Union (IUCN) lists two species of anoplans and enoplans as Vulnerable and one as Lower Risk/Near Threatened. Vulnerable means facing high risk of extinction in the wild. Low Risk/Near Threatened means at risk of becoming threatened with extinction in the future.

WORMS IN A BUCKET

An easy way to collect anoplans and enoplans is to place seaweed and smaller algae in a bucket of seawater. In a few hours to a couple of days any worms in the seaweed will crawl to the sides of the bucket and be easy to see.

WRESTLING FOR DINNER

When prey, such as a crab, comes along, an enoplan hiding in the sand sticks out its long snout, rapidly wraps it around the crab, and injects immobilizing toxins and digestive enzymes into the prey. When the crab stops struggling, the worm pulls in its snout, comes out of its hole, and enters the prey, whose tissues are drained from the shell in about an hour.

Oerstedia dorsalis

NO COMMON NAME
Oerstedia dorsalis

Physical characteristics: *Oerstedia dorsalis* worms are 0.4 to 0.6 inch (10 to 15 millimeters) long and 0.04 to 0.08 inch (1 to 2 millimeters) wide. They have four eyes. Most of these worms are brown to reddish brown and have a white stripe on the back. Some have light or dark brown speckles; some have yellowish dots; some are cream colored without spots; and some have dark bands on a light background. The belly usually is paler than the back.

Geographic range: *Oerstedia dorsalis* (abbreviated as *O. dorsalis*) worms live along both coasts of North America, around Iceland, along the western coast of Europe, and in the Mediterranean Sea.

Habitat: *O. dorsalis* worms live in the sea close to shore. They usually live among algae.

Diet: *O. dorsalis* worms eat small crustaceans and worms.

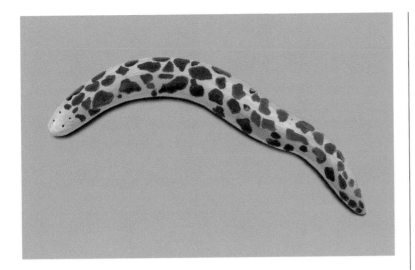

Oerstedia dorsalis *live in the sea close to shore. They usually live among algae. (Illustration by Emily Damstra. Reproduced by permission.)*

Behavior and reproduction: Scientists do not know how *O. dorsalis* worms behave. The sexes are separate. Fertilization takes place outside the body after the worms release eggs and sperm into the water.

Oerstedia dorsalis and people: *O. dorsalis* worms have no known importance to people.

Conservation status: *O. dorsalis* worms are not considered threatened or endangered. ■

FOR MORE INFORMATION

Books:

Carson, Rachel. *The Edge of the Sea.* 1955. Reprint, Boston: Mariner, 1998.

Niesen, Thomas M. *The Marine Biology Coloring Book.* 2nd ed. New York: HarperResource, 2000.

Web site:

Shimek, Ronald L. "Tie A Yellow Ribbon (Worm) around the Old Reef Rock." *Reefkeeping.* http://www.reefkeeping.com/issues/2004-01/rs/ (accessed on February 9, 2005).

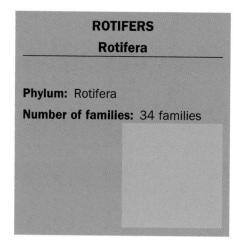

ROTIFERS

Rotifera

Phylum: Rotifera
Number of families: 34 families

phylum

CHAPTER

■ **phylum**

class

subclass

order

monotypic order

suborder

family

PHYSICAL CHARACTERISTICS

Rotifers (ROH-tuh-fuhrs) are microscopic animals that have complex jaws and a wheel organ, which is used for movement and feeding. Most rotifers are 0.006 to 0.02 inch (150 to 500 micrometers) long. The body usually is divided into a head, a trunk, and a foot. The largest organ in the head is the wheel organ, which is made up of beating hairlike fibers arranged in bands around the mouth. The jaw has a single sharp tooth or a plate with several strong teeth used to grab and pierce food. The trunk shape varies from long to spherical or baglike. The foot has one or several sections, and it often has two toes with sticky glands at the tips.

GEOGRAPHIC RANGE

Rotifers live all over the world.

HABITAT

Most rotifers live in freshwater in sand or mud at the bottom, in plants, or in open water. Several species live in saltwater, usually among plants but sometimes between grains of sand on beaches.

DIET

Rotifers eat algae and other protists, bacteria, and even other rotifers. Algae (AL-jee) are plantlike growths that live in water and have no true roots, stems, or leaves. Protists (PROH-tists) are one-celled living things that have a nucleus (NOO-klee-uhs), which is the control center of a cell.

BEHAVIOR AND REPRODUCTION

Most rotifers collect food by beating the wheel organ to make a water current. Swimming rotifers move gently through the water in a spiral motion. Crawling rotifers use sticky glands on their foot and head to move much the way inchworms do.

WHAT'S IN A NAME?

The name rotifer comes from the Latin words *rota*, meaning "wheel," and *ferre*, meaning "to carry." When these animals are swimming or feeding, the beating of their hairlike fibers gives the illusion that the animal carries two small, rotating wheels.

Some species of rotifers use only sexual reproduction; some use only asexual reproduction, and others have both a sexual and an asexual phase. Asexual (ay-SEK-shuh-wuhl) means without and sexual means with the uniting of egg and sperm for the transfer of DNA from two parents. In species that use only asexual reproduction, all the rotifers are females. The female produces eggs that develop into new embryos without fertilization (FUR-teh-lih-ZAY-shun), or the joining of egg and sperm to start development. The daughters are genetically identical to the mother.

In rotifers that use only sexual reproduction the males store sperm in a bag that they transfer to females during mating. Fertilization takes place inside the females. Later the females attach the eggs to crustaceans called sea fleas, where they stay until the young hatch. Crustaceans (krus-TAY-shuns) are water-dwelling animals that have jointed legs and a hard shell but no backbone.

Among rotifers that have two reproductive phases, the asexual phase has only females that produce more females without fertilization. Certain physical events, however, can produce sexually reproducing females, whose eggs can be fertilized (FUR-teh-lyzed) by a male. If not fertilized, the eggs develop into dwarf males. These males do not live long and immediately after hatching seek a female and fertilize her eggs by injecting her with sperm. The thick-shelled egg that results can survive extreme conditions such as freezing and drying out. After a resting period, an asexually reproducing female hatches from the egg.

ROTIFERS AND PEOPLE

Many species of rotifers are cultured as fish food for aquariums and fish farms. They also can be used in tests for water pollution.

CONSERVATION STATUS

Rotifers are not considered threatened or endangered.

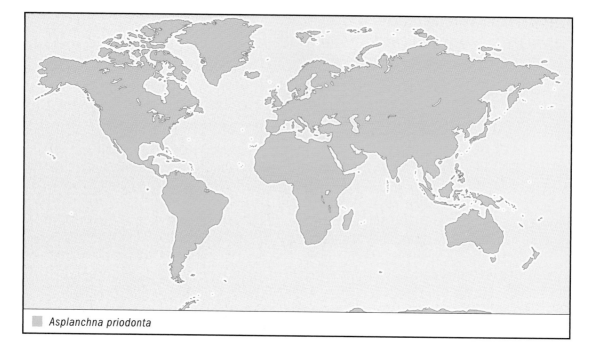

Asplanchna priodonta

SPECIES ACCOUNTS

NO COMMON NAME
Asplanchna priodonta

Physical characteristics: Female *Asplanchna priodonta* rotifers are 0.01 to 0.06 inch (250 to 1,500 micrometers) long, and males are 0.008 to 0.02 inch (200 to 500 micrometers) long. The shape is long in summer and baglike in spring and autumn. The hard parts of the jaw are large, curved, sharply pointed, and tweezerlike.

Geographic range: *Asplanchna priodonta* (abbreviated as *A. priodonta*) rotifers live all over the world.

Habitat: *A. priodonta* rotifers live in freshwater.

Diet: *A. priodonta* rotifers eat algae, other protists, and other rotifers.

Behavior and reproduction: *A. priodonta* rotifers produce sexual and asexual females. Fertilization takes place inside the body. These rotifers also may have a third type of female, which can produce eggs that hatch into asexually producing females and eggs that hatch into dwarf males.

Asplanchna priodonta and people: *A. priodonta* rotifers have no known importance to people.

Conservation status: *A. priodonta* rotifers are not considered threatened or endangered.   ■

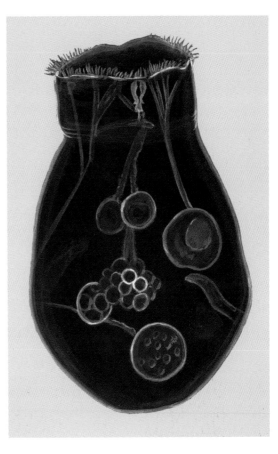

The shape of Asplanchna priodonta *is long in summer and baglike in spring and autumn. (Illustration by Joseph E. Trumpey. Reproduced by permission.)*

Seison nebaliae

NO COMMON NAME
Seison nebaliae

Physical characteristics: *Seison nebaliae* rotifers are 0.03 to 0.1 inch (800 to 2,500 micrometers) long. Males and females are the same size. The head is egg shaped and has a long neck made up of parts that can retract like the sections of a telescope. The trunk is oval, and the foot is long and made up of sections. Rather than toes, these rotifers have a sticky disk they use to attach themselves to sea fleas.

Geographic range: *Seison nebaliae* (abbreviated as *S. nebaliae*) rotifers live in the Atlantic Ocean off the coast of Europe and in the Mediterranean Sea.

Habitat: *S. nebaliae* rotifers live on sea fleas.

Diet: *S. nebaliae* rotifers eat bacteria.

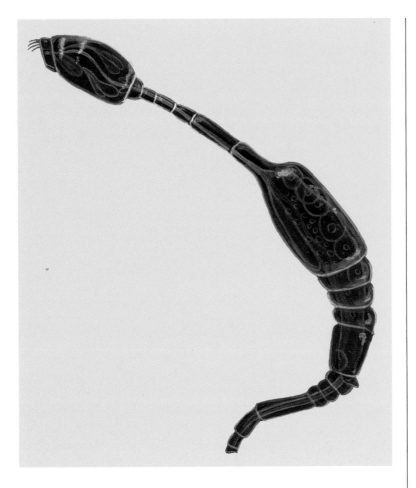

Seison nebaliae *rotifers live on sea fleas. (Illustration by Joseph E. Trumpey. Reproduced by permission.)*

Behavior and reproduction: Except that *S. nebaliae* rotifers live on sea fleas, scientists do not know how they behave. These rotifers use sexual reproduction.

Seison nebaliae and people: *S. nebaliae* rotifers have no known importance to people.

Conservation status: *S. nebaliae* rotifers are not considered threatened or endangered. ■

FOR MORE INFORMATION

Books:

Smith, Douglas Grant. *Pennak's Freshwater Invertebrates of the United States: Porifera to Crustacea.* 4th ed. New York: Wiley, 2001.

Web sites:

"Rotifers."   http://www.micrographia.com/specbiol/rotife/homebdel/bdel0100.htm (accessed on February 11, 2005).

Russell, Bruce J. "Whirling Animals." *Biomedia.* http://ebiomedia.com/gall/rotifers/rotifermain.html (accessed on February 11, 2005).

Phylum: Gastrotricha
Number of families: 13 families

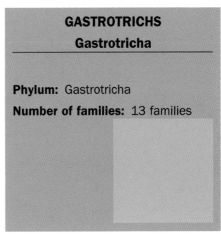

phylum
CHAPTER

PHYSICAL CHARACTERISTICS

Gastrotrichs (GAS-truh-tricks) are microscopic water-dwelling worms shaped like straps, bowling pins, or various forms in between. They are 0.002 to 0.1 inch (50 micrometers to 3.5 millimeters) long. The body is flat on the bottom and arched on the top. The body covering is almost see-through, like fogged-up glass. The belly is covered with hairlike fibers. The body is divided into head and trunk regions. The head has a mouth at the tip and sometimes eyes, tentacles, or both. The trunk contains a straight intestine, reproductive organs, at least one pair of simple waste-filtering organs, and an anus (AY-nuhs). Muscles on the trunk run in the circular, lengthwise, and spiral directions. There is no body cavity. Some gastrotrichs have sticky tubes on the head or trunk.

GEOGRAPHIC RANGE

Gastrotrichs live all over the world.

HABITAT

All gastrotrichs live in water. About one-half of all species live in the sea between sand grains on beaches and the continental shelf. Some species live in the deep sea. Freshwater gastrotrichs live on submerged or floating plants, drift in open water, or live between grains of sand.

DIET

Gastrotrichs eat algae, other protists, and bacteria. Algae (AL-jee) are plantlike growths that live in water and have no true

■ **phylum**

class

subclass

order

monotypic order

suborder

family

roots, stems, or leaves. Protists (PROH-tists) are one-celled living things that have a nucleus (NOO-klee-uhs), which is the control center of a cell.

BEHAVIOR AND REPRODUCTION

Gastrotrichs glide by beating the hairlike fibers on their bellies and use muscles to change direction while gliding. Sea-dwelling species move toward and along solid objects such as sand or gravel and use sticky tubes to attach to the bottom. Some species use creeping movements like those inchworms make. Most gastrotrichs move away from light.

Gastrotrichs make both sperm and eggs. They place sperm in each other while mating. Fertilization (FUR-teh-lih-ZAY-shun), or the joining of egg and sperm to start development, takes place inside the body, but the embryos, or fertilized eggs, are released and develop outside the body. When they hatch, the young gastrotrichs look like small adults. There is no larva stage. A larva (LAR-vuh) is an animal in an early stage that changes form before becoming an adult.

GASTROTRICHS AND PEOPLE

Gastrotrichs may help beaches by eating washed-up waste, preventing decay and the odor that comes with it.

CONSERVATION STATUS

Gastrotrichs are not considered threatened or endangered.

Lepidodermella squamata

NO COMMON NAME
Lepidodermella squamata

Physical characteristics: *Lepidodermella squamata* (abbreviated as *L. squamata*) gastrotrichs are shaped like bowling pins and grow to a length of 0.007 inch (190 micrometers). The head is separated from the body by a short neck. The trunk has a forked tail and two sticky tubes. The body covering is made up of scales. Hairlike fibers are present on the sides of the head and in two rows on the belly.

Geographic range: *L. squamata* gastrotrichs live in the United States, Brazil, Uruguay, Japan, and much of Europe.

Habitat: *L. squamata* gastrotrichs live on plants in lakes, ponds, swamps, and streams. They also may live between grains of sand.

Diet: *L. squamata* gastrotrichs eat algae, bacteria, and waste.

Behavior and reproduction: *L. squamata* gastrotrichs glide slowly and are sensitive to blue light. The life cycle begins with development of eggs without fertilization. Up to four of these eggs are laid. Some

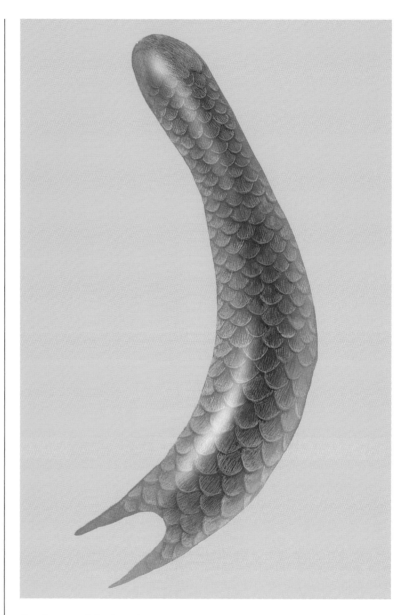

Lepidodermella squamata *gastrotrichs live on plants in lakes, ponds, swamps, and streams. They also may live between grains of sand. (Illustration by John Megahan. Reproduced by permission.)*

develop quickly, but the eggs usually develop slowly and can survive drying out and freezing. A few days after hatching, the gastrotrich develops both female and male reproductive organs.

***Lepidodermella squamata* and people:** *L. squamata* gastrotrichs are sold for use in laboratory studies.

Conservation status: *L. squamata* gastrotrichs are not considered threatened or endangered. ■

FOR MORE INFORMATION

Books:

Burnie, David. *How Nature Works.* Pleasantville, NY: Reader's Digest, 1991.

Cushing, Colbert E., and J. David Allan. *Streams.* San Diego, CA: Academic, 2001.

Reid, George K. *Pond Life.* New York: St. Martin's, 2001.

Web sites:

"Chaetonotus (Gastrotricha) Movies." Florida State University. http://micro.magnet.fsu.edu/moviegallery/pondscum/gastrotrich/chaetonotus/index.html (accessed on February 2, 2005).

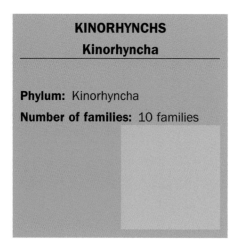

KINORHYNCHS

Kinorhyncha

Phylum: Kinorhyncha

Number of families: 10 families

phylum

CHAPTER

phylum

class

subclass

order

monotypic order

suborder

family

PHYSICAL CHARACTERISTICS

Kinorhynchs (KIH-nuh-rinks) are tiny, spiny worms that live in the sea. Adult kinorhynchs are 0.008 to 0.05 inch (200 micrometers to 1.2 millimeters) long. Most kinorhynchs are clear, but some are yellowish or reddish. Kinorhynchs have 13 body segments: a head, a neck, and 11 trunk segments. The head is spherical, can be drawn into the trunk, and has 5 to 7 rings and as many as 91 spines that face backward. The mouth, which is at the tip of the head, contains sharp teeth and is surrounded by bristles. There are more bristles inside the mouth. The head is joined to the trunk by a neck that has plates that close over the head when it is pulled back into the trunk. The trunk is covered by armor and spines and contains glands that release mucus.

GEOGRAPHIC RANGE

Kinorhynchs live all over the world.

HABITAT

Kinorhynchs live in all seas from polar to tropical and at all depths. Most live in mud or mud mixed with sand.

DIET

Kinorhynchs eat diatoms, waste material, and bacteria. Diatoms (DYE-uh-tahms) are a type of algae that have a shell. Algae (AL-jee) are plantlike growths that live in water and have no true roots, stems, or leaves.

128   Grzimek's Student Animal Life Resource

BEHAVIOR AND REPRODUCTION

Kinorhynchs move by contracting the muscles on the top and bottom of their body. The contraction increases pressure on the fluid in the trunk. This process plows the spines into the sand or mud and pushes the worm forward, at the same time forcing its head out of the trunk. When the worm relaxes its muscles, the head is pulled back into the trunk.

Kinorhynchs collect diatoms by using their rigid bristles as tweezers to pinch an end of the diatom's shell, manipulate the diatom into their mouth, and break the shell. Then they suck out the insides.

Kinorhynchs have separate sexes. A male places a bag of sperm in a female, where fertilization (FUR-teh-lih-ZAY-shun), or the joining of egg and sperm to start development, takes place. The female then attaches the egg sac to sand grains. In about ten days the young kinorhynchs tear open the egg sac by straightening their bodies and thrusting out their heads. Young kinorhynchs shed their outer layer five or six times before reaching adult size.

KINORHYNCHS AND PEOPLE

Kinorhynchs have no known importance to people.

CONSERVATION STATUS

Kinorhynchs are not considered threatened or endangered.

Echinoderes sensibilis

NO COMMON NAME
Echinoderes sensibilis

Physical characteristics: The trunk of *Echinoderes sensibilis* kinorhynchs is 0.012 to 0.014 inch (320 to 350 micrometers) long and yellowish. The head has 91 spines arranged in seven circles. There are hairlike fibers on some trunk segments.

Geographic range: *Echinoderes sensibilis* (abbreviated as *E. sensibilis*) kinorhynchs live on the Pacific coast of Japan.

Habitat: *E. sensibilis* kinorhynchs live in saltwater pools in areas that are exposed at low tide.

Diet: *E. sensibilis* kinorhynchs eat diatoms.

Behavior and reproduction: Scientists do not know how *E. sensibilis* kinorhynchs behave. The young shed six times as they grow into adults.

Echinoderes sensibilis and people: *E. sensibilis* kinorhynchs have no known importance to people.

Conservation status: *E. sensibilis* kinorhynchs are not considered threatened or endangered. ◼

FOR MORE INFORMATION

Books:

Valentine, James W. *On the Origin of Phyla.* Chicago: University of Chicago Press, 2004.

Web sites:

"Evolution and Biogeography of Benthic Deep-Sea Fauna in the East of New Zealand." *Geomar.* http://www.geomar.de/projekte/zealandia/english/hintergrund.html#evolution (accessed on February 2, 2005).

Kinorhynchs move by contracting the muscles on the top and bottom of their body. This process plows the spines into the sand or mud and pushes the worm forward, at the same time forcing its head out of the trunk. When the worm relaxes its muscles, the head is pulled back into the trunk. (Illustration by Amanda Humphrey. Reproduced by permission.)

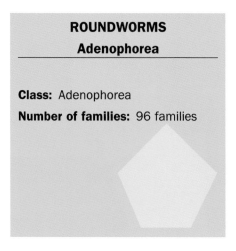

ROUNDWORMS

Adenophorea

Class: Adenophorea

Number of families: 96 families

class

CHAPTER

phylum

● **class**

subclass

order

monotypic order

suborder

family

PHYSICAL CHARACTERISTICS

The size of roundworms ranges from microscopic to as long as 3.3 feet (1 meter). Most roundworms have a hard, sharp spear on their head, and some have bristles on the head. The body of roundworms is protected by a flexible but strong, grooved body covering. A layer beneath this covering releases fluids that harden to form the covering. The body has three tissue layers and a fluid-filled false body cavity, meaning the cavity is between the inner and middle layers rather than the middle layer and the outer layer, as it is in complex animals. The sensing system of roundworms is made up of holes behind, or in some cases on, the lips.

GEOGRAPHIC RANGE

Roundworms live all over the world.

HABITAT

Roundworms live in water and soil everywhere except the desert. A few species are parasites of plants and animals. Parasites (PAIR-uh-sites) are animals or plants that live on or in other animals or plants, or hosts, without helping them and usually harming them.

DIET

Most roundworms eat bacteria, fungi, and tiny growths in the soil. The parasite species feed on blood, body fluids, intestinal contents, and mucus in their hosts.

BEHAVIOR AND REPRODUCTION

Roundworms move their spear in and out of their prey, puncturing the cells and emptying the contents. Most species of roundworms have two sexes, but in a few species the worms make both eggs and sperm. Fertilization (FUR-teh-lih-ZAY-shun), or the uniting of egg and sperm to start development, takes place inside the females, who then lay the eggs.

ROUNDWORMS AND PEOPLE

Roundworms that infect people can cause disease and death. Roundworm plant parasites damage crops. Roundworms that are not parasites help keep soil healthy, which helps the growth of crops. It may be possible to control mosquitoes with roundworms that kill mosquito larvae. Larvae (LAR-vee) are animals in an early stage that change form before becoming adults.

CONSERVATION STATUS

Roundworms are not considered threatened or endangered.

THAT'S A LOT OF WORMS

Nematodes (NEE-muh-toads), the group that includes roundworms, are second only to insects as having the largest number of animals on earth. Scientists estimate the total number of nematode species is eighty thousand to one million. The total number of species of roundworms is estimated to be about twelve thousand.

NO COMMON NAME
Desmoscolex squamosus

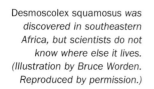

Desmoscolex squamosus *was discovered in southeastern Africa, but scientists do not know where else it lives. (Illustration by Bruce Worden. Reproduced by permission.)*

Physical characteristics: *Desmoscolex squamosus* worms have a small body that is tapered at both ends. Females are longer than males. The body covering has about 70 rings that have a row of holes. Bristles on the body are arranged in pairs. The head is wider than it is long and has a wide front end. The tail has two main rings, and females also have two partial rings.

Geographic range: *Desmoscolex squamosus* (abbreviated as *D. squamosus*) was discovered in southeastern Africa, but scientists do not know where else it lives.

Habitat: *D. squamosus* worms live mainly in the sea, but some live in freshwater and soil.

Diet: Scientists do not know what *D. squamosus* worms eat.

Behavior and reproduction: Scientists do not know how *D. squamosus* worms behave. They have two sexes, and fertilization takes place inside the female's body.

***Desmoscolex squamosus* and people:** *D. squamosus* worms have no known importance to people.

Conservation status: *D. squamosus* worms are not considered threatened or endangered. ∎

NO COMMON NAME
Mermis nigrescens

Physical characteristics: *Mermis nigrescens* worms are free living as adults. As larvae they are parasites that infect the body cavity of grasshoppers. These worms are thin and 2 to 8 inches (5 to 20 centimeters) long. Females are longer than males. Adult females are reddish brown at the front.

Geographic range: *Mermis nigrescens* (abbreviated as *M. nigrescens*) worms live in the British Isles, Europe, and North America. Specific distribution map not available.

Habitat: While they are larvae, *M. nigrescens* worms live mainly in grasshoppers and locusts but may also infect other insects. Once they burrow out of a host, the larvae dig into the soil, where they transform into adults.

Diet: *M. nigrescens* larvae feed on nutrients in their host. The free-living adults do not eat, so the worms must gain all of their nutrients while in the insect host.

Behavior and reproduction: Adult *M. nigrescens* worms easily climb plants, especially during rainy seasons. Females may stay in the soil for several years before coming out to lay eggs on grass and plants, which are then eaten by grasshoppers. Even though they sometimes move toward light, the worms die if they receive continued exposure to direct sunlight.

After the eggs hatch, *M. nigrescens* larvae bore through the host insect's intestinal wall into its body cavity and feed on the host's nutrients. Many worms can infect the same grasshopper. By late summer, the grasshopper is packed with the parasites and dies. The larvae leave the dead insect's body, and the worms spend the rest of their lives in the soil transforming into adults and growing to reproductive age.

Mermis nigrescens and people: Because the larvae kill their hosts, it may be possible to use *M. nigrescens* worms to control grasshoppers, which harm crops.

Conservation status: *M. nigrescens* worms are not considered threatened or endangered. ∎

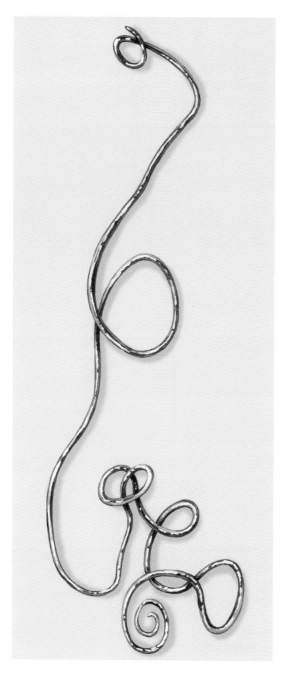

While they are larvae, Mermis nigrescens *worms live mainly in grasshoppers and locusts but may also infect other insects. Once they burrow out of a host, the larvae dig into the soil, where they transform into adults. (Illustration by Bruce Worden. Reproduced by permission.)*

FOR MORE INFORMATION

Books:

Aaseng, Nathan. *Invertebrates.* New York: Venture, 1993.

Niesen, Thomas M. *The Marine Biology Coloring Book.* 2nd ed. New York: HarperResource, 2000.

Web sites:

"Nematodes: Worms of the World." *Medical Laboratory Observer.* http://www.findarticles.com/p/articles/mi_m3230/is_1_33/ai_69759773 (accessed on February 2, 2005).

Class: Secernentea

Number of families: 60–89 families

class

CHAPTER

PHYSICAL CHARACTERISTICS

Secernenteans (seck-uhr-NEHN-shuns) are land-dwelling parasites of plants and animals. Parasites (PAIR-uh-sites) are animals or plants that live on or in other animals or plants, or hosts, without helping them and usually harming them. Secernenteans can be microscopic to several feet long. The body of secernenteans consists of a flexible cylinder with a pointed tail and a blunt head. A flexible but tough covering with a system of crosswise grooves from head to tail protects the insides of secernenteans. Lengthwise ridges run along most of the body. Most secernenteans have a hard, sharp spear on the head. They use muscles to move the spear in and out to puncture their host's cells and empty the contents.

GEOGRAPHIC RANGE

Secernenteans live all over the world.

HABITAT

Most secernenteans live in plant and animal hosts in all types of land habitats. They are rarely found in the sea or in freshwater habitats. Species that are not parasites often live in the soil.

DIET

Secernenteans feed on blood, body fluid, intestinal contents, and mucus in their hosts. They eat bacteria, fungi, and other growths in the soil.

CLASSIFYING WORMS

Are there 60 families of secernenteans or 89 or a number in-between? On the basis of the number of species found and studied so far—about eight thousand—scientists believe a huge number of species have yet to be discovered. Until they know more about the worms, scientists are not ready to assign them to a particular group.

CARE FOR YOUR PET

One dog can be infected with 25 to 100 heartworms. The heart swells, and lung, liver, and kidney damage can occur. Drugs and surgery are used to remove the worms from an infected dog. People can protect their pets by giving them medication regularly to prevent heartworm.

BEHAVIOR AND REPRODUCTION

The life cycle of secernenteans generally goes from fertilization (FUR-teh-lih-zay-shun), or the joining of egg and sperm to start development, in the females through four stages of young and into adulthood. The young worms that hatch from the eggs usually resemble adults except they are smaller and their sex organs are not yet mature. Each of the four stages of young is separated from one another by complete shedding of the outer body layer. Most species of secernenteans have males and females, but in some species male and female organs are in the same worm.

SECERNENTEANS AND PEOPLE

Parasitic secernenteans cause disease and death in people, their food animals, their pets, and their crops. On the other hand, secernenteans that are not parasites are important to the health and survival of humans because they help keep soil healthy.

CONSERVATION STATUS

Secernenteans are not considered threatened or endangered.

CANINE HEARTWORM
Dirofilaria immitis

Physical characteristics: Female canine heartworms are 10 to 12 inches (25 to 30 centimeters) long and about 0.2 inch (5 millimeters) wide. Males are about half the size of females.

Geographic range: Canine heartworms live all over the world. Because they are found throughout the world, no distribution map is provided.

Habitat: Canine heartworms live mainly in warm areas. The primary hosts, also called final hosts, are dogs, cats, ferrets, foxes, wolves, sea lions, and humans. In their hosts adult worms live in the right ventricle of the heart and the blood vessels that connect to it. The intermediate hosts are mosquitoes.

Diet: Canine heartworms feed on their hosts' nutrients, primarily through blood in and around the heart and lungs.

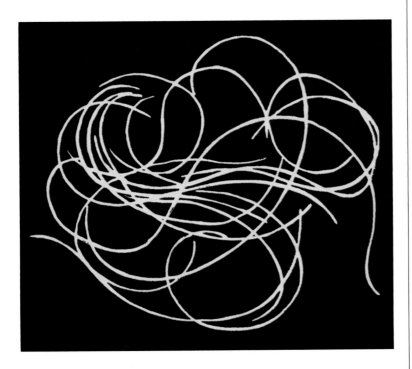

In their hosts adult canine heartworms live in the right ventricle of the heart and the blood vessels that connect to it. (Illustration by John Megahan. Reproduced by permission.)

Behavior and reproduction: Adult canine heartworms live in the pulmonary arteries of their primary hosts. The pulmonary (PULL-muh-NAIR-ee) arteries take blood from the heart to the lungs. Rather than releasing eggs, the females release large numbers of microscopic young worms—as many as five thousand a day—into the host's bloodstream. These microscopic worms can stay in the host for a year or more but cannot develop further until they enter a mosquito. A mosquito bites the host and sucks in the worms with the hosts' blood. The worms start maturing inside the mosquito, which bites another animal and injects the young worms into it. The worms travel to the heart, become adults, and start releasing microscopic young in the new host. Adults can live in a host and continue to produce microscopic young for several years.

Canine heartworms and people: Canine heartworms are dangerous to people and their animals.

Conservation status: Canine heartworms are not considered threatened or endangered. ■

RAT LUNGWORM
Angiostrongylus cantonensis

Physical characteristics: Adult rat lungworms are 0.8 to 1.3 inches (20 to 34 millimeters) long and 0.01 to 0.02 inch (320 to 560 micrometers) wide. The females are larger than the males.

Geographic range: Rat lungworms live all over the world in warm areas. Because they are found throughout the world, no distribution map is provided.

Habitat: The primary hosts of rat lungworms are rats. The intermediate hosts are animals such as snails, oysters, slugs, and crabs.

Diet: Rat lungworms feed on nutrients in the blood of their hosts, specifically around the lungs and brains of rodents and the lungs of humans.

Behavior and reproduction: Adult rat lungworms live in the blood vessels of the lungs of their hosts. Young worms in their first developmental stage enter the respiratory tract, move up the breathing tubes to the mouth, and then are swallowed. The worms move through the digestive tract and are passed in the host's feces (FEE-seez). They

The primary hosts of rat lungworms are rats. The intermediate hosts are animals such as snails, oysters, slugs, and crabs. (Illustration by John Megahan. Reproduced by permission.)

enter intermediate hosts, such as snails, which are eaten by rodents and humans. In rodents the worms travel to the pulmonary arteries and the lungs, where they mature. The adults eventually travel to the brain and travel back to the lungs through veins. In humans, the parasites enter the brain but do not develop further and die.

Rat lungworms and people: Rat lungworms are dangerous to humans because they rupture blood vessels in the brain, causing headache, fever, nerve damage, coma, and death.

Conservation status: Rat lungworms are not considered threatened or endangered. ■

FOR MORE INFORMATION

Books:

Zimmer, Carl. *Parasite Rex.* New York: Free Press, 2000.

Web sites:

"Filarial Nematodes." *Worm Learn.* http://home.austarnet.com.au/wormman/nemacont.htm (accessed on February 16, 2005).

"Heartworm: The Parasite." Mar Vista Animal Medical Center. http://www.marvistavet.com/html/heartworm_-_the_parasite.html (accessed on February 16, 2005).

"Illinois, Iowa, Ohio and Wisconsin Warned of Giant African Snails." News-Medical.Net. http://www.news-medical.net/?id=1301 (accessed on February 16, 2005).

Phylum: Nematomorpha
Number of families: 2 families

phylum
C H A P T E R

PHYSICAL CHARACTERISTICS

Hair worms are long and thin—2 to 118 inches (5 to 300 centimeters) long and 0.02 to 0.4 inch (0.5 to 10 millimeters) wide. They are black, brown, yellow, white, or gray. The front end of most of these worms has a white tip with a thin dark band behind it. Some hair worms have raised bumps on their surface. Young hair worms are parasites (PAIR-eh-sites) and live on or in other animals, or hosts, without helping them and usually harming them, but adults live freely.

GEOGRAPHIC RANGE

Hair worms live all over the world except Antarctica.

HABITAT

One type of hair worm lives in sea animals such as crabs and shrimp. The other type lives in insects such as crickets, grasshoppers, and beetles.

The worms that live in insects usually are found in slow-moving freshwater streams or ponds. In streams the worms are either attached to plants hanging over the banks or live between rocks on the bottom. In the sea, hair worms live anywhere from beaches to the sea floor.

DIET

Adult hair worms do not eat. Young worms absorb nutrients from their hosts.

■ **phylum**

class

subclass

order

monotypic order

suborder

family

BEHAVIOR AND REPRODUCTION

Adult hair worms that live in insects emerge from their hosts in late spring or summer. Some species mate immediately, but others wait a few months. After mating, females lay as many as six million eggs and then die. The worm larvae (LAR-vee) hatch from the eggs and bore into the larvae of water flies. When these larvae transform into adults, they fly to land, taking the hair worm larvae with them. The crickets and beetles and crabs and shrimp are infected when they eat flies containing hair worm larvae.

HAIR WORMS AND PEOPLE

Hair worms do not infect humans.

CONSERVATION STATUS

Hair worms are not considered threatened or endangered.

Paragordius varius

NO COMMON NAME
Paragordius varius

Physical characteristics: The color of *Paragordius varius* worms ranges from light yellow to nearly black. These worms are 4 to 14 inches (100 to 350 millimeters) long and about 0.03 inch (700 micrometers) wide. The tip of the male's tail is split in two and the tip of the female's tail in three.

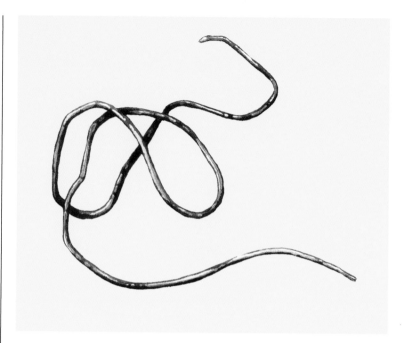

Adult Paragordius varius *worms live in and near slower streams, puddles, and places where rainwater collects. (Illustration by Bruce Worden. Reproduced by permission.)*

Geographic range: *Paragordius varius* (abbreviated as *P. varius*) worms live in North and South America.

Habitat: Adult *P. varius* worms live in and near slower streams, puddles, and places where rain water collects. The larvae live in crickets and grasshoppers.

Diet: *P. varius* larvae absorb nutrients from their hosts. The adults do not eat.

Behavior and reproduction: In the spring, water insects carrying *P. varius* larvae transform into flying adults. Crickets and grasshoppers are infected when they eat dead insects containing worm larvae. Development to adult worms inside the host takes about one month. With this fast development, as many as three generations are produced in a single year.

***Paragordius varius* and people:** *P. varius* worms do not infect humans.

Conservation status: *P. varius* worms are not considered threatened or endangered. ■

FOR MORE INFORMATION

Books:

Thorp, J. H., and A. P. Covich, eds. *Ecology and Classification of North American Freshwater Invertebrates.* San Diego, CA: Academic, 1991.

Web sites:

Hanelt, Ben. "General Gordian Worm Information." University of Nebraska, Lincoln. http://bsweb.unl.edu/emb/janovy/ben/info.html (accessed on February 3, 2005).

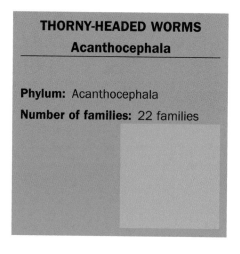

THORNY-HEADED WORMS
Acanthocephala

Phylum: Acanthocephala
Number of families: 22 families

phylum
CHAPTER

■ **phylum**

class

subclass

order

monotypic order

suborder

family

PHYSICAL CHARACTERISTICS

Thorny-headed worms are parasites that live in vertebrates as adults and in insects and crustaceans as larvae. Parasites (PAIR-uh-sites) are animals or plants that live on or in other animals or plants, or hosts, without helping them and usually harming them. Vertebrates (VER-teh-brehts) are animals with a backbone. Crustaceans (krus-TAY-shuns) are water-dwelling animals that have jointed legs and a hard shell but no backbone. Larvae (LAR-vee) are animals in an early stage that change form before becoming adults.

Adult thorny-headed worms are tubular or slightly flat. Most are white or colorless, but some are yellow, brown, red, or orange. Adult thorny-headed worms are less than 1 inch (a few millimeters) to more than 2 feet (60 centimeters) long. Females usually are larger than males. The snout has hooks arranged in rows or lengthwise lines. The worm can retract the snout into its body. In some species the body is armed with spines. Inside their bodies, thorny-headed worms have a network of fluid-filled cavities. They have no digestive tract.

GEOGRAPHIC RANGE

Thorny-headed worms live all over the world.

HABITAT

Adult thorny-headed worms live in the intestines of mammals, birds, fishes, amphibians, and reptiles. Larvae live in crustaceans and insects.

DIET

Thorny-headed worms absorb nutrients from their hosts' intestines.

BEHAVIOR AND REPRODUCTION

When they attach themselves to the intestinal wall of their hosts, thorny-headed worms can cause serious, sometimes fatal, internal damage. In most cases, the more worms there are, the more serious is the damage.

Female and male thorny-headed worms mate in the intestines of their primary hosts. Fertilization (FUR-teh-lih-ZAY-shun), the joining of egg and sperm to start development, takes place inside the female's body. She releases the fertilized (FUR-teh-lyzed) eggs into the host's intestine, and they leave the host in its feces (FEE-seez). Outside the host, the eggs are eaten by intermediate hosts. The larvae hatch, bore into the intermediate host's intestinal wall, and develop there through two more stages. When a primary host, such as a bird, eats the intermediate host, such as an insect, the larvae enter the primary host and develop into adults.

Some species of thorny-headed worms have transport hosts. These hosts are vertebrates that eat intermediate hosts containing final-stage larvae but in which the larvae cannot develop into adult worms. The larvae do not die but stay in the transport host until it is eaten by a suitable primary host.

DRIVING THE HOST CRAZY

To make sure their life cycle is complete, thorny-headed worms can change the behavior of their hosts. For example, one species of crustacean normally swims to the bottom of the water when a duck is near. When infected with thorny-headed worms, however, this crustacean swims up and attaches itself to a rock, making itself easy prey for the duck, which becomes the primary host.

THORNY-HEADED WORMS AND PEOPLE

Very few species of thorny-headed worms cause disease in humans.

CONSERVATION STATUS

Thorny-headed worms are not considered threatened or endangered.

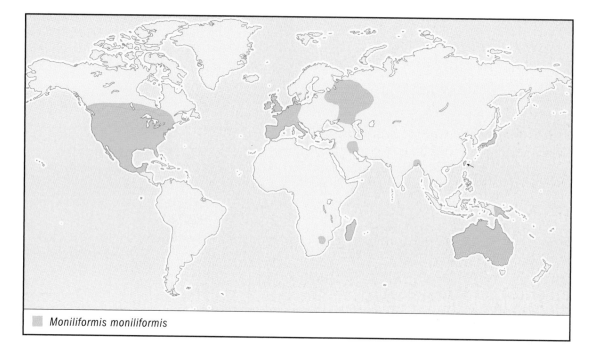

Moniliformis moniliformis

SPECIES ACCOUNTS

NO COMMON NAME
Moniliformis moniliformis

Physical characteristics: *Moniliformis moniliformis* worms are long, threadlike, and often coiled. Females are 4 to 11 inches (10 to 27 centimeters) long. Males are 1.6 to 2 inches (4 to 5 centimeters) long. The snouts of these worms have 12 lengthwise rows of seven to eight hooks.

Geographic range: *Moniliformis moniliformis* (abbreviated as *M. moniliformis*) worms live all over the world.

Habitat: The primary hosts of *M. moniliformis* worms are dogs, cats, and wild rodents, especially rats. The intermediate hosts are beetles and cockroaches. The transport hosts are toads and lizards.

Diet: *M. moniliformis* worms absorb nutrients from their hosts.

Behavior and reproduction: Adult *M. moniliformis* worms mature in five to six weeks in the intestines of primary hosts. Hatching of the first-stage larvae occurs 15 minutes to 48 hours after ingestion by

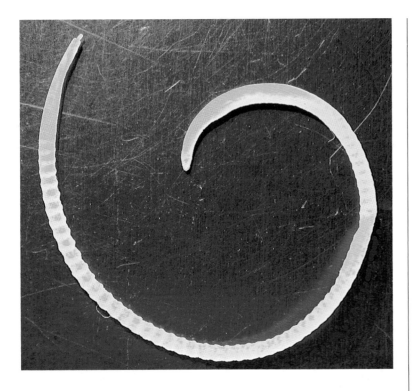

The primary hosts of Monilifromis moniliformis *worms are dogs, cats, and wild rodents, especially rats. (Allen Shostak)*

the intermediate host. The larvae develop to their final stage in the intermediate host in about two months.

***Moniliformis moniliformis* and people:** *M. moniliformis* worms cause disease in people. The symptoms include tiredness, ringing in the ears, and diarrhea.

Conservation status: *M. moniliformis* worms are not considered threatened or endangered. ■

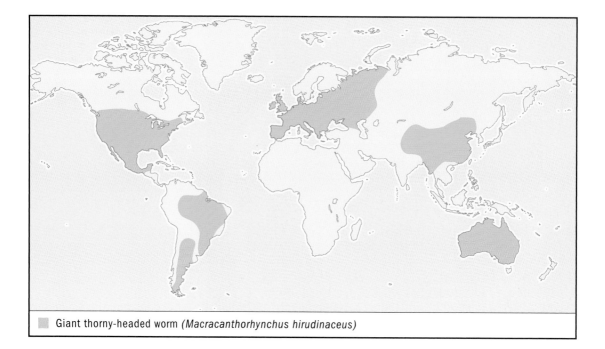

Giant thorny-headed worm (*Macracanthorhynchus hirudinaceus*)

GIANT THORNY-HEADED WORM
Macracanthorhynchus hirudinaceus

Physical characteristics: Female giant thorny-headed worms are as long as 26 inches (65 centimeters) and are 0.3 to 0.4 inch (8 to 9 millimeters) wide. Males are as long as 4 inches (10 centimeters). The body is grayish brown with deep grooves on the surface. The snout has six spiral rows of six hooks each.

Geographic range: Giant thorny-headed worms live all over the world.

Habitat: Adult giant thorny-headed worms live in hogs, squirrels, moles, hyenas, and dogs. The larvae live in cockroaches and beetles.

Diet: Giant thorny-headed worms absorb nutrients from their hosts.

Behavior and reproduction: Female giant thorny-headed worms release a huge number of eggs that can survive more than three years in the primary host. The larvae develop for four to five months in the

intermediate host. The worms reach adulthood two to three months after entering the primary host.

Giant thorny-headed worms and people: Giant thorny-headed worms cause disease in people and hogs. Hogs become infected when they ingest beetles while rooting for grubs. Humans become infected mainly in rural Asia, where people eat beetles and use them for medicine.

Conservation status: Giant thorny-headed worms are not considered threatened or endangered. ■

FOR MORE INFORMATION

Books:

Moore, Janice. *Parasites and the Behavior of Animals.* New York: Oxford University Press, 2002.

Zimmer, Carl. *Parasite Rex.* New York: Free Press, 2000.

Web sites:

Cole, Rebecca A. "Acanthocephaliasis." *Field Manual of Wildlife Diseases.* http://212.187.155.84/pass_06june/Subdirectories_for_Search/Glossary& References_Contents/BooksContents/BookRef36_FieldManualofWildlife Diseases/33/chapter33.htm (accessed on February 18, 2005).

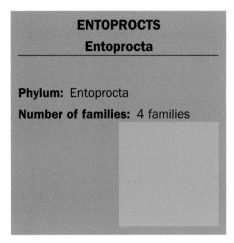

ENTOPROCTS
Entoprocta

Phylum: Entoprocta
Number of families: 4 families

phylum C H A P T E R

PHYSICAL CHARACTERISTICS

Entoprocts are tiny bottom-dwelling animals that have a crown of tentacles and a thin stalk. Both the mouth and anus (AY-nuhs) open inside the crown. Some entoprocts live in colonies and are attached to one another by a branch at the base of their stalks.

GEOGRAPHIC RANGE

Entoprocts live all over the world.

HABITAT

Most entoprocts live at the bottom of warm, moderate, and cold seas from the shore to deep water. One species lives in freshwater. Colonies live on rocks, shell remains, human-made objects such as dock pilings, and sometimes on other animals. Most species not in colonies live on the bodies of animals such as sponges.

DIET

Entoprocts eat drifting microscopic plant particles.

BEHAVIOR AND REPRODUCTION

When they are touched, entoprocts contract their tentacles and bend at the stalk. Some species that live alone rather than in colonies can glide over the bottom. Others somersault across the bottom, and one can walk using a foot with two leglike extensions.

phylum

class
subclass
order
monotypic order
suborder
family

Entoprocts that live in colonies are either male or female, but both sexes are present in a single colony. Entoprocts that do not live in colonies make both eggs and sperm. They are males first and then turn into females. Male entoprocts release sperm into the water. The sperm is taken up by females and joins with eggs inside them. Larvae develop inside the females. Larvae (LAR-vee) are animals in an early stage that change form before becoming adults.

All entoprocts can reproduce by budding. Buds develop at the base of entoprocts that live in colonies or at the base or crown of entoprocts that live alone. The buds grows to full size and then break off to live as new individuals.

ENTOPROCTS AND PEOPLE

Entoprocts have no known importance to humans.

CONSERVATION STATUS

Entoprocts are not considered threatened or endangered.

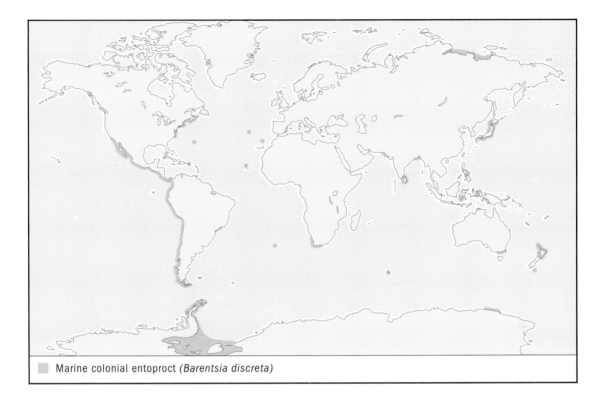

Marine colonial entoproct (*Barentsia discreta*)

MARINE COLONIAL ENTOPROCT
Barentsia discreta

Physical characteristics: Marine colonial entoprocts are 0.1 to 0.2 inch (3 to 6 millimeters) long and have about 20 tentacles. The stalks are three to eight times longer than the crown and have a muscular swelling at the base. The bases are attached to a branch that connects the colony members.

Geographic range: Marine colonial entoprocts live all over the world except northern Europe.

Habitat: Marine colonial entoprocts live on rocks, stones, dock pilings, and worm tubes in shallow or deep sea water.

Diet: Marine colonial entoprocts eat drifting microscopic plant particles.

Behavior and reproduction: When disturbed, marine colonial entoprocts bend from the base, but the stalk itself does not curve. When

Marine colonial entoprocts live on rocks, stones, dock pilings, and worm tubes in shallow or deep sea water. (Illustration by Emily Damstra. Reproduced by permission.)

one member of the colony bends, those around it also bend. Marine colonial entoprocts bud from the branch that connects the colony members. A single colony has both male and female members. Embryos develop into larvae inside the females.

Marine colonial entoprocts and people: Marine colonial entoprocts have no known importance to people.

Conservation status: Marine colonial entoprocts are not considered threatened or endangered. ■

FOR MORE INFORMATION

Books:

Valentine, James W. *On the Origin of Phyla.* Chicago: University of Chicago Press, 2004.

Web sites:

Badorf, Michelle, Courtney Lewis, Bridget O'Malley, Kimberly Owen, and Shelly Zimmerman. "Reclassification of Entoprocta into the Subkingdom Proterostomata." *Journal of Systematic Biology.* http://comenius.susqu .edu/bi/202/Journal/Vol8/number1/1zoobls.html (accessed on February 3, 2005).

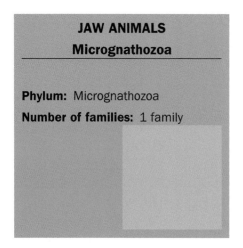

JAW ANIMALS
Micrognathozoa

Phylum: Micrognathozoa
Number of families: 1 family

phylum
CHAPTER

- phylum
- class
- subclass
- order
- monotypic order
- suborder
- family

PHYSICAL CHARACTERISTICS

Limnognathia maerski is the only species of jaw animals. These animals are 0.004 to 0.006 inch (100 to 150 micrometers) long. The body is divided into a head, an accordion-like chest, and an abdomen. Jaw animals have plates between the cells of the body covering of their back and sides. The bottom surface of the animals is covered with hairlike fibers. The sensing system is a series of bristles. The digestive system is made up of a highly complex jaw, a simple intestine, and an anus (AY-nuhs) that rarely opens.

GEOGRAPHIC RANGE

Jaw animals live in Greenland and between Africa and Australia 1,500 miles (2,400 kilometers) north of Antarctica.

HABITAT

Jaw animals live in moss or sand at the bottom of cold running or still freshwater.

DIET

Jaw animals eat bacteria, algae, and diatoms. Algae (AL-jee) are plantlike growths that live in water and have no true roots, stems, or leaves. Diatoms (DYE-uh-tahms) are a type of algae that have a shell.

BEHAVIOR AND REPRODUCTION

During their search for food, jaw animals move their head slowly from side to side, while the fibers on the head beat food particles toward the animal's mouth. Food that reaches the mouth is quickly grabbed by the bottom jaws, dragged into the mouth, and processed by the main jaws.

When they move, jaw animals either crawl or swim. While swimming, they move slowly in a spiral. When crawling, they glide slowly on the bottom. If disturbed, a crawling jaw animal stops and attaches to the bottom by using a sticky pad on its belly.

Jaw animals produce two kinds of eggs: a thin-shelled type and a thick-shelled type. Scientists believe the thin-shelled eggs are made by asexual reproduction and that the thick-shelled eggs are made by sexual reproduction, even though males have never been seen. One possibility is that jaw animals produce dwarf males that live only for a very short period and therefore have not yet been found. Another possibility is that jaw animals hatch as males and then quickly develop into females. Asexual (ay-SEK-shuh-wuhl) means without and sexual means with the uniting of egg and sperm for the transfer of DNA from two parents.

JAW ANIMALS AND PEOPLE

Jaw animals have no known importance to people.

CONSERVATION STATUS

Jaw animals are not considered threatened or endangered.

FOR MORE INFORMATION

Books:

Ruppert, Edward E., Richard S. Fox, and Robert D. Barnes. *Invertebrate Zoology*. 7th ed. Belmont, CA: Thomson-Brooks/Cole, 2004.

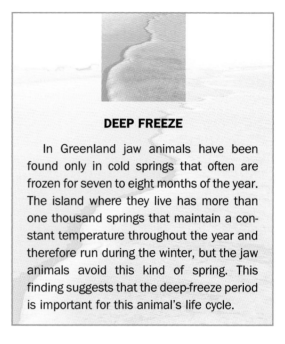

DEEP FREEZE

In Greenland jaw animals have been found only in cold springs that often are frozen for seven to eight months of the year. The island where they live has more than one thousand springs that maintain a constant temperature throughout the year and therefore run during the winter, but the jaw animals avoid this kind of spring. This finding suggests that the deep-freeze period is important for this animal's life cycle.

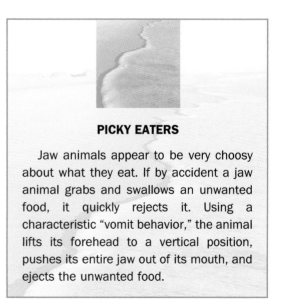

PICKY EATERS

Jaw animals appear to be very choosy about what they eat. If by accident a jaw animal grabs and swallows an unwanted food, it quickly rejects it. Using a characteristic "vomit behavior," the animal lifts its forehead to a vertical position, pushes its entire jaw out of its mouth, and ejects the unwanted food.

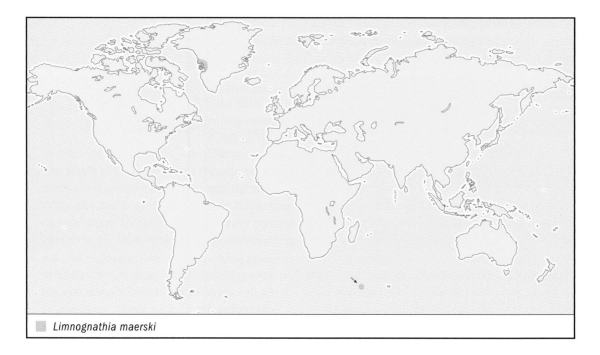

Limnognathia maerski

When they move, jaw animals either crawl or swim. While swimming, they move slowly in a spiral. When crawling, they glide slowly on the bottom. (Illustration by Emily Damstra. Reproduced by permission.)

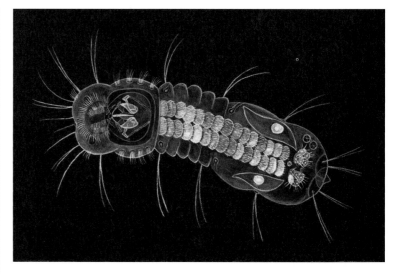

Web sites:

"Jaws: New Animal Discovered." *Science Now*. http://www.calacademy .org/science_now/archive/headline_science/new_critter_120700.htm (accessed on February 20, 2005).

"Micrognathozoa: A New Microscopic Animal Group from Greenland." Zoological Museum in Copenhagen. http://www.zmuc.dk/InverWeb/Dyr/ Limnognathia/Limno_intro_UK.htm (accessed on February 20, 2005).

phylum
CHAPTER

PHYSICAL CHARACTERISTICS

Gnathostomulids (NATH-oh-STOH-muh-lids) are tiny sea worms. They are thread shaped and 0.01 to 0.1 inch (0.3 to 3.5 millimeters) long. Most are colorless or transparent, but some are bright red. The front end of some gnathostomulids is pointed, but that of others is rounded. The rear end is rounded or forms a tail. Each cell of the body covering has a single, long hairlike fiber used for movement. Some of these fibers also may have sensing functions.

The nervous system is at the base of the body covering and consists of a brain and a structure from which paired nerves originate. The muscles are simple and weak, except for a complex feeding tube. The mouth is on the bottom of the worm near the front, and there is no anus (AY-nuhs). In most species the complex, muscular, feeding tube contains hard mouthparts consisting of a plate in the lower lip and paired jaws. In most species, the inner, front parts of the jaw have groups or rows of teeth.

GEOGRAPHIC RANGE

Gnathostomulids live all over the world but mainly in the northern part of the Atlantic Ocean and the southern part of the Pacific Ocean.

HABITAT

Gnathostomulids live on sheltered beaches, near sea grasses and mangroves, and between coral reefs.

phylum

class

subclass

order

monotypic order

suborder

family

DIET

Gnathostomulids graze on bacteria and threads of fungus attached to sand grains.

BEHAVIOR AND REPRODUCTION

Gnathostomulids glide between sand grains. They contract when disturbed. Some species spin a cocoon of mucus. Gnathostomulids make both eggs and sperm. Sperm is transferred by mating and is stored either between the digestive tract and outer tissue layer or in a storage pouch. Only one large egg matures at a time. The egg joins with sperm and then is laid by bursting through the worm's back. The eggs hatch directly into young animals, which grow to adults.

GNATHOSTOMULIDS AND PEOPLE

Gnathostomulids have no known importance to people.

CONSERVATION STATUS

Gnathostomulids are not considered threatened or endangered.

Red haplognathia (Haplognathia ruberrima)

RED HAPLOGNATHIA
Haplognathia ruberrima

Physical characteristics: Red haplognathia are 0.1 inch (3.5 millimeters) long and 0.006 in (140 micrometers) in diameter. They are one of the largest gnathostomulids. Most of these worms are brick red, reddish brown, or pink. The head is pointed, and the rear is rounded. The jaws are solid and have large winglike structures and many sharp feelers. The bottom plate of the jaw is shieldlike and has thorns.

Geographic range: Red haplognathia live on the coasts of Australia, Fiji, Hawaii, eastern North America, western Europe, and countries surrounding the Mediterranean Sea.

Habitat: Red haplognathia live in waste-rich sand in shallow water near the shore.

Diet: Red haplognathia graze on fungus threads and bacteria among sand grains.

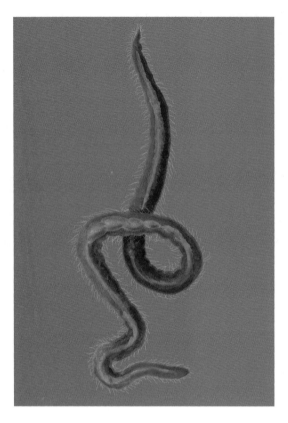

Red haplognathia graze on fungus threads and bacteria among sand grains. (Illustration by Amanda Smith. Reproduced by permission.)

Behavior and reproduction: Red haplognathia coil up by muscular action, then uncoil using their hairlike fibers, often from both ends at the same time, the head pulling forward and the rear pulling backward. Red haplognathia lay a single egg, which bursts through the worm's back. The egg then sticks to a sand grain until the young worm emerges.

Red haplognathia and people: Red haplognathia have no known importance to people.

Conservation status: Red haplognathia are not considered threatened or endangered. ∎

FOR MORE INFORMATION

Books:

Valentine, James W. *On the Origin of Phyla.* Chicago: University of Chicago Press, 2004.

Web sites:

Tyler, Seth. "Platyhelminthes and Acoelomorpha: Phyla of Controversy." University of Maine. http://devbio.umesci.maine.edu/styler/globalworming/platyhelm.htm (accessed on February 3, 2005).

phylum
C H A P T E R

PHYSICAL CHARACTERISTICS

The body of priapulans (PRYE-uh-PUH-luhns) is divided into three parts: introvert (IN-troh-vert), trunk, and tail. The animals use a pair of muscles to pull the introvert completely into the trunk. Spines of various sizes and shapes cover the entire surface of the introvert. Inside the introvert is a muscular feeding tube armed with teeth.

The trunk houses the internal body organs, in particular the digestive system and reproductive organs. The body is filled with fluid that serves as a skeleton to support the body when the muscles of the body wall contract. When priapulans move, the fluid moves around in the body cavity and serves the functions of circulation, waste removal, and respiration. The tail is continuous with the body cavity of the trunk and may be used for respiration.

GEOGRAPHIC RANGE

Priapulans live all over the world.

HABITAT

Priapulans live in sand and mud in all oceans at all depths. Larger priapulans live in colder waters. Small priapulans are most common in shallow tropical waters.

DIET

Priapulans eat sea worms.

███ **phylum**

class

subclass

order

monotypic order

suborder

family

The skeleton of pria-
pulans is nothing but fluid.

BEHAVIOR AND REPRODUCTION

With the introvert fully extended, priapulans grasp prey with their teeth and rapidly roll it inward. Priapulans depend on their fluid skeleton for movement. They use their extended introvert and the muscles of the front part of their trunk to anchor themselves in the sand. Once anchored, priapulans can pull themselves through the sand by contracting their body wall muscles.

Priapulans have separate sexes. They release their eggs and sperm into the water, where fertilization (FUR-teh-lih-zay-shun), or the uniting of egg and sperm to start development, takes place and larvae develop. Larvae (LAR-vee) are animals in an early stage that change form before becoming adults.

PRIAPULANS AND PEOPLE

Because they are considered living fossils, priapulans are important for research.

CONSERVATION STATUS

Priapulans are not considered threatened or endangered.

Priapulus caudatus

NO COMMON NAME
Priapulus caudatus

Physical characteristics: *Priapulus caudatus* is large, as long as 8 inches (200 millimeters). The body is strongly tubular and ringed. The introvert can be quite long when extended, as much as one-third the length of the trunk.

Geographic range: *Priapulus caudatus* (abbreviated as *P. caudatus*) lives in the Northern Hemisphere, from the Arctic Ocean to the Mediterranean Sea in the eastern Atlantic Ocean and to California in the eastern Pacific Ocean.

Habitat: *P. caudatus* lives in the sea on soft, muddy bottoms.

Diet: *P. caudatus* eats waste when young and is a predator of worms as an adult.

Behavior and reproduction: *P. caudatus* uses its fluid skeleton for movement. The introvert and forward part of the trunk act as an anchor in the mud. Once anchored, the animal pulls itself through the

Priapulans   169

Priapulus caudatus *eats waste when young and is a predator of worms as an adult. (Illustration by John Megahan. Reproduced by permission.)*

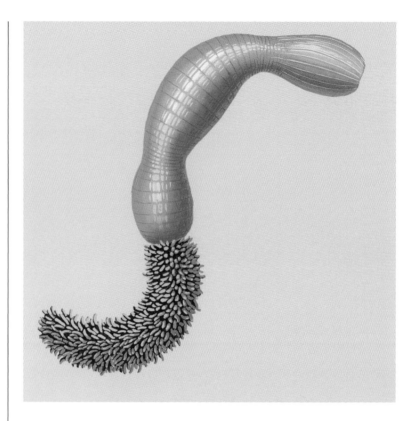

mud by contracting body wall muscles. *P. caudatus* has separate sexes. Eggs and sperm are released into the water, where they unite. The larvae live in the bottom mud. As the larvae grow, they shed their outer covering and gradually grow into young animals.

Priapulus caudatus and people: *P. caudatus* has no known importance to people.

Conservation status: *P. caudatus* is not considered threatened or endangered. ■

FOR MORE INFORMATION

Books:

Nielsen, Claus. *Animal Evolution.* New York: Oxford University Press, 2001.

Valentine, James W. *On the Origin of Phyla.* Chicago: University of Chicago Press, 2004.

Young, Craig M., ed. *Atlas of Marine Invertebrate Larvae.* San Diego, CA: Academic, 2002.

Web sites:

"The Priapulida." Lamont-Doherty Earth Observatory. http://www.ldeo .columbia.edu/edu/dees/ees/life/slides/phyla/priapulida.html (accessed on February 3, 2005).

"Priapulid Evolution." Seattle University. http://classes.seattleu.edu/ biology/biol235/hodin/nematodePriapulidGroup/priapulid/evolution.htm (accessed on February 3, 2005).

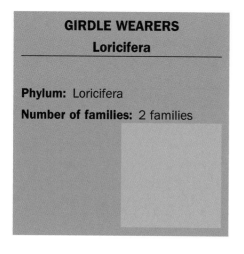

GIRDLE WEARERS
Loricifera

Phylum: Loricifera
Number of families: 2 families

phylum

CHAPTER

■ **phylum**
class
subclass
order
monotypic order
suborder
family

PHYSICAL CHARACTERISTICS

Girdle wearers are 0.008 to 0.02 inch (200 to 400 micrometers) long. The body is divided into five sections: a mouth cone, a head that can be drawn into the body, a neck, a thorax, and an abdomen. The mouth cone consists of six to 16 ridges and a tube. Some girdle wearers have six sharp spears in the mouth. The head consists of nine rows of spines used for movement and sensing. The neck consists of three rows of plates with 15 plates in each row and 15 spines. The thorax has no spines.

The abdomen consists of an armored band, or girdle, with six to ten strong plates or 22 to 40 folds. There are sense organs toward the rear of the abdomen. Girdle wearers have a digestive system, a reproductive system, a simple waste-removal system, a complex muscular system, and a nervous system with a large brain and a nerve cord with groups of nerve cells outside the brain.

GEOGRAPHIC RANGE

Girdle wearers live all over the world.

HABITAT

Girdle wearers live in the sea at all depths. They are common around the North Pole and the South Pole, especially in the deep sea. Girdle wearers live in the spaces between sand grains or in mud.

172   Grzimek's Student Animal Life Resource

DIET

Girdle wearers eat algae and bacteria. Algae (AL-jee) are plantlike growths that live in water and have no true roots, stems, or leaves.

BEHAVIOR AND REPRODUCTION

Girdle wearers attach themselves to sand or mud with a kind of glue made by glands located toward the rear of adults and on the toes of larvae. Larvae (LAR-vee) are animals in an early stage that change form before becoming adults. Adults crawl by using their spines and their mouth cones. The mouth cone telescopes out to its full length, fastens itself to a sand grain, and then draws in again so that the animal's body is pulled forward. The larvae use spines and bristles to crawl between grains of sand. They can also swim by using their toes. Girdle wearers eat by piercing bacteria and algae with their mouth spears and sucking out the contents.

Girdle wearers have separate sexes. Fertilization (FUR-teh-lih-ZAY-shun), or the joining of egg and sperm to start development, takes place either inside or outside the body. The primary larvae hatch from the fertilized (FUR-teh-lyzed) eggs and grow by shedding their outer layer. After two to five of these shedding stages, the larvae go into a resting stage and never feed. A male or female with fully developed reproductive organs emerges from the resting stage, and the life cycle repeats itself.

Some girdle wearers also have a cycle in which the larvae develop from eggs without fertilization. These larvae develop either into new larvae that develop without fertilization or into resting-stage larvae that shed their outer layer and transform into adult males or females.

GIRDLE WEARERS AND PEOPLE

Scientists may be able to use girdle wearers as indicators of pollution.

CONSERVATION STATUS

Girdle wearers are not considered threatened or endangered.

WHAT'S IN A NAME?

The lorica (luh-RYE-kuh) was the metal or leather plated body armor worn by Roman soldiers. The plated band or belt on loriciferans looks like this armor. In the old days a belt was called a girdle.

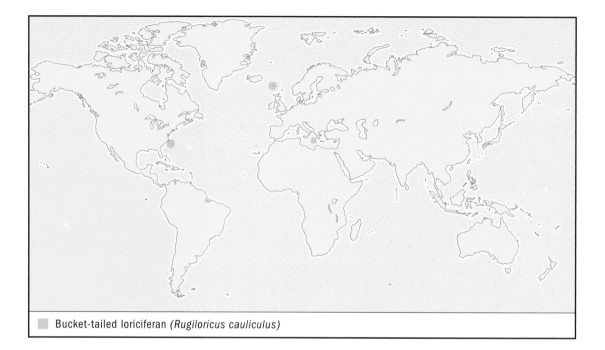

Bucket-tailed loriciferan (*Rugiloricus cauliculus*)

SPECIES ACCOUNT

BUCKET-TAILED LORICIFERAN
Rugiloricus cauliculus

Physical characteristics: Adult bucket-tailed loriciferans (LAW-ruh-SIH-fuh-ruhns) are 0.007 to 0.01 inch (180 to 264 micrometers) long. The head has nine rows of spines. The armored band has 60 folds. The anal (AY-nuhl) cone is pointed.

Geographic range: Bucket-tailed loriciferans live off the coast of North Carolina and South Carolina, United States; in the Mediterranean Sea; and around a small group of islands north of the United Kingdom.

Habitat: Bucket-tailed loriciferans live on sand at a depth of 660 to 1,640 feet (200 to 500 meters).

Diet: Bucket-tailed loriciferans eat bacteria.

Behavior and reproduction: Scientists do not know how bucket-tailed loriciferans behave. They have sexual and asexual life cycles.

Asexual (ay-SEK-shuh-wuhl) means without and sexual means with the uniting of egg and sperm for the transfer of DNA from two parents.

Bucket-tailed loriciferans and people: Bucket-tailed loriciferans have no known importance to people.

Conservation status: Bucket-tailed loriciferans are not considered threatened or endangered. ■

FOR MORE INFORMATION

Books:

Valentine, James W. *On the Origin of Phyla.* Chicago: University of Chicago Press, 2004.

Young, Craig M., ed. *Atlas of Marine Invertebrate Larvae.* San Diego, CA: Academic, 2002.

Web sites:

"Between the Grains." *The Why Files.* http://whyfiles.org/022critters/meiofauna.html (accessed on February 4, 2005).

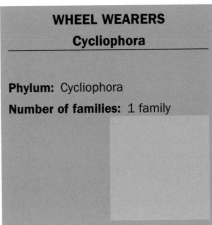

WHEEL WEARERS

Cycliophora

Phylum: Cycliophora
Number of families: 1 family

phylum
C H A P T E R

PHYSICAL CHARACTERISTICS

Wheel wearers are microscopic animals that live in the mouths of Norway lobsters. *Symbion pandora* is the only fully described species. Scientists have found two other species, but do not have enough details to describe them thoroughly.

The main phase in the life cycle of wheel wearers is the feeding stage. Wheel wearers in this stage are about 0.01 inch (350 micrometers) long. The body is made up of a bell-shaped mouth funnel, a trunk, and a stalk with an attachment disk. The rim of the funnel is made up of hairlike fibers alternating with muscle cells. The fibers are used to collect food, and the muscle cells close the mouth when the animal stops feeding. The inside of the funnel is covered with hairlike fibers. The funnel connects to the trunk with a narrow, movable neck. The trunk is slightly egg shaped and contains a U-shaped digestive system that runs from the mouth through the stomach to the anus, which is close to the neck. The trunk narrows to a stalk that leads to the attachment disk.

GEOGRAPHIC RANGE

Wheel wearers live in the northeastern part of the Atlantic Ocean, including the Mediterranean Sea.

HABITAT

Wheel wearers live only on bristles in the mouths of Norway lobsters.

phylum

class

subclass

order

monotypic order

suborder

family

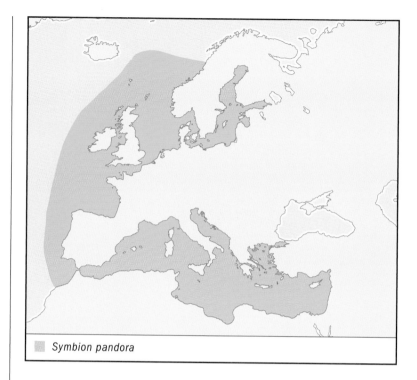

Symbion pandora

DIET

Wheel wearers eat particles of the lobster's prey, usually mollusks and crustaceans. Mollusks (MAH-lusks) are animals with a soft, unsegmented body that may or may not have a shell. Crustaceans (krus-TAY-shuns) are water-dwelling animals that have jointed legs and a hard shell but no backbone.

BEHAVIOR AND REPRODUCTION

When a lobster seizes its prey, food particles and nutrients are suspended in the water around its mouthparts. The hairlike fibers in the wheel wearer's funnel beat and make a current, which causes water containing food particles to flow into the funnel, where the food particles are grabbed by the hairlike fibers and moved toward the stomach.

Feeding-stage wheel wearers use internal budding to replace their body organs several times. While the organ replacement is going on, the wheel wearers also use internal budding to produce larvae that contain miniature feeding-stage animals. Larvae (LAR-vee) are animals in an early stage that change form before becoming adults. When fully developed, these larvae leave the wheel wearer through the mother's anus (AY-nuhs) and settle on the lobster's mouth bristles. A bag develops, the larva (LAR-vuh, the singular of larvae) breaks down, and the miniature feeding-stage animal starts to grow inside the bag. After a short time, the funnel emerges through the bag, and the new wheel wearer starts to feed.

Sometimes feeding-stage wheel wearers produce either females or larvae that give rise to males. The male-producing larvae can move only short distances. Immediately after they are released, these larvae seek the closest feeding-stage wheel wearer with a developing female inside and attach to the wheel wearer close to its anal opening. One or two dwarf males then begin to develop inside the larva. When the female leaves through the anus of the wheel wearer, the dwarf males emerge from the larva. Being good swimmers, the dwarf males quickly find and mate with the female, which contains a single large egg. The female then settles on the lobster's mouth. After settling, the female starts to break down and form a bag in which a new larva starts to develop. Larvae in this stage have a dense layer of hairlike fibers on the belly and are much better swimmers than wheel wearers in any of the other stages of the life cycle. They swim to a new lobster or stay free in the water while the lobster is shedding its shell. When the larvae have settled, a bag forms, and a new feeding-stage wheel wearer starts to develop.

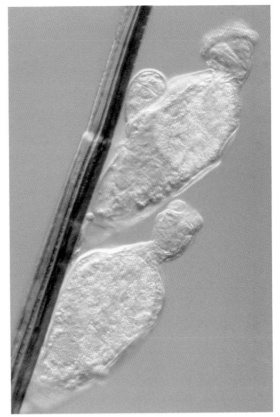

Wheel wearers are microscopic animals that live in the mouths of Norway lobsters. (Scanning micrograph by Reinhardt M. Kristensen. Reproduced by permission.)

WHEEL WEARERS AND PEOPLE

Wheel wearers have no known importance to people. Because they do not harm their lobster hosts, wheel wearers are not a problem for people who make their living catching and selling lobsters.

CONSERVATION STATUS

Wheel wearers are not considered threatened or endangered.

OUT WITH THE OLD, IN WITH THE NEW

A bud forms inside a feeding-stage wheel wearer. Inside this bud, a new set of organs, including the digestive system, nervous system, and mouth funnel, starts to develop. When fully developed, the new organs slowly move forward and push out all the old organs, until the new funnel can emerge through the neck and replace the old one. The only parts of the old wheel wearer that are used again are the trunk and the attachment disk. A feeding-stage wheel wearer can repeat this self-renewal process several times, and scientists are uncertain why it is necessary. Some believe that because the feeding-stage animals do not have a waste-removal system, waste accumulates, and the self-renewal enables the animal to eliminate these wastes before they become toxic.

FOR MORE INFORMATION

Books:

Valentine, James W. *On the Origin of Phyla.* Chicago: University of Chicago Press, 2004.

Young, Craig M., ed. *Atlas of Marine Invertebrate Larvae.* San Diego, CA: Academic, 2002.

Web sites:

Walker, Dave. "A Lobster's Microscopic Friend: *Symbion pandora*: A New Life Form and a New Phylum." *Microscopy UK.* http://www.microscopy-uk.net/mag/indexmag.html?http://www.microscopy-uk.net/mag/articles/pandora.html (accessed on February 24, 2005).

Class: Crinoidea
Number of families: 25 families

class

CHAPTER

phylum
● **class**
subclass
order
monotypic order
suborder
family

PHYSICAL CHARACTERISTICS

Sea lilies and feather stars are sea animals with five arms and a mouth that faces up. The main body part is the crown, which holds the mouth, digestive tract, and anus (AY-nuhs). The arms grow out of the crown. Sea lilies have a stalk below the crown and look like flowers. Feather stars have a cluster of tentacles below the crown and look like ferns. The arms of both animals usually have branches, as many as two hundred in some species. Each arm and branch has a food groove lined with grabbers called tube feet. The arms of sea lilies and feather stars are 0.4 to 14 inches (1 to 35 centimeters) long. The sea lily stalk is about 3.3 feet (1 meter) long. Feather stars are white, black, purple, red, green, brown, violet, or a combination of colors. The deeper the animals live, the paler is the color. Sea lilies are white.

GEOGRAPHIC RANGE

Sea lilies and feather stars live in the western part of the Pacific Ocean and on both sides of the Atlantic Ocean.

HABITAT

Most sea lilies live in deep water, and most feather stars live on coral reefs. Both animals usually live on hard surfaces.

DIET

Sea lilies and feather stars eat plankton and waste. Plankton is microscopic plants and animals drifting in water.

BEHAVIOR AND REPRODUCTION

Sea lilies and feather stars stand upright in the water current and extend their branches so that their food grooves can catch plankton. Feather stars usually live in clumps, attaching themselves to crevices and other places in which they can hide most of their body. Most species come out at night, exposing part or all of their arms, or even the entire body. Sea lilies also live in clusters but because of the lack of light in deep water do not have a day-and-night pattern of coming out.

Feather stars use their arms to crawl. Some swim by alternating their arms up and down. They go down through the water by extending their arms like parachutes. Only a few sea lilies can crawl, and none can swim.

Sea lilies and feather stars can regrow lost body parts. Feather stars can regrow their arms as long as at least one arm and a nerve center are intact. Sea lilies can regrow an entire crown.

Sea lilies and feather stars have separate sexes. The males release sperm into the water, and females of most species release their eggs into the water. In some feather stars, the eggs stay on the female for days and then are released into the water or enter pouches. After joining with sperm, the eggs of almost all sea lilies and feather stars develop into non-feeding, drifting larvae (LAR-vee), which are animals in an early stage that change form before becoming adults. These larvae transform into bottom-dwelling, non-feeding, stalked larvae that transform into bottom-dwelling, stalked young animals. The young are ready to reproduce in twelve to eighteen months.

SEA LILIES, FEATHER STARS, AND PEOPLE

Sea lilies and feather stars have no known importance to people.

CONSERVATION STATUS

Sea lilies and feather stars are not considered threatened or endangered.

Orange sea lily *(Nemaster rubiginosa)*

ORANGE SEA LILY
Nemaster rubiginosa

Physical characteristics: Orange sea lilies are feather stars with twenty to thirty-five arms that are 4 to 8 inches (10 to 20 centimeters) long. They are bright orange with a black stripe along the top of each arm.

Geographic range: Orange sea lilies live in the western part of the Atlantic Ocean from Florida to Brazil.

Habitat: Orange sea lilies live in shallow water attached to hard surfaces.

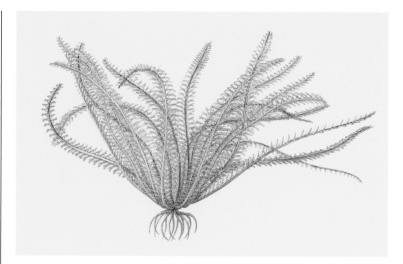

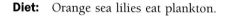

Diet: Orange sea lilies eat plankton.

Behavior and reproduction: Orange sea lilies hide their crown during the day, only the arms and branches showing. The entire body may come out at night. The males release sperm and the females release eggs into the water, where they join. The fertilized (FUR-teh-lyzed) eggs develop into larvae, which transform into young orange sea lilies, which mature into adults.

Orange sea lilies and people: Orange sea lilies have no known importance to people.

Conservation status: Orange sea lilies are not considered threatened or endangered. ■

West Atlantic stalked crinoid (*Endoxocrinus parrae*)

WEST ATLANTIC STALKED CRINOID
Endoxocrinus parrae

Physical characteristics: West Atlantic stalked crinoids (CRY-noyds) are sea lilies with a stalk less than 3.3 feet (1 meter) long. Each arm has eight branches. Hairlike fibers on a curved stalk anchor the lilies to the material on which they live.

Geographic range: West Atlantic stalked crinoids live in the Atlantic Ocean near Florida, the Bahamas, and Cuba.

Habitat: West Atlantic stalked crinoids live in water 500 to 3,200 feet (150 to 975 meters) deep. They anchor themselves to hard surfaces.

Diet: West Atlantic stalked crinoids eat plankton.

Behavior and reproduction: West Atlantic stalked crinoids wave their arms rapidly up and down to prevent other animals and undesired particles from settling on the crown. They move from place to place by crawling over the bottom using their arms. Scientists do not know how these sea lilies reproduce.

West Atlantic stalked crinoids and people: West Atlantic stalked crinoids have no known importance to people.

Conservation status: West Atlantic stalked crinoids are not considered threatened or endangered. ■

FOR MORE INFORMATION

Books:

Carson, Rachel. *The Edge of the Sea.* 1955. Reprint, Boston: Mariner, 1998.

Niesen, Thomas M. *The Marine Biology Coloring Book.* 2nd ed. New York: HarperResource, 2000.

Web sites:

"Class Crinoidea." Palaeos. http://www.palaeos.com/Invertebrates/Echinoderms/Crinoidea/Crinoidea.htm (accessed on February 25, 2005).

Messing, Charles Garrett. "Introduction to Comatulids." *Charles Messing's Comatulid Crinoid Page.* http://www.nova.edu/ocean/messing/crinoids/w3introduction.html (accessed on February 25, 2005).

West Atlantic stalked crinoids wave their arms rapidly up and down to prevent other animals and undesired particles from settling on the crown. They move from place to place by crawling over the bottom using their arms. (Illustration by Emily Damstra. Reproduced by permission.)

class
CHAPTER

phylum
◆ **class**
subclass
order
monotypic order
suborder
family

PHYSICAL CHARACTERISTICS

Sea stars have spiny skin and at least five arms large enough to hold digestive and reproductive organs. Some species of sea stars have as many as thirty arms. Sea stars are 0.4 inch (1 centimeter) to almost 3 feet (91 centimeters) across. The bottom of each arm is covered with rows of tube feet along a groove. Depending on the species, tube feet have suckers that help the sea star stick to hard surfaces or assist in prying open the shells of its prey.

The skeleton of sea stars consists of small plates that act as a firm but flexible skeleton. The upper and lower body surfaces also are covered with pinchers that range from simple spines to hooks. The upper surface is covered with many small, clear sacs used for exchanging oxygen, that is, for breathing. Sea stars have a nerve net but no brain. Even so, they are advanced enough to change on the basis of previous experiences and to stop behaviors, usually feeding behaviors, that continue to be unsuccessful.

GEOGRAPHIC RANGE

Sea stars live in the Pacific, Atlantic, and Indian oceans, including the Antarctic regions.

HABITAT

Sea stars live in the sea from the shore to the deepest ocean. They live in sea grass beds, under rock rubble, on coral reefs and rocky underwater cliffs, and in sand and mud.

Sand stars can swallow hundreds of live young mollusks in one feeding trip.

DIET

Sea stars eat anything that is too slow to escape, such as mollusks, crustaceans, sponges, worms, and even other sea stars and their relatives. Mollusks (MAH-lusks) are animals with a soft, unsegmented body that may or may not have a shell. Crustaceans (krus-TAY-shuns) are water-dwelling animals that have jointed legs and a hard shell but no backbone.

BEHAVIOR AND REPRODUCTION

Flexible bodies and suckered tube feet keep sea stars firmly in place so they can withstand the force of crashing waves. Their flexibility also allows the stars to assume a variety of positions to capture and handle prey and closely follow irregular surfaces in search of food. The flexibility also helps sea stars upright themselves if they are overturned.

Sea stars use two different feeding methods. In one method the star takes the prey into its stomach alive. In the other the star uses its tube feet and arms to pull apart the shells of a prey animal. Then it turns its own stomach inside out and pushes it out through its mouth. Digestion begins when the stomach comes in contact with the soft body of the opened animal.

Sea stars swarm in large numbers at certain times of the year, usually for releasing eggs and sperm, feeding frenzies, or group travel to deeper water offshore. Some species of sea stars are active at dawn and dusk. Others are active during high and low tide, when the water is quiet enough for success in finding food.

Most sea stars have separate sexes with no visible differences between them. Each arm contains a pair of organs that fill with eggs or sperm. Most species release eggs and sperm into the water, where fertilization (FUR-teh-lih-ZAY-shun), or the joining of egg and sperm to start development, takes place. To increase the chances of fertilization, sea stars swarm when they are ready to release eggs and sperm. Fertilized (FUR-teh-lyzed) eggs rapidly develop into drifting larvae (LAR-vee), or animals in an early stage that change form before becoming adults. These larvae transform into another type of larvae, which transform into young sea stars that settle on the bottom and grow into adults.

In some species of sea stars, females hold their fertilized eggs in a space under an arm, in the stomach, or in the reproductive organs. After development in the stomach or reproductive organs, the young escape through the small openings in the female's body wall.

Some sea stars use asexual reproduction by splitting into two new stars or regrowing an entire animal from part of an arm. Asexual (ay-SEK-shuh-wuhl) means without the uniting of egg and sperm for the transfer of DNA from two parents.

SEA STARS AND PEOPLE

Sea star swarms eat so many mollusks, they harm the livelihood or earnings of people who catch and sell shellfish. Coral reefs also often fall victim to the destructive feeding power of sea stars. However, sea stars do have some benefit to people. In some places, sea stars are used as an ingredient in fish meal, which is fed to poultry. Some companies collect sea stars for biological supplies to schools and collectors. The dried bodies of sea stars also are important to people who make a living selling souvenirs.

CONSERVATION STATUS

Sea stars are not considered threatened or endangered.

YOU THOUGHT YOU WERE HUNGRY?

Sea stars can go for months without food. One species can survive for eighteen months without eating.

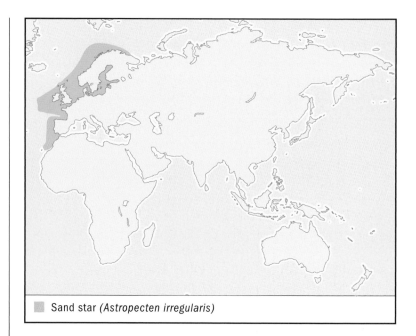

Sand star (*Astropecten irregularis*)

SPECIES ACCOUNTS

SAND STAR
Astropecten irregularis

Physical characteristics: Most sand stars are 2 to 4 inches (5 to 10 centimeters) across, but those in deep water can be as large as 8 inches (20 centimeters) across. Sand stars are pale violet to yellowish and have five arms that form stiff angles. These stars have upper and lower plates fringed with small spines. The tube feet are pointed and have no suckers.

Geographic range: Sand stars live in the western part of the Atlantic Ocean from Norway to Morocco.

Habitat: Sand stars live in water 16 to 3,280 feet (5 to 1,000 meters) deep. They live on bottoms ranging from coarse gravel to fine mud, although they usually live on sand.

Diet: Sand stars are greedy predators of mollusks, worms, crustaceans, and other sea stars and their relatives. They dig up their prey and swallow it whole.

Behavior and reproduction: Sand stars live partially or completely buried. They travel into deeper water during the winter and swarm

Sand stars are greedy predators of mollusks, worms, crustaceans, and other sea stars and their relatives. They dig up their prey and swallow it whole. (© Richard Herrmann/SeaPics.com)

closer to shore when the seawater warms between May and July. They then release their eggs and sperm into the water, where fertilization takes place.

Sand stars and people: Arm damage to sand stars is used as an indicator of damage caused by fishing boats that drag their nets along the bottom.

Conservation status: Sand stars are not considered threatened or endangered. ■

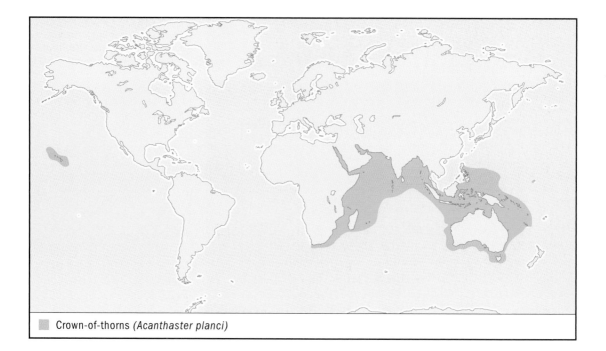

Crown-of-thorns (*Acanthaster planci*)

CROWN-OF-THORNS
Acanthaster planci

Physical characteristics: Crowns-of-thorns are about 16 inches (40 centimeters) across and have ten to thirty arms covered in thorn-like spines, which are venomous. These sea stars are red and green, and the spines have reddish tips. Young crowns-of-thorns have camouflage coloring.

Geographic range: Crowns-of-thorns live in the Pacific and Indian oceans.

Habitat: Adult crowns-of-thorns live on open sand and feed among coral. The young hide among the coral, under rocks, and in coral rubble.

Diet: Crowns-of-thorns are greedy predators of coral.

Behavior and reproduction: Crowns-of-thorns feed at night. Large swarms appear suddenly, feed on coral, and then disappear. These

Grzimek's Student Animal Life Resource

sea stars turn their stomach inside out over coral, releasing an enzyme that turns the coral tissue to liquid, and then absorb the liquid. Crowns-of-thorns can survive without food for six months and feed on about 3 square miles (8 square kilometers) of coral per year. Crowns-of-thorns can regrow broken arms to form another star. These animals have separate sexes and reproduce by releasing eggs and sperm into the water, where fertilization takes place. There are two stages of larvae.

Crowns-of-thorns and people: Crowns-of-thorns have caused widespread damage to coral reefs. The stings of these sea stars are painful and cause nausea.

Conservation status: Crowns-of-thorns are not considered threatened or endangered. ■

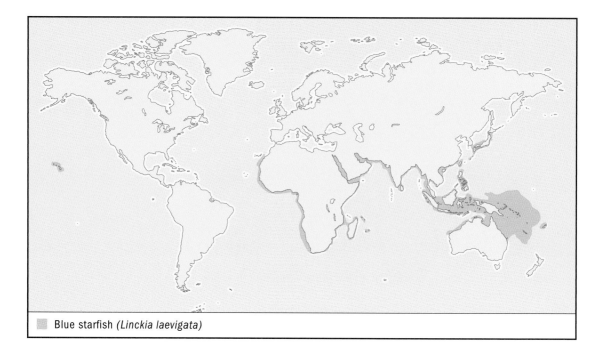

Blue starfish (*Linckia laevigata*)

BLUE STARFISH
Linckia laevigata

Physical characteristics: Blue starfish have five arms and can be as large as 12 inches (30 centimeters) across. Adults are brilliant blue. The young are bluish green or purplish with dark spots.

Geographic range: Blue starfish live in the Indian and Pacific oceans.

Habitat: Blue starfish live on coral gravel in direct sunlight, in sand, and under rocks.

Diet: Blue starfish graze on waste and small animals.

Behavior and reproduction: Adult blue starfish hide during the day in coral and rocky crevices. They turn their stomachs inside out to feed on coral. Blue starfish use asexual reproduction, but scientists do not know the details.

Blue starfish have five arms and can be as large as 12 inches (30 centimeters) across. Adults are brilliant blue. The young are bluish green or purplish with dark spots. (Patricia Jordan/Peter Arnold, Inc.)

Blue starfish and people: Blue starfish are used in home aquariums and are the most commonly imported sea star.

Conservation status: Blue starfish are not considered threatened or endangered. ■

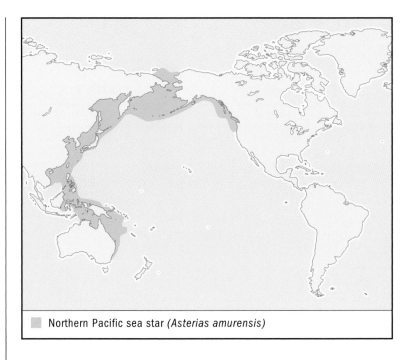

Northern Pacific sea star (*Asterias amurensis*)

NORTHERN PACIFIC SEA STAR
Asterias amurensis

Physical characteristics: Northern Pacific sea stars are 16 to 20 inches (40 to 50 centimeters) across. They have five arms that are turned up at the tips. These sea stars are rosy brown, yellowish brown, red, or purple. Their underside is very flat. The skin is covered with unevenly arranged spines that have jagged ends.

Geographic range: Northern Pacific sea stars live in the western, northern, and eastern parts of the Pacific Ocean.

Habitat: Northern Pacific sea stars live in shallow water on sheltered coasts in sand and mud and among rocks and algae thickets. Algae (AL-jee) are plantlike growths that live in water and have no true roots, stems, or leaves.

Diet: Northern Pacific sea stars eat scallops, oysters, mussels, shrimp, and other sea stars.

Behavior and reproduction: Northern Pacific sea stars feed by using their tube feet and arms to pull apart the shells of their prey before turning their stomachs inside out. When it is time to release eggs and sperm, the swarms are so dense that the females lift themselves above the ground on their arms and release eggs between the arms while the male sea stars crawl beneath. The females release about twenty million eggs, which when fertilized develop into drifting larvae.

Northern Pacific sea stars and people: Northern Pacific sea stars accidentally introduced into Australia and Tasmania have caused damage to the shellfish business.

Conservation status: Northern Pacific sea stars are not considered threatened or endangered.   ■

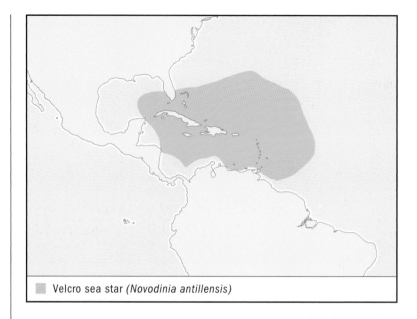

Velcro sea star (*Novodinia antillensis*)

VELCRO SEA STAR
Novodinia antillensis

Physical characteristics: Velcro sea stars have ten to fourteen arms with rows of spines and teethlike pinchers. The arms are long and thin. These sea stars are brick red.

Geographic range: Velcro sea stars live in the Atlantic Ocean near the West Indies.

Habitat: Velcro sea stars live in water 1,970 to 2,625 feet (600 to 800 meters) deep. They attach themselves to steep rocky surfaces in areas where the current is strong. They often live near large sponges, sea fans, and hard corals.

Diet: Velcro sea stars eat animal plankton, which is microscopic animals drifting in the water.

Behavior and reproduction: Velcro sea stars look like baskets when they extend their arms and curl the tips inward over their mouth. They stay still while waiting for prey but slowly bend their arms to capture prey, which becomes stuck on arm spines and hooks. Velcro sea stars release eggs and sperm into the water, where fertilization takes place.

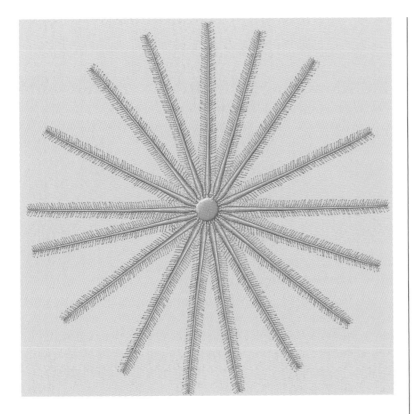

Velcro sea stars look like baskets when they extend their arms and curl the tips inward over their mouth. They stay still while waiting for prey but slowly bend their arms to capture prey, which becomes stuck on arm spines and hooks. (Illustration by Barbara Duperron. Reproduced by permission.)

Velcro sea stars and people: Velcro sea stars have no known importance to people.

Conservation status: Velcro sea stars are not considered threatened or endangered. ■

FOR MORE INFORMATION

Books:

Carson, Rachel. *The Edge of the Sea.* 1955. Reprint, Boston: Mariner, 1998.

Niesen, Thomas M. *The Marine Biology Coloring Book.* 2nd ed. New York: HarperResource, 2000.

Web sites:

"Echionoderms: The Spiny Animals." *Oceanic Research Group.* http://www.oceanicresearch.org/echinoderm.html (accessed on February 28, 2005).

"Sea Stars." *OceanLink.* http://oceanlink.island.net/oinfo/biodiversity/seastars.html (accessed on February 28, 2005).

SEA DAISIES
Concentricycloidea

Class: Concentricycloidea
Number of families: 1 family

PHYSICAL CHARACTERISTICS

Sea daisies are small, circular animals related to sea stars. There are only two species. Sea daisies have no arms, but the circle is rimmed with flat spines that look like daisy petals. The upper surface of the animal is delicately plated. The bottom surface has a mouth frame that leads to a shallow stomach and has a single ring of tube feet. Sea daisies are 0.4 to 0.6 inches (10 to 14 millimeters) across. They are see-through but not clear, like fogged-up glass. These animals have a water circulation system arranged in rings. The sexes are separate.

GEOGRAPHIC RANGE

Sea daisies live near New Zealand and the Bahamas.

HABITAT

Sea daisies live on sunken wood in water deeper than 3,280 feet (1,000 meters).

DIET

Sea daisies eat bacteria, dissolved nutrients on sunken wood, waste, and possibly microscopic mollusks. Mollusks (MAH-lusks) are animals with a soft, unsegmented body that may or may not have a shell.

BEHAVIOR AND REPRODUCTION

To move to new habitats, sea daisies use pulsing actions of their stomach or drift like parachutes. Sea daisies have separate sexes and mate rather than releasing eggs and sperm into the water. In one species the fertilized (FUR-teh-lyzed) eggs, those that have joined with sperm, develop inside a female, who gives birth to live young. In the other species the fertilized eggs are laid, and the young develop outside the female's body. The developing young are cone-shaped or flat.

SEA DAISIES AND PEOPLE

Sea daisies have no known importance to people.

CONSERVATION STATUS

Sea daisies are not considered threatened or endangered.

■ Medusiform sea daisy *(Xyloplax medusiformis)*

MEDUSIFORM SEA DAISY
Xyloplax medusiformis

Physical characteristics: Medusiform (mih-DOO-seh-form) sea daisies are circular and slightly inflated. The body is 0.4 inches (9 millimeters) across, including the spines around the rim. The spines are all one length: 0.002 to 0.003 inches (40 to 75 micrometers). The mouth frame has ten to thirty bones. Medusiform sea daisies do not have a stomach. Instead there is a thin, flexible sheet on the bottom surface of the daisy that is supported by the mouth frame.

Geographic range: Medusiform sea daisies live on the east and west coasts of New Zealand.

Habitat: Medusiform sea daisies live on sunken wood in deep water.

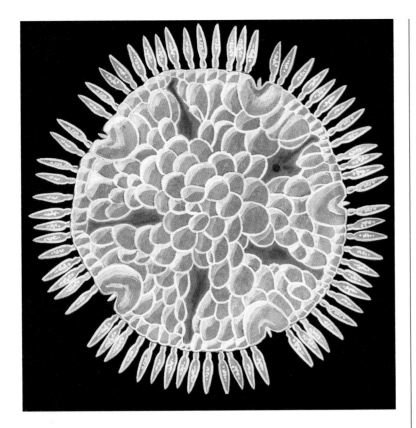

To move to new habitats, sea daisies use pulsing actions of their stomach or drift like parachutes. (Illustration by Barbara Duperron. Reproduced by permission.)

Diet: Medusiform sea daisies absorb dissolved nutrients from decomposing wood.

Behavior and reproduction: Scientists do not know how medusiform sea daisies behave. They have separate sexes and mate. The young develop inside the females.

Medusiform sea daisies and people: Medusiform sea daisies have no known importance to people.

Conservation status: Medusiform sea daisies are not considered threatened or endangered. ■

FOR MORE INFORMATION

Books:

Brusca, Richard C., Gary J. Brusca, and Nancy Haver. *Invertebrates.* 2nd ed. Sunderland, MA: Sinauer, 2002.

Periodicals:

Voight, Janet R. "How to Study Animals in Habitiats You've Never Seen." *In the Field* (spring 2005): 16–17.

Web sites:

"The Echinoderm Phylum." University of Washington School of Aquatic and Fishery Sciences. http://www.fish.washington.edu/classes/fish310/PDF/echino.pdf (accessed on March 9, 2005).

Tropical brittle star (Ophiactis savignyi)

TROPICAL BRITTLE STAR
Ophiactis savignyi

Physical characteristics: Tropical brittle stars usually have six arms. The body is 0.04 to 0.1 inches (1 to 3 millimeters) across. These stars are green with darker markings.

Geographic range: Tropical brittle stars live all over the world.

Habitat: Tropical brittle stars live among algae and sponges and hide in reef crevices.

Diet: Tropical brittle stars eat small particles from the surface they live on or from the open water.

Behavior and reproduction: Tropical brittle stars use both sexual reproduction and splitting. When these brittle stars split, the body softens, forms a groove, and tears into jagged halves, which grow into new six-armed stars. Tropical brittle stars begin reproducing sexually when they are larger than 0.1 inch (3 millimeters) across. The larvae drift freely and feed on microscopic animals drifting in the water.

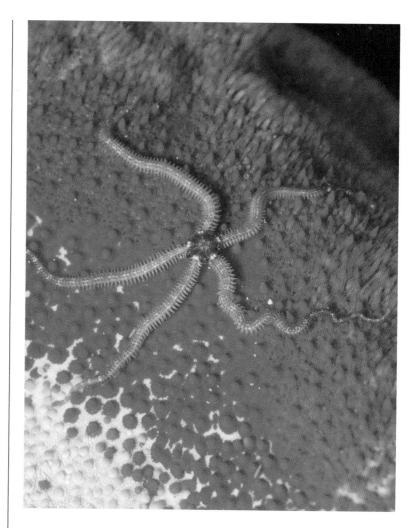

Tropical brittle stars live among algae and sponges and hide in reef crevices. (© DR & TL Schrichte/SeaPics.com)

Tropical brittle stars and people: Tropical brittle stars have no known importance to people.

Conservation status: Tropical brittle stars are not considered threatened or endangered. ■

FOR MORE INFORMATION

Books:

Lichen, Patricia K. *Brittle Stars and Mudbugs: An Uncommon Field Guide to Northwest Shorelines and Wetlands.* Seattle: Sasquatch, 2001.

Niesen, Thomas M. *The Marine Biology Coloring Book.* 2nd ed. New York: HarperResource, 2000.

Web sites:

"Class Ophiuroidea." *Palaeos.* http://www.palaeos.com/Invertebrates/ Echinoderms/Ophiuroidea/Ophiuroidea.htm (accessed on February 28, 2005).

Morris, M., and D. Fautin. "Ophiuroidea." *Animal Diversity Web.* http:// animaldiversity.ummz.umich.edu/site/accounts/information/Ophiuroidea .html (accessed on February 28, 2005).

SEA URCHINS AND SAND DOLLARS
Echinoidea

Class: Echinoidea
Number of families: 46 families

PHYSICAL CHARACTERISTICS

Sea urchins and sand dollars are spine-covered sea animals with five arms and prickly skin. Most sea urchins are almost spherical and have five-way symmetry. Sand dollars usually are flat and have two-way symmetry. Sea urchins and sand dollars have rows of tube feet that run from the anus (AY-nuhs), which is on the top of the animal, to the mouth, which is on the bottom of the animal. At the top of the shell is a small plate with holes that allow seawater to pass into a system of tubes running through the body to the tube feet. Muscles contract to draw seawater into the tubes and send it to the tube feet, which then extend under the force of the water pressure.

The shell of sea urchins and sand dollars is made up of tightly packed plates. This design keeps cracks from spreading if the shell is damaged. The shell of the smallest urchin is 0.2 inches (5 millimeters) across, and that of the largest is about 15 inches (38 centimeters) across.

All sea urchins are covered with moveable spines, but the structure of the spines varies among species. Some spines are thick and blunt; others are long, pointed, and venomous. Spines are used for movement, for fighting predators, for camouflage from predators, and to make shade for protection from direct sunlight.

GEOGRAPHIC RANGE

Sea urchins and sand dollars live all over the world.

HABITAT

Sea urchins live on wave-exposed rocks, in crevices within rocks, in rock pools, on coral reefs, in sandy lagoons, in sea grass beds, and in kelp forests. Sand dollars live in sand and coarse gravel.

DIET

Some sea urchins eat only algae, sea grass, and seaweed. Algae (AL-jee) are plantlike growths that live in water and have no true roots, stems, or leaves. Others also eat small animals and waste particles. Sand dollars eat diatoms and plant particles that accumulate in sand. Diatoms (DYE-uh-tahms) are a type of algae that have a shell.

STRENGTH IN NUMBERS

On wave-exposed shores, sea urchins group together and interlock spines with one another, thus reducing the risk of being swept away by strong waves.

BEHAVIOR AND REPRODUCTION

Sea urchins move slowly and usually search for food at night to avoid predators. They use their teeth to bite and scrape their food. Sand dollars sift the sand for food while burrowing. Their spines are dense enough to prevent sand grains from falling through yet are fine enough to allow food particles to drop out onto strings of mucus before being placed in the mouth. Sea urchins and sand dollars use their tube feet for trapping food particles, for movement, for prey capture, for attaching to the material they live on, and for breathing.

Sea urchins and sand dollars have separate sexes. Females release millions of eggs into the water, where they unite with sperm from the males and develop into larvae. Larvae (LAR-vee) are animals in an early stage that change form before becoming adults. Sea urchin and sand dollar larvae drift before settling to the bottom and transforming into young animals with a body form that looks like that of adults. In a few species of sea urchins and sand dollars the young develop inside the females. These species do not have free-floating larvae.

SEA URCHINS, SAND DOLLARS, AND PEOPLE

In the United States, red, purple, and green sea urchins are harvested for their eggs, which people eat. In Japan, urchin eggs and reproductive organs are eaten as delicacies. In areas where predators of sea urchins have been over-fished, huge numbers of sea urchins damage the environment. In the Caribbean Sea,

for example, sea urchins have caused ninety percent of the erosion of coral reefs. Because they are so efficient at consuming unwanted algae and waste, sea urchins are used in aquariums. Sand dollar shells are prized by beachcombers and collectors.

CONSERVATION STATUS

The World Conservation Union (IUCN) lists one species of sea urchins and sand dollars as Low Risk/Near Threatened, or at risk of becoming threatened with extinction in the future.

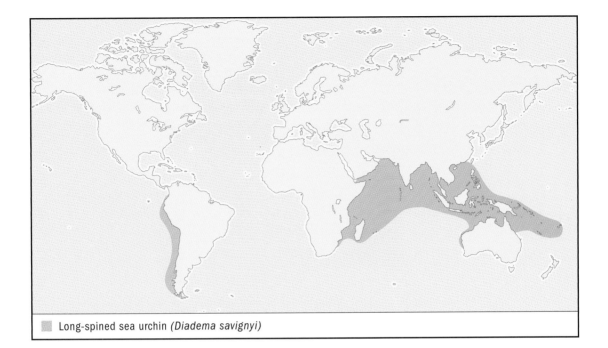

Long-spined sea urchin (*Diadema savignyi*)

LONG-SPINED SEA URCHIN
Diadema savignyi

Physical characteristics: The body of long-spined sea urchins is somewhat flattened and is about 3 inches (8 centimeters) in diameter. The long, thin, black or white spines are 2 to 4 inches (5 to 10 centimeters) long. The shell and spines are fragile. There is a shiny blue ring around the anus.

Geographic range: Long-spined sea urchins live in the Indian Ocean and in the Pacific Ocean from Australia to Southeast Asia and along the western coast of South America.

Habitat: Long-spined sea urchins live in shallow water on rocks in sheltered areas of coral reefs, in sandy lagoons, and sometimes in sea grass beds. Darker urchins live in the open on sand; paler urchins live in crevices or in cloudy water.

Diet: Long-spined sea urchins eat algae.

Behavior and reproduction: Long-spined sea urchins hide during the day in rocky crevices but look for food at night. These urchins

Long-spined sea urchins hide during the day in rocky crevices but look for food at night. These urchins are greedy grazers of algae. (Gregory Ochocki/Photo Researchers, Inc.)

are greedy grazers on algae. When large numbers of the urchins die, algae grow rapidly and harm coral reefs. The shell color of long-spined sea urchins often changes according to changes in light. To protect themselves from predators, a variety of sea animals, such as shrimps and young fish, live among the spines of long-spined sea urchins. Long-spined sea urchins form groups when it is time to release eggs and sperm.

Long-spined sea urchins and people: The spines of long-spined sea urchins are poisonous and easily puncture human skin, often causing infection. Long-spined sea urchins protect coral reefs from overgrowth of algae.

Conservation status: Long-spined sea urchins are not considered threatened or endangered.   ■

Pea urchin (*Echinocyamus pusillus*)

PEA URCHIN
Echinocyamus pusillus

Physical characteristics: Pea urchins are one of the smallest urchins. The tiny egg-shaped shell is only about 0.6 inches (1.5 centimeters) long. These urchins are usually grayish green to bright green and have very short spines, which give the animal a velvety texture.

Geographic range: Pea urchins live in the coastal waters of northern Europe.

Habitat: Pea urchins live buried in gravel and sand.

Diet: Pea urchins eat food particles they find in the sand or gravel.

Behavior and reproduction: Scientists know little about how pea urchins behave. These urchins release eggs and sperm into the water,

where they unite and develop into free-living larvae, which transform into young urchins that grow into adults.

Pea urchins and people: Pea urchins have no known importance to people.

Conservation status: Pea urchins are not considered threatened or endangered. ■

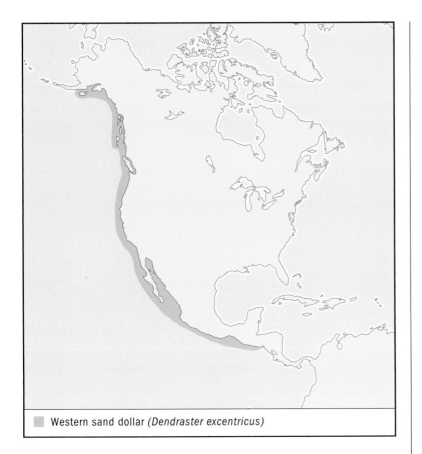

■ Western sand dollar *(Dendraster excentricus)*

WESTERN SAND DOLLAR
Dendraster excentricus

Physical characteristics: Western sand dollars have a rigid shell about 3.5 inches (9 centimeters) across and covered with moveable spines. These sand dollars are pale grayish lavender to dark purplish black. They have a five-way petal-shaped pattern of tube feet on the upper surface of the shell.

Geographic range: Western sand dollars live along the west coast of North America from southern Alaska to Mexico.

Habitat: Western sand dollars live on sandy bottoms in sheltered bays, lagoons, and open coastal areas.

Western sand dollars live in groups that form a thick carpet of animals. Scientists believe these sand dollars form the groups to influence the water current so that more food flows toward them. (Illustration by Bruce Worden. Reproduced by permission.)

Diet: Western sand dollars eat plankton, or microscopic plants and animals drifting in water.

Behavior and reproduction: Western sand dollars live in groups that form a thick carpet of animals. Scientists believe these sand dollars form the groups to influence the water current so that more food flows toward them. Mucus strands help the sand dollars trap food particles. Young Western sand dollars take in sand when feeding to help weigh them down.

Western sand dollars release sperm and eggs into the water, where they unite and develop into larvae, which transform into young animals that grow into adults. Some scientists believe adult Western sand dollars eat their larvae but not the eggs, which have a protective coating. Western sand dollars live about fifteen years.

Western sand dollars and people: Western sand dollars are prized by beachcombers and collectors.

Conservation status: Western sand dollars are not considered threatened or endangered. ∎

Six keyhole sand dollar (*Leodia sexiesperforata*)

SIX KEYHOLE SAND DOLLAR
Leodia sexiesperforata

Physical characteristics: Six keyhole sand dollars are thin, flat disks with six slot-like holes and a five-way petal-like pattern of tube feet on the top side. They are about 4 inches (10 centimeters) across and are yellow to light brown.

Geographic range: Six keyhole sand dollars live along the east coast of North and South America from North Carolina to Uruguay.

Six keyhole sand dollars burrow several inches (centimeters) straight down into the sand. They use mucus strands to collect food. (Andrew J. Martinez/Photo Researchers, Inc.)

Habitat: Six keyhole sand dollars live in open sandy areas clear of algae.

Diet: Six keyhole sand dollars eat algae and waste particles.

Behavior and reproduction: Six keyhole sand dollars burrow several inches (centimeters) straight down into the sand. They use mucus strands to collect food. Six keyhole sand dollars release eggs and sperm during the rainy season between late summer and autumn.

Six keyhole sand dollars and people: Six keyhole sand dollars are prized by beachcombers and collectors.

Conservation status: Six keyhole sand dollars are not considered threatened or endangered. ∎

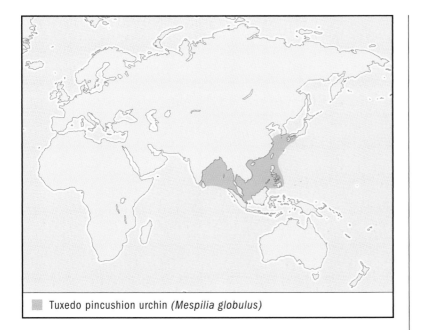

Tuxedo pincushion urchin (*Mespilia globulus*)

TUXEDO PINCUSHION URCHIN
Mespilia globulus

Physical characteristics: The shell of tuxedo pincushion urchins is about 2.5 inches (6 centimeters) across and has five to ten broad bands of bright blue with bands of reddish brown spines.

Geographic range: Tuxedo pincushion urchins live in the coastal waters of Asia from India to southern Japan.

Habitat: During the day tuxedo pincushion urchins live among rocks and rubble as well as in crevices on coral reefs.

Diet: Tuxedo pincushion urchins eat algae and coral.

Behavior and reproduction: Tuxedo pincushion urchins hide during the day and look for food at night. They live alone rather than in groups. They camouflage their shell with found shell fragments and algae held on with hairlike fibers between their spines. These urchins reproduce by releasing sperm and eggs into the water, where they unite and develop into larvae which transform into young urchins that grow into adults.

Tuxedo pincushion urchins hide during the day and look for food at night. They live alone rather than in groups. They camouflage their shell with found shell fragments and algae held on with hairlike fibers between their spines. (Fred Connaughey/Photo Researchers, Inc.)

Tuxedo pincushion urchins and people: Tuxedo pincushion urchins are used in home aquariums.

Conservation status: Tuxedo pincushion urchins are not considered threatened or endangered. ■

FOR MORE INFORMATION

Books:

Carson, Rachel. *The Edge of the Sea.* 1955. Reprint, Boston: Mariner, 1998.

Niesen, Thomas M. *The Marine Biology Coloring Book.* 2nd ed. New York: HarperResource, 2000.

Periodicals:

Samarri, Fariss. "Helping Urchins May Benefit Coral." *Sea Frontiers* (winter 1995): 16–17.

Web sites:

Fautin, Daphne G., and Judy Follo. "Echinoidea." *Animal Diversity Web.* http://animaldiversity.ummz.umich.edu/site/accounts/information/Echinoidea.html (accessed on March 1, 2005).

"Sand Dollars." *Seashells.org.* http://www.seashells.org/identcatagories/sanddollarstypes.htm (accessed on March 1, 2005).

Class: Holothuroidea
Number of families: 25 families

class

CHAPTER

PHYSICAL CHARACTERISTICS

Sea cucumbers are soft-bodied sea animals that have a circle of five to twenty tentacles around the mouth. Some sea cucumbers have a thick, muscular body wall, but others are clear and jellylike. Most sea cucumbers look like thick worms or slugs, but some are U-shaped. Depending on the species, the tentacles are simple, fingerlike, featherlike, or flat and shovel- or shieldlike. The large tube feet of some sea cucumbers make them look prickly. Most sea cucumbers are about 20 inches (51 centimeters) long, although some are only a fraction of an inch (millimeters) long and others are longer than 10 feet (3 meters). Sea cucumbers that live in warm, shallow water usually are bright green, red, orange, or yellow. Most sea cucumbers that live in deep, open water are dark. Those that live in deep water but burrow in the bottom are pale gray to white, although some are clear, light purple, or pink.

The water-circulating system that powers the tube feet of sea cucumbers is made up of a ring canal around the throat and long canals that run from the ring to the rear of the animal. In sea stars and other relatives of sea cucumbers, the water-circulating system exchanges water with the environment through a strainer plate that opens to the outside. In most sea cucumbers, however, the strainer plate is inside the animal and opens into the body cavity.

In almost all sea cucumbers, the skeleton of the body wall is made up of microscopic bonelike parts that look like rods, roses, crosses, buttons, tables, or wheels and anchors, among other shapes. In some sea cucumbers, these parts are large and

platelike and make the animal rigid. Another important feature of the skeleton is a hard ring around the throat. This ring is an attachment surface for the muscles that move the mouth tentacles and for the forward ends of the muscles that contract the body lengthwise.

GEOGRAPHIC RANGE

Sea cucumbers live all over the world.

HABITAT

Sea cucumbers live in all sea habitats, ranging from areas exposed at low tide to the bottom of the deepest part of the ocean. Some species live on wave-hammered reef crests and rocky shorelines. Many species live on hard bottoms. Others burrow in sand or mud. Some species swim miles above the sea floor.

DIET

Sea cucumbers eat algae, plankton, bacteria, and waste particles. Algae (AL-jee) are plantlike growths that live in water and have no true roots, stems, or leaves. Plankton is microscopic plants and animals drifting in water.

BEHAVIOR AND REPRODUCTION

Most sea cucumbers are slow-moving animals. Some rear up and extend their front ends into the water when releasing eggs and sperm. Some twist violently or inflate when they meet a predator. Some deep-sea species can swim. Bottom dwellers wander in an apparently random way as they feed. Many tropical species of sea cucumbers are active at night, staying in crevices or under the sand during the day.

Some sea cucumbers have toxins in their body wall that generate a taste that keeps fishes away. Other sea cucumbers defend themselves by shooting tubes out their anus (AY-nuhs). The tubes become very long and sticky, entangling predators or scaring them away. Some sea cucumbers defend themselves by ejecting their internal organs—some through the head by breaking off the tentacle crown and others through the anus. The sea cucumbers survive the organ ejection, and the organs grow back.

Sea cucumbers use their tentacles for eating. Some sea cucumbers scoop up sand or mud with shovel-shaped tentacles. Others lash the surface with featherlike tentacles. Still others scoop up food particles as they burrow with fingerlike tentacles. Some sea cucumbers have branched tentacles that are lightly coated in mucus and extend into the current to capture algae and plankton. Food sticks to the mucus, and the sea cucumber brings the tentacles into its mouth one at a time to wipe them clean by contracting muscles around its throat.

Some species of sea cucumbers have separate sexes, and others make both sperm and eggs. At least one deep-sea species forms pairs. Some sea cucumbers, mainly those that live in warm water and those that live in the deep sea, release eggs and sperm into the water, where they unite and larvae develop. Larvae (LAR-vee) are animals in an early stage that change form before becoming adults. In other species, mainly those that live near the shore or in cold water, females use their tentacles to gather up the eggs as they are being released and keep them on their bellies or in special pouches for development. In a few species the larvae develop inside the female's body cavity.

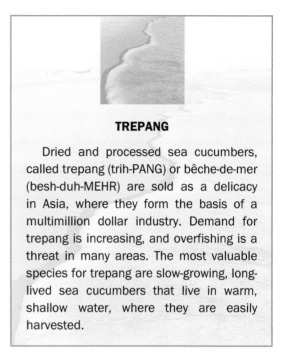

TREPANG

Dried and processed sea cucumbers, called trepang (trih-PANG) or bêche-de-mer (besh-duh-MEHR) are sold as a delicacy in Asia, where they form the basis of a multimillion dollar industry. Demand for trepang is increasing, and overfishing is a threat in many areas. The most valuable species for trepang are slow-growing, long-lived sea cucumbers that live in warm, shallow water, where they are easily harvested.

Some sea cucumber larvae are non-feeding but have fat stored in them and develop directly into adults. Other sea cucumber larvae have a feeding stage in which they drift in the water. They then transform from a two-sided to a five-armed body plan and settle on the bottom as miniature adults. Adults of some warm-water species of sea cucumbers may also reproduce by splitting in half.

SEA CUCUMBERS AND PEOPLE

People in several Asian and Pacific Island countries eat sea cucumbers in a dish called trepang. Sea cucumbers also are used in aquariums. The toxins in sea cucumber skin are being studied for use as drugs.

CONSERVATION STATUS

Sea cucumbers are not considered threatened or endangered.

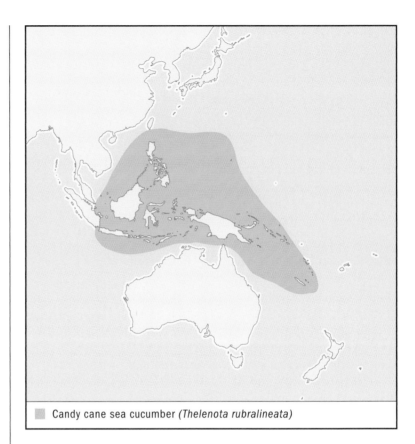

Candy cane sea cucumber (*Thelenota rubralineata*)

CANDY CANE SEA CUCUMBER
Thelenota rubralineata

Physical characteristics: Candy cane sea cucumbers are colorful and large, as long as 20 inches (51 centimeters). The entire body is covered with pointed tube feet. Candy cane sea cucumbers have a bright red pattern of stripes on a white background and have about twenty dull red shield-shaped tentacles.

Geographic range: Candy cane sea cucumbers live in the south-western part of the Pacific Ocean.

Habitat: Candy cane sea cucumbers live on sand patches on reefs 20 to 200 feet (6 to 60 meters) deep.

Diet: Candy cane sea cucumbers eat food particles they find in the sand.

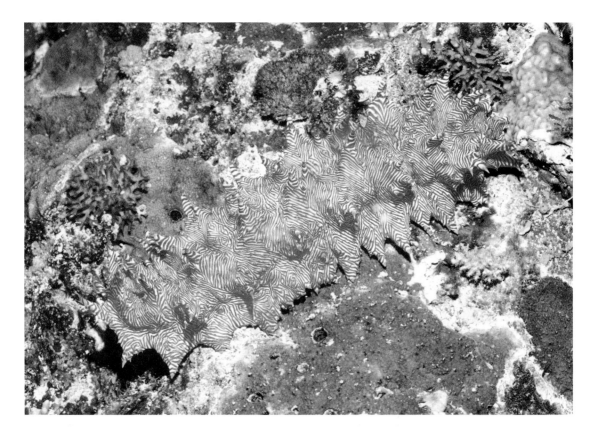

Behavior and reproduction: Candy cane sea cucumbers crawl exposed on the reef during the day and at night. When disturbed they curl up by bringing their front and back ends together. Candy cane sea cucumbers release their eggs and sperm into the water, where they unite and develop into larvae, which transform into young sea cucumbers that develop into adults.

Candy cane sea cucumbers and people: Candy cane sea cucumbers are harvested by accident with sea cucumbers that are used to make trepang.

Conservation status: Candy cane sea cucumbers are not considered threatened or endangered. ■

Candy cane sea cucumbers are colorful and large, as long as 20 inches (51 centimeters). The entire body is covered with pointed tube feet. (Fred McConnaughey/Photo Researchers, Inc.)

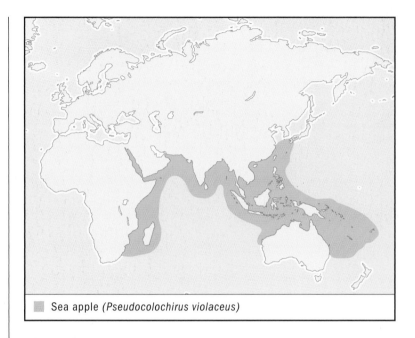

Sea apple (*Pseudocolochirus violaceus*)

SEA APPLE
Pseudocolochirus violaceus

Physical characteristics: Sea apples are colorful sea cucumbers about 7 inches (18 centimeters) long. They usually are purple. Three rows of tube feet run along the bottom side of the animal. The top side has two rows of tube feet as well as small scattered tube feet. The body is curved so that the mouth and anus point upward. The ten tentacles are bushy purple to red and have white tips. The pieces of the body wall skeleton are rounded, smooth plates with a few holes.

Geographic range: Sea apples live in the Indian Ocean and the western part of the Pacific Ocean.

Habitat: Sea apples live on hard material, such as coral reefs, in water as deep as 40 feet (12 meters) in areas with a current.

Diet: Sea apples eat plant plankton.

Behavior and reproduction: Sea apples live partly hidden to fully exposed with tentacles expanded, even during the day. They feed continuously, capturing large food particles with outstretched branching

Sea apples live on hard material, such as coral reefs, in water as deep as 40 feet (12 meters) in areas with a current. (© A. Flowers & L. Newman/ Photo Researchers, Inc. Reproduced by permission.)

tentacles that are lightly coated in mucus. Sea apples have separate sexes. Males release sperm and females release eggs into the water, where they unite and where the larvae develop. The larvae transform into young sea apples that develop into adults.

Sea apples and people: Sea apples have no known importance to people.

Conservation status: Sea apples are not considered threatened or endangered.   ■

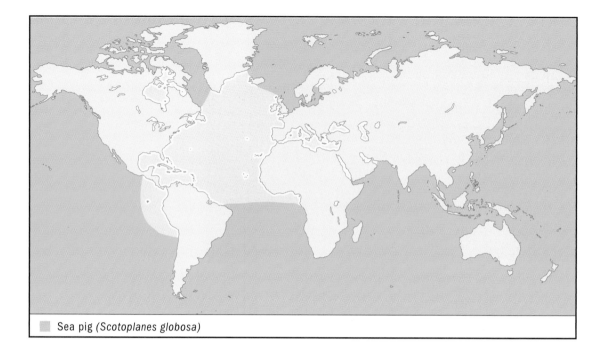

Sea pig (*Scotoplanes globosa*)

SEA PIG
Scotoplanes globosa

Physical characteristics: Sea pigs are clear sea cucumbers 2 to 4 inches (5 to 10 centimeters) long. They have ten tentacles and a few large tube feet. The tube feet on the top side of sea pigs are two widely spaced antennalike pairs. The other tube feet are arranged in a row around the edge of the bottom side of the animal. The pieces of the body wall skeleton are smooth to spiny rods and smaller C-shaped rods. Sea pigs are also called sea cows because the tube feet on the top side of the body look like cattle horns.

Geographic range: Sea pigs live all over the world except the northern part of the Atlantic Ocean and the eastern part of the Pacific Ocean near Central and South America.

Habitat: Sea pigs live in the deep ocean.

Diet: Sea pigs eat food particles they find in the sand.

Behavior and reproduction: Sea pigs move above the bottom using long tube feet. These sea cucumbers form large groups. Sea pigs feed

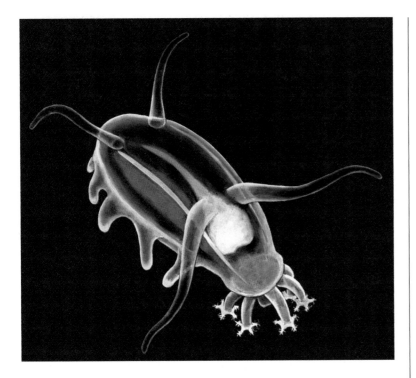

by using their tentacles to push sand or mud into their mouth. Scientists do not know how sea pigs reproduce.

Sea pigs and people: Sea pigs have no known importance to people.

Conservation status: Sea pigs are not considered threatened or endangered. ■

FOR MORE INFORMATION

Books:

Carson, Rachel. *The Edge of the Sea.* 1955. Reprint, Boston: Mariner, 1998.

Niesen, Thomas M. *The Marine Biology Coloring Book.* 2nd ed. New York: HarperResource, 2000.

Periodicals:

Summers, Adam. "Catch and Release: Sea Cucumbers Might Put a Torn Achilles Tendon Back Together Again." *Natural History* (November 2003): 36–37.

Web sites:

"Frequently Asked Questions of the Sea Cucumber." *Charles Darwin Research Station.* http://www.darwinfoundation.org/marine/FAQcuke .html (accessed on March 14, 2005).

"Sea Cucumbers." *Thinkquest.* http://library.thinkquest.org/J001418/ seacuc.html (accessed on March 2, 2005).

phylum
C H A P T E R

phylum

class

subclass

order

monotypic order

suborder

family

PHYSICAL CHARACTERISTICS

Arrow worms are long, straight, narrow sea worms that use hooks for catching prey. Arrow worms that live near the surface are clear, which helps them avoid predators. The intestines of species that live in middle depths often are yellow or red because they eat prey of those colors. Species that live in deeper water are more muscular and less clear than those that live near the surface. Folds of the body wall in the neck region form a hood that folds over the head, helping the worms to swim smoothly. Tufts of bristles on the body are used for detecting prey. The worms have tail fins and one or two pairs of fins on the sides of the body.

Arrow worms are 0.1 to 6 inches (3 to 150 millimeters) long. The largest species lives in Antarctic waters and is about 3 inches (70 millimeters) long. The bottom-dwelling species are the smallest, one species reaching maturity at a length of about 0.1 inches (3 millimeters).

The body cavity of arrow worms is filled with fluid that is surrounded by muscles and a tough covering. The head has complex muscles that support the grasping hooks. Arrow worms have a mouth, one or two rows of teeth, and eyes.

GEOGRAPHIC RANGE

Arrow worms live in all the oceans of the world.

HABITAT

Arrow worms live in every part of the ocean. Most drift in open water close to the surface. Bottom-dwelling species live attached to objects such as sea grass and rocks.

DIET

Arrow worms eat plankton, including tiny crustaceans, fish larvae, and other arrow worms. Digestion is rapid. Scientists believe each arrow worm eats two to fifty prey animals each day. Plankton is tiny plants and animals drifting in water. Crustaceans (krus-TAY-shuns) are water-dwelling animals that have jointed legs and a hard shell but no backbone. Larvae (LAR-vee) are animals in an early stage that change form before becoming adults.

BEHAVIOR AND REPRODUCTION

Arrow worms position themselves at an angle in the water. When their side bristles detect something moving in the water, the worms quickly sweep their tail, swim rapidly in the direction of the prey, and grab the prey using hooks. Scientists believe arrow worms use venom to immobilize their prey after capturing it. Arrow worms that live in middle depths usually swim to the surface at night to feed and sink to deeper water during the day.

Arrow worms make both eggs and sperm. The male reproductive organs are in the tail, and the female organs are in the trunk. The sperm develop first. Fertilization (FUR-teh-lih-ZAY-shun), or the joining of egg and sperm to start development, takes places inside the body after one worm places a sperm pouch on another worm, and the sperm move into the second worm's body. In some species the fertilized (FUR-teh-lyzed) eggs are released into the water. In deep-water species the young develop in sacs hanging from the worm. Arrow worms do not have larvae. Small arrow worms hatch from the eggs and then continue to grow.

ARROW WORMS AND PEOPLE

Arrow worms are used as indicators to determine the level of water from the Atlantic Ocean moving into the North Sea.

CONSERVATION STATUS

Arrow worms are not considered threatened or endangered.

Pterosagitta draco

NO COMMON NAME
Pterosagitta draco

Physical characteristics: *Pterosagitta draco* worms have eight to ten hooks, six to ten front teeth, and eight to eighteen back teeth. The body length reaches 0.4 inches (11 millimeters), and the tail length is about one-third the length of the body. These worms have one pair of fins on the tail. The eyes are small with T-shaped color spots.

Geographic range: *Pterosagitta draco* (abbreviated to *P. draco*) worms live in the Atlantic, Pacific, and Indian oceans.

Habitat: *P. draco* worms live in warm and cool areas of the open ocean close to the surface.

Diet: *P. draco* worms eat tiny crustaceans.

Behavior and reproduction: *P. draco* worms feed at night. They make quick movements over short distances to catch prey. The worms make both eggs and sperm. Fertilized eggs are released into the water, where the worms hatch and grow into adults.

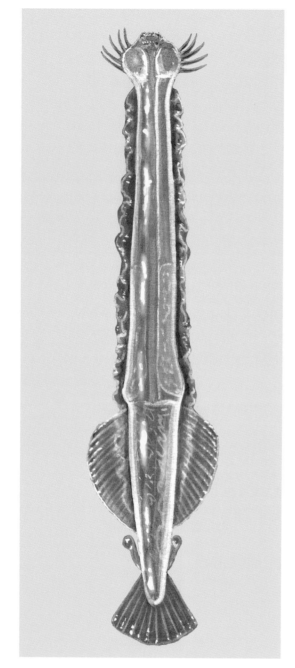

Pterosagitta draco *worms feed at night. They make quick movements over short distances to catch prey. (Illustration by Joseph E. Trumpey. Reproduced by permission.)*

Pterosagitta draco and people: *P. draco* worms have no known importance to people.

Conservation status: *P. draco* worms are not considered threatened or endangered. ∎

Eukrohnia fowleri

NO COMMON NAME
Eukrohnia fowleri

Physical characteristics: *Eukrohnia fowleri* worms have eight to fourteen hooks and two to thirty-one back teeth. There are no front teeth. The body reaches a length of about 1.5 inches (40 millimeters), and the tail length is about one-fourth the length of the body. The neck is narrower than the division between the trunk and the tail. There are long fins on the sides of both the trunk and the tail. The head is small with large oval eyes that have diamond-shaped color spots.

Geographic range: *Eukrohnia fowleri* (abbreviated to *E. fowleri*) worms live in the Atlantic, Pacific, and Indian oceans.

Habitat: *E. fowleri* worms live in open water in the middle depths of the sea. They do not live in extremely cold water.

Diet: *E. fowleri* worms eat tiny crustaceans.

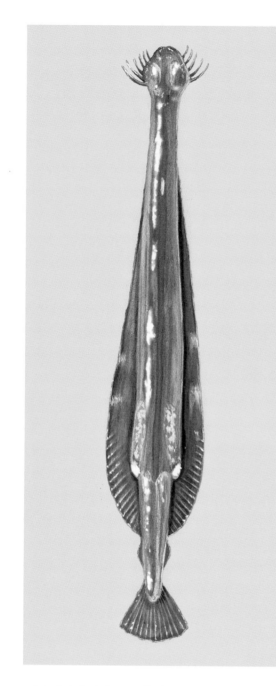

Behavior and reproduction: Scientists do not know how *E. fowleri* worms behave. These worms grow and reproduce very slowly. The fertilized eggs develop in a sac hanging from the worm.

***Eukrohnia fowleri* and people:** *E. fowleri* worms have no known importance to people.

Conservation status: *E. fowleri* worms are not considered threatened or endangered. ■

FOR MORE INFORMATION

Books:

Brusca, Richard C., Gary J. Brusca, and Nancy Haver. *Invertebrates.* 2nd ed. Sunderland, MA: Sinauer, 2002.

Niesen, Thomas M. *The Marine Biology Coloring Book.* 2nd ed. New York: HarperResource, 2000.

Periodicals:

Davis, Cabell S., Carin J. Ashjian, and Philip Alatalo. "Zooplankton Diversity: A Bizarre—and Changing—Array of Life Forms." *Oceanus* (spring-summer 1996): 7–11.

Web sites:

Sutton, Tracey. "Today's Highlights." *Mar-Eco.* http://www.mar-eco.no/Shiptoshore/g._o._sars/cruise_journal_gosars/20June (accessed on March 2, 2005).

Thuesen, Erik V. "Chaetognatha." Evergreen State College. http://academic.evergreen.edu/t/thuesene/chaetognaths/chaetognaths.htm (accessed on March 2, 2005).

Eukrohnia fowleri *worms live in open water in the middle depths of the sea. They do not live in extremely cold water. (Illustration by Joseph E. Trumpey. Reproduced by permission.)*

phylum
C H A P T E R

PHYSICAL CHARACTERISTICS

Hemichordates (heh-mee-COOR-duhts) are wormlike sea animals that live alone or in colonies. The type that lives alone, called acorn worms because of the shape of their heads, is a few inches (centimeters) to several feet (meters) long. They have a three-part body plan of a snout, a simple collar, and a trunk. Hairlike fibers covering the body are used for movement and for distributing mucus. The type of hemichordates that lives in colonies is only about 0.04 inches (1 millimeter) long. They also have a three-part body plan, but the snout is short and shield-shaped and the collar is complex, in some species having tentacled arms. Colony-forming hemichordates live in a network of tubes built with mucus from each animal's snout. A third type of hemichordates has only one species, and only its larvae have been found. Larvae (LAR-vee) are animals in an early stage that change form before becoming adults.

GEOGRAPHIC RANGE

Hemichordates live in all the oceans of the world.

HABITAT

Adult acorn worms usually live in shallow water in burrows at the bottom, but sometimes they live in the sand inside shells, under rocks, in thick seaweed, or between root tangles. Colony-forming hemichordates usually live in deep water in the tubes they make from mucus.

■ **phylum**

class

subclass

order

monotypic order

suborder

family

DIET

Hemichordates eat bacteria, microscopic algae, diatoms, and nutrients they scrape from particles of sand and mud or collect from the water. Algae (AL-jee) are plantlike growths that live in water and have no true roots, stems, or leaves. Diatoms (DYE-uh-tahms) are a type of algae that have a shell.

BEHAVIOR AND REPRODUCTION

Acorn worms live alone sheltered in their burrows, under rocks, or in thick tangles of plants. The burrowing species use their snout for digging. They line the U-shaped burrows with mucus to strengthen the walls. One end of the "U" is a cone-shaped dent, and the other is a pile of feces (FEE-seez) a short distance away. The rest of the burrow is underground and sometimes has a few side tunnels. Burrowing acorn worms sometimes stretch their snout and collar out of the tunnel, but they spend most of their time underground.

Some hemichordates gather their meals by stirring up currents with the hairlike fibers on their body and drawing in nutrients from the water. Others take in particles of sand or mud and eat the nutrients sticking to them. Scientists are not sure whether hemichordates use mucus to capture prey. Some scientists believe food sticks to the mucus-covered snout and that hairlike fibers on the animal's body beat in a pattern that draws the mucus and the food together to the mouth. Other scientists have found that the animals use their hairlike fibers to change the direction of their movements and direct food particles to the mouth.

Hemichordates have separate sexes. They release their eggs and sperm into the water, where fertilization (FUR-teh-lih-ZAY-shun), or the joining of egg and sperm to start development, takes place. In some species the fertilized (FUR-teh-lyzed) eggs develop directly into adults. In most species, however, the fertilized eggs develop into free-floating larvae, which eventually settle on the bottom and transform into adults. Burrow dwellers develop tails that they use to anchor themselves in their mucus-lined tunnels. In some species of hemichordates reproduction is asexual and accomplished by the breaking up of the adult's body or by budding. Asexual (ay-SEK-shuh-wuhl) means without the uniting of egg and sperm for the transfer of DNA from two parents. In budding a bump develops on an animal, grows to full size, and then breaks off to live as a new individual.

HEMICHORDATES AND PEOPLE

Hemichordates have no known importance to people.

CONSERVATION STATUS

Hemichordates are not considered threatened or endangered.

Hawaiian acorn worm (*Ptychodera flava*)

SPECIES ACCOUNTS

HAWAIIAN ACORN WORM
Ptychodera flava

Physical characteristics: Hawaiian acorn worms are yellowish brown and have a small cone-shaped snout, short collar, and long trunk.

Geographic range: Hawaiian acorn worms live in the Pacific Ocean near Japan, Australia, Hawaii, and the Galápagos Islands and in the Indian Ocean near Mauritius and Maldives.

Habitat: Hawaiian acorn worms live in the sea near coastlines.

Diet: Hawaiian acorn worms eat nutrient particles.

Behavior and reproduction: Female Hawaiian acorn worms release mucus-covered eggs into the water, and the males respond by releasing sperm. Fertilization takes place in the water. The eggs hatch into larvae in about two days.

Hawaiian acorn worms and people: Hawaiian acorn worms have no known importance to people.

Conservation status: Hawaiian acorn worms are not considered threatened or endangered. ■

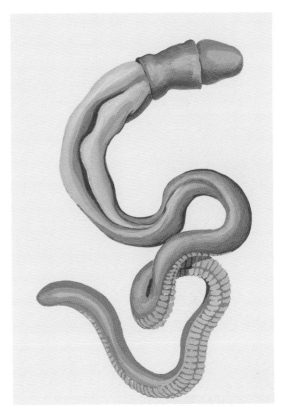

Hawaiian acorn worms live in the sea near coastlines. (Illustration by John Megahan. Reproduced by permission.)

Spaghetti worm (Saxipendium coronatum)

SPAGHETTI WORM
Saxipendium coronatum

Physical characteristics: Spaghetti worms are thin and yellowish white. They can be as long as 10 feet (3 meters). The snout tapers to a soft point toward the front, and the collar is short.

Geographic range: Spaghetti worms live in the Pacific Ocean near the Galápagos Islands.

Habitat: Spaghetti worms live in the deepest ocean loosely attached to rocks near hydrothermal (high-druh-THUR-muhl) vents, which are openings in the ocean floor that serve as smokestacks for releasing extremely hot gases from under Earth's crust.

Diet: Scientists do not know what spaghetti worms eat.

Behavior and reproduction: Spaghetti worms live in tangled coils covered with mucus. Except that fertilization takes place outside the body, scientists do not know how spaghetti worms reproduce.

Spaghetti worms and people: Spaghetti worms have no known importance to people.

Conservation status: Spaghetti worms are not considered threatened or endangered. ■

FOR MORE INFORMATION

Books:

Valentine, James W. *On the Origin of Phyla.* Chicago: University of Chicago Press, 2004.

Web sites:

Scott, Susan. "Elusive Acorn Worms Are Ocean's Vacuum Cleaners." *Ocean Watch.* http://www.susanscott.net/OceanWatch2001/aug17-01.html (accessed on March 2, 2005).

Scott, Susan. "Spaghetti Worms Utilize Tentacles in Amazing Ways." *Ocean Watch.* http://www.susanscott.net/OceanWatch1998/jan19-98.html (accessed on March 2, 2005).

Spaghetti worms live in the deepest ocean loosely attached to rocks near hydrothermal vents. (Illustration by John Megahan. Reproduced by permission.)

Class: Ascidiacea

Number of families: 24 families

phylum

● **class**

subclass

order

monotypic order

suborder

family

PHYSICAL CHARACTERISTICS

Some sea squirts look like large, upright tubes and live alone. Others live in colonies and form a crust on rocks and other hard surfaces. Both types of sea squirts have a protective body covering. This layer is clear or brightly colored, usually red, brown, or yellow but sometimes blue. In some species the body covering is coated with spines. Most sea squirts are 0.04 to 6 inches (1 millimeter to 15 centimeters) long, but some are much larger. Some species that live alone can be as tall as 20 inches (50 centimeters), and some colonies grow to an area of about 10 square feet (1 square meter).

Sea squirts have two body openings: one for taking water in and one for pumping, or squirting, water out. The water-intake opening leads to a large chamber that takes up most of the inside of the sea squirt and is lined with slits. Seawater, which contains food particles and oxygen, is drawn into the large chamber and then is pumped into a second chamber. The slits are small enough to keep the food particles inside the first chamber, which leads to the digestive system. After entering the second chamber, the water is pumped out of the animal through the exit hole.

In colony-forming sea squirts, the body covering forms a sheet that holds the individual sea squirts. Each sea squirt in the colony has its own water-intake opening and main chamber, but several individuals in a system share a second chamber and water-exit hole. The shape of the systems varies. In some species the individual sea squirts are arranged in a circular system around the shared opening. In other species the individual sea squirts form long double rows along a canal of water-exit openings.

GEOGRAPHIC RANGE

Sea squirts live in all oceans and seas.

HABITAT

Sea squirts live at all depths. Most live in shallow water. Some even survive on open shores under strong wave action. Some sea squirts live in ocean trenches as deep as 28,000 feet (8,400 meters). Most species of sea squirts live on rocks, shells, or algae (AL-jee), which are plantlike growths that live in water and have no true roots, stems, or leaves. Some sea squirts live on soft muddy or sandy bottoms. A few species of sea squirts live between gravel grains.

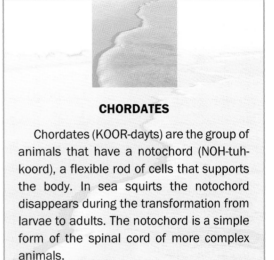

CHORDATES

Chordates (KOOR-dayts) are the group of animals that have a notochord (NOH-tuh-koord), a flexible rod of cells that supports the body. In sea squirts the notochord disappears during the transformation from larvae to adults. The notochord is a simple form of the spinal cord of more complex animals.

DIET

Sea squirts eat bacteria, plankton, and small swimming invertebrates. Plankton is microscopic plants and animals drifting in the water. Invertebrates (in-VER-teh-brehts) are animals without a backbone.

BEHAVIOR AND REPRODUCTION

Most sea squirts firmly attach themselves to the material on which they live. Species that are not firmly attached have threads on their body covering for anchoring themselves. The species that live between grains of gravel are not fixed and can move.

Sea squirts use muscle contractions to draw in seawater and to pump it out, opening and closing their intake and exit holes as they do so. For most sea squirts these movements are slow, but species that live in the deepest part of the ocean, where food is scarce, can quickly contract their muscles and close their large intake opening to catch small invertebrates.

Sea squirts make both eggs and sperm. In some colony-forming species fertilization (FUR-teh-lih-ZAY-shun), or the joining of egg and sperm to start development, takes place inside an individual squirt, but development takes place in the

The Greek philosopher
Aristotle studied sea squirts
more than 2,300 years ago.

chamber the system shares, in special pockets in the body wall of the individual sea squirts, or in the sheet that holds the colony. Colony-forming sea squirts release freely swimming larvae. Larvae (LAR-vee) are animals in an early stage that change form before becoming adults. Some colony-forming sea squirts use asexual reproduction by budding to form colonies. Asexual (ay-SEK-shuh-wuhl) means without the uniting of egg and sperm for the transfer of DNA from two parents. In budding a bump develops on an animal, grows to full size, and then breaks off to live as a new individual.

Sea squirts that live alone either give birth to live young or release fertilized (FUR-teh-lyzed) eggs, which hatch into larvae. The larvae never feed but swim for a short time and then attach to the material on which they will live and transform into young sea squirts that have the same form as adults.

SEA SQUIRTS AND PEOPLE

Sea squirts may be a source for chemicals used to make medicines. In some countries, people eat sea squirts. Sea squirts that grow on the bottoms of ships interfere with mussel and oyster farming.

CONSERVATION STATUS

Sea squirts are not considered threatened or endangered.

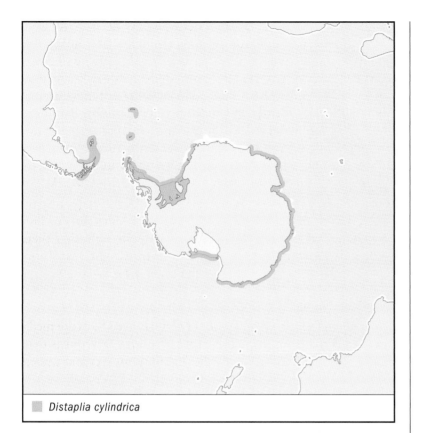

Distaplia cylindrica

NO COMMON NAME
Distaplia cylindrica

Physical characteristics: *Distaplia cylindrica* sea squirts form sausage-shaped colonies that reach a length of 23 feet (7 meters) and a width of 3 inches (8 centimeters). The colony is white or yellowish and has a soft texture. It is attached at one end to rocks and grows upward. The individual sea squirts in the colony are small and are located only in the surface layer of the colony, where they form many small, oval systems.

Geographic range: *Distaplia cylindrica* (abbreviated to *D. cylindrica*) sea squirts live in the Antarctic regions.

Habitat: *D. cylindrica* sea squirts live on rocky bottoms.

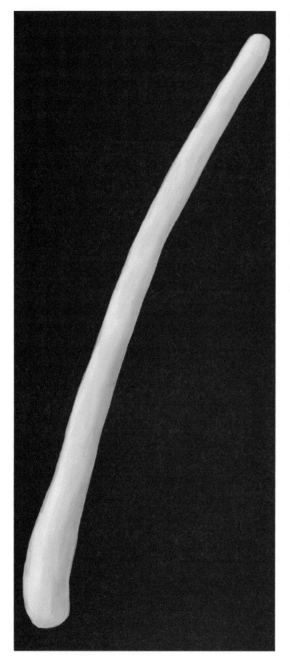

Distaplia cylindrica *sea squirts live in the Antarctic regions. (Illustration by Emily Damstra. Reproduced by permission.)*

Diet: *D. cylindrica* sea squirts eat nutrient particles they strain from the water flowing through them.

Behavior and reproduction: *D. cylindrica* sea squirts attach themselves to rocks. They make both eggs and sperm, but individual sea squirts in different parts of a colony may have better developed male organs and those in another part of the colony may have better developed female organs. Larvae develop in pouches in the parent colony.

***Distaplia cylindrica* and people:** *D. cylindrica* sea squirts have no known importance to people.

Conservation status: *D. cylindrica* sea squirts are not considered threatened or endangered. ■

Botryllus schlosseri

NO COMMON NAME
Botryllus schlosseri

Physical characteristics: *Botryllus schlosseri* sea squirts live in flat colonies on rocks or algae. The colonies reach a width of about 4 inches (10 centimeters). Systems of individual sea squirts are embedded in a soft, slimy dark brown sheet in circular patterns that look like daisies. The system's common opening looks like the center of the flower. The individual sea squirts have a white or yellow stripe on top.

Geographic range: *Botryllus schlosseri* (abbreviated to *B. schlosseri*) sea squirts live on both sides of the Atlantic Ocean.

Habitat: *B. schlosseri* sea squirts live in shallow water on rocks, shells, and algae.

Diet: *B. schlosseri* sea squirts eat nutrient particles they strain from the water flowing through them.

Behavior and reproduction: *B. schlosseri* sea squirts attach themselves to the surface on which they live. Fertilization and the development of larvae take place within the colony.

***Botryllus schlosseri* and people:** *B. schlosseri* sea squirts have no known importance to people.

Conservation status: *B. schlosseri* sea squirts are not considered threatened or endangered. ■

Didemnum studeri

NO COMMON NAME
Didemnum studeri

Physical characteristics: *Didemnum studeri* sea squirts form flat colonies on rocks. The colonies are 3 feet (1 meter) or more in diameter and are less than 0.2 inches (5 millimeters) thick. The colony is white and covered with tiny pieces of a material that looks like bone.

Geographic range: *Didemnum studeri* (abbreviated to D. *studeri*) sea squirts live in the waters just north of the Antarctic regions. They are especially common in the Strait of Magellan.

Habitat: D. *studeri* sea squirts live in shallow water on rocks and on roots or stems of algae.

Diet: D. *studeri* sea squirts eat nutrient particles they strain from the water flowing through them.

Behavior and reproduction: D. *studeri* sea squirts attach themselves to the surface on which they live. The larvae develop inside the colony.

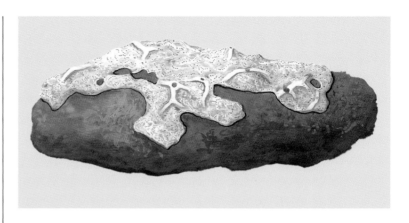

***Didemnum studeri* and people:** *D. studeri* sea squirts have no known importance to people.

Conservation status: *D. studeri* sea squirts are not considered threatened or endangered. ■

FOR MORE INFORMATION

Books:

Byatt, Andrew, Alastair Fothergill, and Martha Holmes. *The Blue Planet.* New York: DK, 2001.

Carson, Rachel. *The Edge of the Sea.* 1955. Reprint, Boston: Mariner, 1998.

Niesen, Thomas M. *The Marine Biology Coloring Book.* 2nd ed. New York: HarperResource, 2000.

Web sites:

Parmentier, Jan, and Wim van Egmond. "Sea Squirts: Our Distant Cousins." *Microscopy UK.* http://www.microscopy-uk.org.uk/mag/indexmag.html?http://www.microscopy-uk.org.uk/mag/artaug98/tuni2.html (accessed on March 3, 2005).

Philipkoski, Kristen. "Sea Squirt Savants Celebrate." *Wired.* http://www.wired.com/news/medtech/0,1286,51840,00.html (accessed on March 3, 2005).

PHYSICAL CHARACTERISTICS

Salps are tiny, drifting sea animals that have a clear cylindrical body with openings at each end. Between the openings is a basketlike structure covered by a sheet of mucus. The jellylike body wall contains bands of muscle. Most salps are 0.2 to 8 inches (5 millimeters to 20 centimeters) long. Some colonies are many feet (meters) long.

GEOGRAPHIC RANGE

Salps live in warm and cool seas.

HABITAT

Most salps live near the surface, but some live in deeper water.

DIET

Salps eat plant plankton, or microscopic plants drifting in water.

BEHAVIOR AND REPRODUCTION

Salps swim through the water by the movement of hairlike fibers on their bodies or by contracting muscles in the body wall to draw water into their intake opening and pump it out through their water-exit opening. Although they swim, salps are at the mercy of ocean currents for their entire lives.

When salps feed, water flows in through the mouth opening, through the mucus sheet covering the internal basket, and

phylum

● **class**

subclass

order

monotypic order

suborder

family

Chains of salps can be as long as a blue whale.

out the exit hole. Plankton and other small particles are caught on the mucus, which is moved to the mouth and eaten.

In some species of salps fertilized (FUR-teh-lyzed) eggs, or those that have been united with sperm, develop and hatch inside the animals. In other species the fertilized eggs hatch into larvae (LAR-vee), which are animals in an early stage that change form before becoming adults. Still other species alternate asexual and sexual stages of reproduction. Asexual (ay-SEK-shuh-wuhl) means without and sexual means with the uniting of egg and sperm for the transfer of DNA from two parents. An asexual generation buds into a sexual generation, which produces the eggs and sperm that fuse to produce the next asexual generation. This method of alternating asexual and sexual stages allows salps to reproduce extremely rapidly.

SALPS AND PEOPLE

There can be so many salps in an area that they use up all the food needed by animals that are eaten by fishes upon which humans rely. The fishes disappear from the area, and the humans lose their food and their work.

CONSERVATION STATUS

Salps are not considered threatened or endangered.

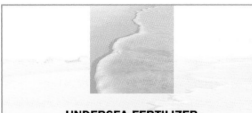

UNDERSEA FERTILIZER

Vast swarms of salps eat huge amounts of plant plankton and produce massive amounts of feces (FEE-seez). The sinking feces supply carbon, an element essential to life, to the deep ocean.

PYROSOME
Pyrosoma atlanticum

Physical characteristics: Individual pyrosomes (PYE-ruh-sohms) are about 0.3 inches (8 millimeters) long and are embedded in a thick, clear tube that forms the base for a colony as long as 24 inches (60 centimeters). Colonies are pink or yellowish pink. The mouth openings of the pyrosomes face out from the tube, and the water-exit holes point toward the inside of the colony. Pyrosomes produce light, which appears in waves of a brilliant glow along the colony.

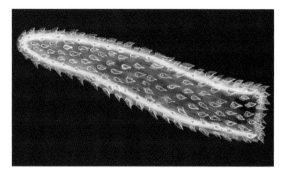

Pyrosomes produce light, which appears in waves of a brilliant glow along the colony. (Illustration by Emily Damstra. Reproduced by permission.)

Geographic range: Pyrosomes live all over the world in warm to cool seas. Because they are found throughout the world, no distribution map is provided.

Habitat: Pyrosomes live in surface waters but each day travel down more than 2,500 feet (750 meters) and then return to the surface.

Diet: Pyrosomes eat plant plankton.

Behavior and reproduction: Water enters individual pyrosomes through the mouth holes and empties into the colony's common tube. The water exits the tube through an opening at one end of the colony, propelling the colony through the water. The water-pumping system also is used for feeding. Water entering each pyrosome passes through a mucus sheet that filters particles of plant plankton into the digestive system. Pyrosomes form swarms that produce huge amounts of feces.

Pyrosomes make both eggs and sperm. In each pyrosome of a colony a single egg is fertilized and then grows to a four-animal stage that leaves the parent to start a new colony by budding, which is a method of asexual reproduction by which a bump develops on an animal, grows to full size, and then breaks off to live as a new individual. This fast method of alternating asexual and sexual reproduction results in giant swarms of pyrosome colonies.

Pyrosomes and people: The brilliant light displays given off by colonies of pyrosomes have bewildered and fascinated sailors for generations.

Conservation status: Pyrosomes are not considered threatened or endangered. ■

SALP
Thalia democratica

Physical characteristics: Salps in the asexual stage are about 0.5 inches (12 millimeters) long and have a pair of tentacles at their hind end. Salps in the sexual stage are about 0.2 inches (6 millimeters) long. The body covering is thick and has five muscle bands.

Geographic range: Salps live all over the world in warm to cool seas. Because they are found throughout the world, no distribution map is provided.

Habitat: Salps usually live in surface waters.

Diet: Salps eat plant plankton.

Behavior and reproduction: Salps swim actively through the water by contracting their muscles. Salps are one of the fastest growing many-celled animals. Their body length more than doubles within an hour. Salps in the asexual stage produce a tail on which bud rows of the sexual stage stay connected to one another, forming chains several feet (meters) long. Fertilized salp eggs develop directly into the asexual stage. New generations of salps are produced in as fast as a few days, resulting in huge swarms covering hundreds of square miles (kilometers) of open ocean.

Salps and people: Salps have no known importance to people.

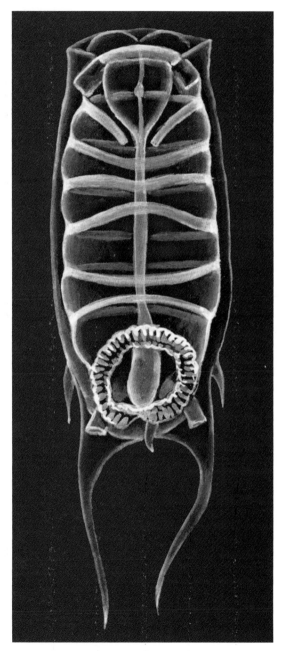

Salps are one of the fastest growing many-celled animals. Their body length more than doubles within an hour. (Illustration by Emily Damstra. Reproduced by permission.)

Conservation status: Salps are not considered threatened or endangered. ■

FOR MORE INFORMATION

Books:

Brusca, Richard C., Gary J. Brusca, and Nancy Haver. *Invertebrates*. 2nd ed. Sunderland, MA: Sinauer, 2002.

Byatt, Andrew, Alastair Fothergill, and Martha Holmes. *The Blue Planet*. New York: DK, 2001.

Periodicals:

Erickson, Paul. "Where Sea Jellies Hover." *Sea Frontiers* (fall 1995): 22–25.

Kunzig, Robert. "At Home with the Jellies." *Discover* (September 1997): 64–71.

Vogel, Steven. "Second-Rate Squirts." *Discover* (August 1994): 71–76.

Web sites:

"Hermaphroditic Salps." Monmouth County Department of Health. http://www.shore.co.monmouth.nj.us/health/environmental/coastal/salps.htm (accessed on March 3, 2005).

"Salps: Big Squirts That Swim the Sea." *California Diving News*. http://www.saintbrendan.com/cdnoct00/marine10.html (accessed on March 3, 2005).

class

C H A P T E R

PHYSICAL CHARACTERISTICS

Larvaceans (lar-VAY-shuns) are small, clear sea animals that make a complex net, or house, of mucus. They live their entire lives as tadpoles, or larvae, even when they are adults and ready to reproduce. Larvae (LAR-vee) are animals in an early stage that change form before becoming adults. The body of larvaceans is made up of a trunk containing most of the internal organs and of a tail with a notochord running down the middle. A notochord (NOH-tuh-koord) is a flexible rod of cells that supports the body of some simple animals. The trunk secretes the mucus house, which encloses the entire animal or only the tail, depending on the species. The body and house are jellylike. The body of larvaceans is 0.04 to 1 inches (1 to 25 millimeters) long. The house is 0.2 inches to 7 feet (4 millimeters to 2 meters) across.

Larvaceans have an amazing filtering mechanism. The wall of the house contains two filters, and a filter in the trunk is connected to the animal's mouth. The filters are made of strands of mucus that allow only the smallest food particles, those less than 0.0004 inches (1 micrometer) in diameter, into the tube leading to the mouth.

GEOGRAPHIC RANGE

Larvaceans live in ocean currents all over the world.

HABITAT

Larvaceans live in open ocean and near the shore in surface waters and in middle depths.

phylum
class
subclass
order
monotypic order
suborder
family

DIET

Larvaceans eat plant plankton that they filter from the water that passes through them. Plankton is microscopic plants and animals drifting in water.

BEHAVIOR AND REPRODUCTION

Larvaceans move their tail inside their house to make a current that filters food particles and moves the house through the water. If the filters become clogged or something bumps the house, the larvacean leaves the house through a trap door. The beginnings of a new house lie on the trunk of the animal's body, and the larvacean inflates the new house and flips inside.

Some larvaceans have glowing grains in their house wall. Some scientists believe that predators eat an empty house that is flashing light while the larvacean swims away to make another house. Surface waters of some bays and harbors sometimes glow brilliantly because of the presence of large groups of larvaceans.

Larvaceans make both eggs and sperm, which are released directly into the water. The sperm are released first, and then the eggs burst out of the body wall, a process that results in the death of the animal. Fertilization (FUR-teh-lih-ZAY-shun), or the joining of egg and sperm to start development, and development take place in the open water. These animals reproduce rapidly. If there is a great deal of plant plankton in an area, huge swarms of larvaceans can form, sometimes in a matter of a few days.

LARVACEANS AND PEOPLE

Larvaceans can clear an area of plant plankton, eating the food needed by sea animals that fishes eat. The fishes leave the area, and people lose their food and their jobs.

CONSERVATION STATUS

Larvaceans are not considered threatened or endangered.

NO COMMON NAME
Oikopleura labradoriensis

Physical characteristics: *Oikopleura labradoriensis* larvaceans are about 0.2 inches (6 millimeters) long. The trunk makes up about one-third of the animal's length and the tail about two-thirds of the length. The house is approximately 0.4 inch (9 millimeters) across.

Geographic range: *Oikopleura labradoriensis* (abbreviated to *O. labradoriensis*) larvaceans live all over the world. Because they are found throughout the world, no distribution map is provided.

Habitat: *O. labradoriensis* larvaceans live in cool to cold waters near the surface. They live in the open sea as well as closer to shore.

Diet: *O. labradoriensis* larvaceans eat only the smallest of plant particles, those less than 0.0004 inches (1 micrometer) in diameter.

Behavior and reproduction: *O. labradoriensis* larvaceans have glowing grains in the walls of their houses that may help confuse predators, which eat empty houses rather than animals that have abandoned the houses. *O. labradoriensis* larvaceans make both eggs and sperm. They release sperm first then release eggs by rupturing their body wall, a process that results in the death of the animal. Fertilization and development take place in the open water.

***Oikopleura labradoriensis* and people:** *O. labradoriensis* larvaceans have no known importance to people.

Conservation status: *O. labradoriensis* larvaceans are not considered threatened or endangered. ∎

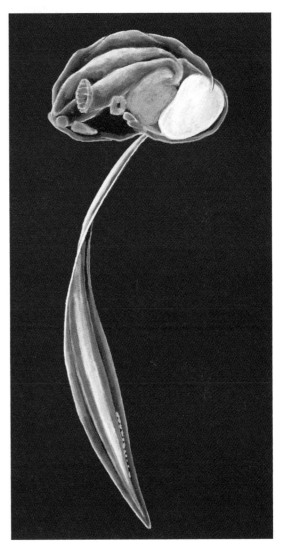

Oikopleura labradoriensis *live in cool to cold waters near the surface. (Illustration by Emily Damstra. Reproduced by permission.)*

FOR MORE INFORMATION

Books:

Byatt, Andrew, Alastair Fothergill, and Martha Holmes. *The Blue Planet.* New York: DK, 2001.

Niesen, Thomas M. *The Marine Biology Coloring Book.* 2nd ed. New York: HarperResource, 2000.

Periodicals:

Dybas, Cheryl Lyn. "Voyagers of Inner Space." *Sea Frontiers* (spring 1996): 18–21.

Morell, Virginia. "Way Down Deep." *National Geographic* (June 2004): 36–55.

Web sites:

"Pelagic Tunicates." *JelliesZone.* http://jellieszone.com/tunicates.htm (accessed on March 3, 2005).

Van Egmond, Wim. "*Oikopleura*'s Fishing House." *Microscopy UK.* http://www.microscopy-uk.net/mag/indexmag.html?http://www.microscopy-uk.net/mag/artjan01/oiko.html (accessed on March 24, 2005).

Class: Sorberacea
Number of families: 1 family

class

CHAPTER

PHYSICAL CHARACTERISTICS

Sorberaceans (soor-buh-RAY-shuns) are a small group of deep-water, bottom-dwelling sea animals related to sea squirts. Some species of sorberaceans have an egg-shaped body, and others are slightly longer than egg-shaped. The outside layer of sorberaceans is covered with short hairlike fibers and with the shells of tiny animals, sand, and mud particles sticking to the fibers. Sorberaceans are 0.1 to 2.4 inches (0.3 to 6.0 centimeters) long. Water intake and outflow openings are on opposite ends of the body and are directed away from each other. The outflow opening is very small. The intake opening is large, is on the front end or the side of the body, and is surrounded by six rounded bulges. The intake opening leads to the mouth cavity, which is lined with the same layer that covers the body. The mouth cavity leads into a small chamber lined with slits and has a few openings that lead to a system of thin-walled tubes that open into a second chamber. Some species of sorberaceans have a very large stomach, which occupies most of the inside of the animal. All species have a kidney.

GEOGRAPHIC RANGE

Sorberaceans live in all the oceans of the world but have not been found in the northernmost waters of the Arctic Ocean or the northern part of the Pacific Ocean.

HABITAT

Sorberaceans live at the bottom of the deepest part of the ocean, although some have been found in shallower water. The deep bottom is almost always soft and covered by a thick layer of mud, on which sorberaceans live unattached.

DIET

Sorberaceans probably eat small moving invertebrates (in-VER-teh-brehts), or animals without a backbone.

BEHAVIOR AND REPRODUCTION

Sorberaceans do not survive capture, and scientists have not directly observed their behavior. They do know that sorberaceans live alone rather than in colonies. Although they are not firmly attached to the bottom, it is unlikely that these animals move. The hairlike fibers covering the body are encased in attached particles of mud and shells. This evidence suggests that the animals are anchored in the mud and cannot actively move.

Scientists believe sorberaceans actively search and capture prey using their muscular water-intake opening. The fingerlike bulges on the end of the opening may work as a hand for capturing small invertebrates.

Sorberaceans make both eggs and sperm. The eggs are laid and develop outside the parent's body. Other than that, scientists do not know how sorberaceans reproduce. The larvae have never been found. The youngest sorberaceans found already had the adult form. Larvae (LAR-vee) are animals in an early stage that change form before becoming adults.

SORBERACEANS AND PEOPLE

Sorberaceans have no known importance to people.

CONSERVATION STATUS

Sorberaceans are not considered threatened or endangered.

Oligotrema sandersi

| NO COMMON NAME |
| Oligotrema sandersi |

Physical characteristics: *Oligotrema sandersi* sorberaceans are no longer than 0.2 inches (5 millimeters). The oval body is covered by sparse hairlike fibers with attached mud particles and the shells of tiny animals. The intake and outflow openings are on opposite sides of the body. The intake opening is very muscular, turns inside out, and has six fingerlike bulges. The stomach is very large and occupies most of the animal's body.

Geographic range: *Oligotrema sandersi* (abbreviated to *O. sandersi*) sorberaceans live in the Atlantic Ocean.

Habitat: *O. sandersi* sorberaceans live in the deepest part of the ocean.

Diet: *O. sandersi* sorberaceans eat small invertebrates.

Behavior and reproduction: Scientists do not know how *O. sandersi* sorberaceans behave or reproduce.

Sorberaceans do not survive capture, and scientists have not directly observed their behavior. They do know that sorberaceans live alone rather than in colonies. (Illustration by John Megahan. Reproduced by permission.)

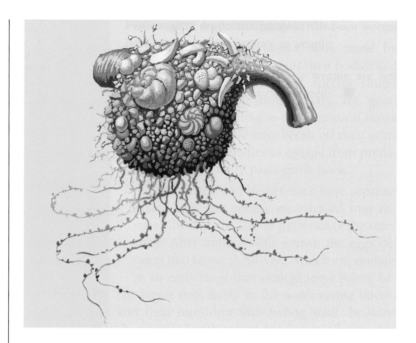

Oligotrema sandersi and people: *O. sandersi* sorberaceans have no known importance to people.

Conservation status: *O. sandersi* sorberaceans are not considered threatened or endangered.   ■

FOR MORE INFORMATION

Books:

Brusca, Richard C., Gary J. Brusca, and Nancy Haver. *Invertebrates.* 2nd ed. Sunderland, MA: Sinauer, 2002.

Gage, John D., and Paul A. Tyler. *Deep-Sea Biology.* New York: Cambridge University Press, 1991.

class

CHAPTER

PHYSICAL CHARACTERISTICS

Lancelets look like slender fish without eyes. They are 0.4 to 3 inches (1 to 8 centimeters) long and whitish to creamy yellow, sometimes with a tint of pink. Mucus secreted by cells in their body covering gives lancelets a pearly sheen. V-shaped lines on the outside of lancelets' bodies outline muscle blocks inside the body. Small bristles surround the mouth. A fin runs along the entire back of the animal and extends forward into a short fin over the snout and backward into a tail fin. There is a fin on the belly toward the rear of the animal. Paired fin-like folds in front of the belly fin extend to the front of the lancelet.

Lancelets have a notochord (NOH-tuh-koord), which is a flexible rod of cells supporting the body. The rest of the skeleton is made up of small, flexible rods between the gill slits and supporting the mouth bristles. A nerve cord runs along the top of the notochord, and various types of sensing cells are distributed in the body covering, especially near the snout. Lancelets have blood vessels but no heart. The chest has about two hundred gill slits that do not open to the outside but empty into a chamber inside the body wall. The chamber empties to the outside through a hole on the belly of the lancelet.

GEOGRAPHIC RANGE

Lancelets live in all the oceans of the world in warm and cool waters.

LANCELETS AND VERTEBRATES

Scientists consider lancelets the closest living relatives to vertebrates (VER-teh-brehts), or animals with a backbone. The two groups share traits such as the organization of the main body muscles into separate segments and the organization of the blood vessels. Lancelets also have a structure that is a simple form of the liver of vertebrates. The nerve cord of lancelets has a central canal that is enlarged at the head end, making it similar to parts of the vertebrate brain.

HABITAT

Lancelets live in sandy bottoms near the shore. The larvae may drift over long distances before settling. Larvae (LAR-vee) are animals in an early stage that change form before becoming adults.

DIET

Lancelets eat plant plankton and diatoms. Plankton is microscopic plants and animals drifting in water. Diatoms (DYE-uh-tahms) are a type of algae that have a shell. Algae (AL-jee) are plantlike growths that live in water and have no true roots, stems, or leaves.

BEHAVIOR AND REPRODUCTION

Lancelets can swim vigorously forward and backward, but they spend most of their time buried halfway in the sand. They live in masses of more than nine thousand animals per square yard (meter). Depending on the coarseness of the sand, lancelets assume different feeding positions. In coarse sand they bury their entire body with only the head exposed to the water. In fine sand they lie on the bottom. Lancelets continuously produce a mucus net that they move over their gill slits to capture food particles in the water. The food particles and mucus net are rolled into a mass that passes into the digestive tract.

Lancelets have separate sexes. There are equal numbers of males and females in a population. Eggs and sperm are released into the water, where the fertilized (FUR-teh-lyzed) eggs, those that have united with sperm, develop into larvae. When twelve to fifteen pairs of gill slits have formed, the larvae sink to the bottom and transform into young lancelets. From that point on the animals grow, and additional gill slits and muscle segments develop while the reproductive organs grow to maturity.

LANCELETS AND PEOPLE

In southern China local fishermen using traditional techniques fish for and eat lancelets. The greatest importance of lancelets to people, however, is in the study of evolution.

CONSERVATION STATUS

Lancelets are not considered threatened or endangered.

Florida lancelet (*Branchiostoma floridae*)

FLORIDA LANCELET
Branchiostoma floridae

Physical characteristics: Florida lancelets are whitish to creamy yellow, sometimes with a tint of pink. They have fifty-six to sixty-four muscle blocks and reach a length of 2.5 inches (6 centimeters).

Geographic range: Florida lancelets live in the Gulf of Mexico.

Habitat: Florida lancelets live on sandy bottoms in shallow seawater.

Diet: Florida lancelets eat plant plankton and diatoms.

Behavior and reproduction: Florida lancelets can swim but spend most of their time buried halfway in the sand. They capture food

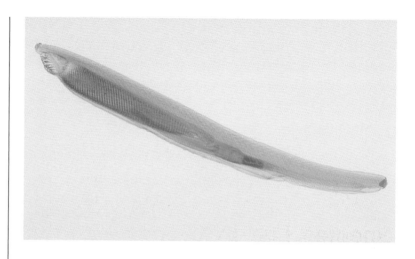

particles with a mucus net. They breed in Tampa Bay, Florida, from late spring to late summer. They can release eggs and produce and release more eggs in the same breeding season.

Florida lancelets and people: Florida lancelets are used for studies of embryonic development.

Conservation status: Florida lancelets are not considered threatened or endangered. ■

FOR MORE INFORMATION

Books:

Gee, Henry. *Before the Backbone.* London, Weinheim, New York: Chapman & Hall, 1996.

Simmer, Carl. *Evolution: The Triumph of an Idea.* New York: HarperCollins, 2001.

Periodicals:

Stokes, M. D., and N. D. Holland. "Ciliary Hovering in Larval Lancelets (Amphioxus)." *Biological Bulletin* (June 1995): 231–233.

Web sites:

"*Branchiostoma belcheri.*" *Community-Based Conservation Management, China and Vietnam.* http://ois.xmu.edu.cn/cbcm/english/resource/save/save04.htm (accessed on March 3, 2005).

"Introduction to the Cephalochordata." University of California, Berkeley, Museum of Paleontology. http://www.ucmp.berkeley.edu/chordata/cephalo.html (accessed on March 3, 2005).

Species List by Biome

CONIFEROUS FOREST
Canine heartworm
Giant thorny-headed worm
Mermis nigrescens
Moniliformis moniliformis

CONTINENTAL MARGIN
Aequorea victoria
Black coral
Blue starfish
Botryllus schlosseri
Bucket-tailed loriciferan
Candy cane sea cucumber
Convulutriloba longifissura
Crown-of-thorns
Deep water reef coral
Desmoscolex squamosus
Dicyemodeca deca
Didemnum studeri
Distaplia cylindrica
Distichopora violacea
Dwarf brittle star
Eukrohnia fowleri
Fire coral
Florida lancelet
Frilled anemone
Hawaiian acorn worm
Long-spined sea urchin
Marine colonial entoproct
Medusiform sea daisy
Nightlight jellyfish
Northern Pacific sea star
Notoplana acticola
Oerstedia dorsalis
Oikopleura labradoriensis
Orange sea lily
Oyster leech
Pea urchin
Portuguese man of war
Priapulus caudatus
Pterosagitta draco
Pyrosome
Red coral
Rhopalura ophiocomae
Salp
Sand star
Sea apple
Sea nettle
Sea walnut
Sea wasp
Seison nebaliae
Six keyhole sand dollar
Soleneiscus radovani
Symbion pandora
Thimble jelly
Trichoplax adhaerens
Tropical brittle star
Tuxedo pincushion urchin
Velcro sea star
West Atlantic stalked crinoid
Western sand dollar

DECIDUOUS FOREST
Canine heartworm
Dog tapeworm
Giant thorny-headed worm
Human blood fluke
Mermis nigrescens
Moniliformis moniliformis
Rat lungworm

DESERT
Dog tapeworm

GRASSLAND
Canine heartworm
Dog tapeworm
Fasciola hepatica
Giant thorny-headed worm
Human blood fluke
Lancet fluke
Mermis nigrescens
Moniliformis moniliformis

LAKE AND POND
Asplanchna priodonta
Broad fish tapeworm
Dactylogyrus vastator

Desmoscolex squamosus
Fasciola hepatica
Freshwater planarian
Freshwater sponge
Human blood fluke
Lepidodermella squamata
Paragordius varius
Polystoma integerrimum
Proteocephalus longicollis

OCEAN
Aequorea victoria
Aglantha digitale
Bird's nest sponge
Deep water reef coral
Dwarf brittle star
Eukrohnia fowleri
Frilled anemone
Nightlight jellyfish
Oikopleura labradoriensis
Oligotrema sandersi
Portuguese man of war
Priapulus caudatus
Pterosagitta draco
Pyrosome
Rhopalura ophiocomae
Salp
Sea pig

Spaghetti worm
Tropical brittle star
Venus's girdle

RAINFOREST
Canine heartworm
Dog tapeworm
Giant thorny-headed worm
Human blood fluke
Rat lungworm

RIVER AND STREAM
Broad fish tapeworm
Dactylogyrus vastator
Desmoscolex squamosus
Freshwater planarian
Freshwater sponge
Human blood fluke
Lepidodermella squamata
Limnognathia maerski
Paragordius varius
Proteocephalus longicollis

SEASHORE
Canine heartworm
Desmoscolex squamosus
Dwarf brittle star

Echinoderes sensibilis
Florida lancelet
Frilled anemone
Giant green anemone
Northern Pacific sea star
Notoplana acticola
Oerstedia dorsalis
Oyster leech
Pea urchin
Rat lungworm
Red haplognathia
Rhopalura ophiocomae
Six keyhole sand dollar
Tropical brittle star
Tuxedo pincushion urchin
Western sand dollar

WETLAND
Canine heartworm
Desmoscolex squamosus
Dog tapeworm
Fasciola hepatica
Human blood fluke
Lepidodermella squamata
Rat lungworm

UNKNOWN
Salinella salve

Species List by Geographic Range

AFGHANISTAN

Asplanchna priodonta
Canine heartworm
Dactylogyrus vastator
Dog tapeworm
Fasciola hepatica
Giant thorny-headed worm
Human blood fluke
Lancet fluke
Lepidodermella squamata
Limnognathia maerski
Oerstedia dorsalis
Paragordius varius
Polystoma integerrimum
Proteocephalus longicollis
Rat lungworm

ALBANIA

Asplanchna priodonta
Bucket-tailed loriciferan
Canine heartworm
Convolutriloba longifissura
Dactylogyrus vastator
Dog tapeworm
Fasciola hepatica
Freshwater sponge
Giant thorny-headed worm
Human blood fluke
Lancet fluke
Lepidodermella squamata

Limnognathia maerski
Mermis nigrescens
Moniliformis moniliformis
Oerstedia dorsalis
Paragordius varius
Polystoma integerrimum
Priapulus caudatus
Proteocephalus longicollis
Pyrosome
Rat lungworm
Red haplognathia
Salp
Sea nettle
Sea walnut
Seison nebaliae
Symbion pandora
Thimble jelly

ALGERIA

Asplanchna priodonta
Bucket-tailed loriciferan
Canine heartworm
Convolutriloba longifissura
Dactylogyrus vastator
Dog tapeworm
Fasciola hepatica
Giant thorny-headed worm
Human blood fluke
Lancet fluke
Lepidodermella squamata

Limnognathia maerski
Nightlight jellyfish
Oerstedia dorsalis
Oikopleura labradoriensis
Paragordius varius
Pea urchin
Polystoma integerrimum
Priapulus caudatus
Proteocephalus longicollis
Pyrosome
Rat lungworm
Red coral
Red haplognathia
Salp
Sea nettle
Sea walnut
Seison nebaliae
Symbion pandora
Thimble jelly

ANDORRA

Asplanchna priodonta
Canine heartworm
Dactylogyrus vastator
Dog tapeworm
Giant thorny-headed worm
Human blood fluke
Lancet fluke
Lepidodermella squamata
Mermis nigrescens

Moniliformis moniliformis
Oerstedia dorsalis
Paragordius varius
Proteocephalus longicollis
Rat lungworm

ANGOLA
Asplanchna priodonta
Botryllus schlosseri
Canine heartworm
Convolutriloba longifissura
Dog tapeworm
Freshwater sponge
Giant thorny-headed worm
Human blood fluke
Lancet fluke
Lepidodermella squamata
Moniliformis moniliformis
Nightlight jellyfish
Oerstedia dorsalis
Oikopleura labradoriensis
Paragordius varius
Pea urchin
Polystoma integerrimum
Proteocephalus longicollis
Rat lungworm
Symbion pandora
Thimble jelly

ANTARCTICA
Asplanchna priodonta
Canine heartworm
Dactylogyrus vastator
Didemnum studeri
Distaplia cylindrica
Dog tapeworm
Human blood fluke
Lancet fluke
Oerstedia dorsalis
Paragordius varius
Polystoma integerrimum
Proteocephalus longicollis
Rat lungworm
Symbion pandora
Venus's girdle

ANTIGUA AND BARBUDA
Asplanchna priodonta
Bucket-tailed loriciferan
Canine heartworm
Convolutriloba longifissura
Dactylogyrus vastator
Dog tapeworm
Fasciola hepatica
Freshwater sponge
Giant thorny-headed worm
Human blood fluke
Lancet fluke
Lepidodermella squamata
Limnognathia maerski
Moniliformis moniliformis
Nightlight jellyfish
Oerstedia dorsalis
Oikopleura labradoriensis
Paragordius varius
Pea urchin
Polystoma integerrimum
Priapulus caudatus
Proteocephalus longicollis
Pyrosome
Rat lungworm
Red haplognathia
Salp
Sea nettle
Sea walnut
Seison nebaliae
Symbion pandora
Thimble jelly
Tropical brittle star

ARCTIC
Asplanchna priodonta
Bucket-tailed loriciferan
Canine heartworm
Dactylogyrus vastator
Dog tapeworm
Fasciola hepatica
Frilled anemone
Human blood fluke
Lancet fluke
Lepidodermella squamata

Limnognathia maerski
Oerstedia dorsalis
Oikopleura labradoriensis
Paragordius varius
Polystoma integerrimum
Priapulus caudatus
Proteocephalus longicollis
Rat lungworm
Red haplognathia
Seison nebaliae
Symbion pandora

ARCTIC OCEAN
Aglantha digitale
Asplanchna priodonta
Dactylogyrus vastator
Frilled anemone
Lepidodermella squamata
Limnognathia maerski
Nightlight jellyfish
Oerstedia dorsalis
Oikopleura labradoriensis
Paragordius varius
Pea urchin
Polystoma integerrimum
Priapulus caudatus
Proteocephalus longicollis
Sea pig
Seison nebaliae
Symbion pandora

ARGENTINA
Asplanchna priodonta
Botryllus schlosseri
Bucket-tailed loriciferan
Canine heartworm
Convolutriloba longifissura
Dactylogyrus vastator
Didemnum studeri
Dog tapeworm
Fasciola hepatica
Freshwater sponge
Giant thorny-headed worm
Human blood fluke
Lancet fluke

Lepidodermella squamata
Limnognathia maerski
Moniliformis moniliformis
Nightlight jellyfish
Oerstedia dorsalis
Oikopleura labradoriensis
Paragordius varius
Pea urchin
Polystoma integerrimum
Priapulus caudatus
Proteocephalus longicollis
Pyrosome
Rat lungworm
Red haplognathia
Salinella salve
Salp
Sea nettle
Sea walnut
Seison nebaliae
Symbion pandora
Tropical brittle star

ARMENIA

Asplanchna priodonta
Bucket-tailed loriciferan
Canine heartworm
Convolutriloba longifissura
Dactylogyrus vastator
Dog tapeworm
Fasciola hepatica
Freshwater sponge
Giant thorny-headed worm
Human blood fluke
Lancet fluke
Lepidodermella squamata
Limnognathia maerski
Moniliformis moniliformis
Oerstedia dorsalis
Oikopleura labradoriensis
Paragordius varius
Pea urchin
Polystoma integerrimum
Priapulus caudatus
Proteocephalus longicollis
Pyrosome

Rat lungworm
Red haplognathia
Seison nebaliae
Symbion pandora

ATLANTIC OCEAN

Aglantha digitale
Asplanchna priodonta
Bird's nest sponge
Botryllus schlosseri
Bucket-tailed loriciferan
Dactylogyrus vastator
Deep water reef coral
Didemnum studeri
Distaplia cylindrica
Dwarf brittle star
Eukrohnia fowleri
Fasciola hepatica
Fire coral
Frilled anemone
Lepidodermella squamata
Limnognathia maerski
Nightlight jellyfish
Oerstedia dorsalis
Oikopleura labradoriensis
Oligotrema sandersi
Paragordius varius
Polystoma integerrimum
Portuguese man of war
Priapulus caudatus
Proteocephalus longicollis
Pterosagitta draco
Pyrosome
Red coral
Red haplognathia
Salp
Sand star
Sea nettle
Sea pig
Sea walnut
Seison nebaliae
Symbion pandora
Thimble jelly
Tropical brittle star
Venus's girdle

AUSTRALIA

Asplanchna priodonta
Blue starfish
Bucket-tailed loriciferan
Candy cane sea cucumber
Canine heartworm
Convolutriloba longifissura
Crown-of-thorns
Dactylogyrus vastator
Distichopora violacea
Dog tapeworm
Eukrohnia fowleri
Fasciola hepatica
Freshwater sponge
Fire coral
Giant thorny-headed worm
Hawaiian acorn worm
Human blood fluke
Lancet fluke
Lepidodermella squamata
Limnognathia maerski
Long-spined sea urchin
Moniliformis moniliformis
Nightlight jellyfish
Oerstedia dorsalis
Oikopleura labradoriensis
Paragordius varius
Pea urchin
Polystoma integerrimum
Portuguese man of war
Priapulus caudatus
Proteocephalus longicollis
Pterosagitta draco
Pyrosome
Rat lungworm
Red haplognathia
Salp
Sea apple
Sea nettle
Sea walnut
Sea wasp
Seison nebaliae
Soleneiscus radovani
Symbion pandora
Thimble jelly
Tropical brittle star

AUSTRIA

Asplanchna priodonta
Canine heartworm
Dog tapeworm
Freshwater sponge
Giant thorny-headed worm
Human blood fluke
Lancet fluke
Lepidodermella squamata
Mermis nigrescens
Moniliformis moniliformis
Oerstedia dorsalis
Paragordius varius
Proteocephalus longicollis
Rat lungworm

AZERBAIJAN

Asplanchna priodonta
Canine heartworm
Convolutriloba longifissura
Dog tapeworm
Freshwater sponge
Giant thorny-headed worm
Human blood fluke
Lancet fluke
Moniliformis moniliformis
Oerstedia dorsalis
Paragordius varius
Proteocephalus longicollis
Rat lungworm

BAHAMAS

Asplanchna priodonta
Botryllus schlosseri
Bucket-tailed loriciferan
Canine heartworm
Convolutriloba longifissura
Dactylogyrus vastator
Dog tapeworm
Fasciola hepatica
Freshwater sponge
Giant thorny-headed worm
Human blood fluke
Lancet fluke
Lepidodermella squamata

Limnognathia maerski
Moniliformis moniliformis
Nightlight jellyfish
Oerstedia dorsalis
Oikopleura labradoriensis
Paragordius varius
Pea urchin
Polystoma integerrimum
Priapulus caudatus
Proteocephalus longicollis
Pyrosome
Rat lungworm
Red haplognathia
Salp
Sea nettle
Sea walnut
Seison nebaliae
Symbion pandora
Thimble jelly
Tropical brittle star
West Atlantic stalked crinoid

BAHRAIN

Asplanchna priodonta
Bucket-tailed loriciferan
Canine heartworm
Convolutriloba longifissura
Dactylogyrus vastator
Dog tapeworm
Fasciola hepatica
Freshwater sponge
Human blood fluke
Lancet fluke
Lepidodermella squamata
Limnognathia maerski
Nightlight jellyfish
Oerstedia dorsalis
Oikopleura labradoriensis
Paragordius varius
Pea urchin
Polystoma integerrimum
Priapulus caudatus
Proteocephalus longicollis
Pyrosome
Rat lungworm
Red haplognathia

Salp
Sea nettle
Sea walnut
Seison nebaliae
Symbion pandora
Thimble jelly
Tropical brittle star

BANGLADESH

Asplanchna priodonta
Blue starfish
Bucket-tailed loriciferan
Canine heartworm
Convolutriloba longifissura
Crown-of-thorns
Dactylogyrus vastator
Distichopora violacea
Dog tapeworm
Eukrohnia fowleri
Fasciola hepatica
Fire coral
Freshwater sponge
Human blood fluke
Lancet fluke
Lepidodermella squamata
Limnognathia maerski
Long-spined sea urchin
Moniliformis moniliformis
Nightlight jellyfish
Oerstedia dorsalis
Oikopleura labradoriensis
Paragordius varius
Pea urchin
Polystoma integerrimum
Portuguese man of war
Priapulus caudatus
Proteocephalus longicollis
Pterosagitta draco
Pyrosome
Rat lungworm
Red haplognathia
Salp
Sea apple
Sea nettle
Sea walnut
Seison nebaliae

Symbion pandora
Thimble jelly
Tropical brittle star
Tuxedo pincushion urchin

BARBADOS

Asplanchna priodonta
Botryllus schlosseri
Bucket-tailed loriciferan
Canine heartworm
Convolutriloba longifissura
Dactylogyrus vastator
Dog tapeworm
Fasciola hepatica
Freshwater sponge
Giant thorny-headed worm
Human blood fluke
Lancet fluke
Lepidodermella squamata
Limnognathia maerski
Moniliformis moniliformis
Nightlight jellyfish
Oerstedia dorsalis
Oikopleura labradoriensis
Paragordius varius
Pea urchin
Polystoma integerrimum
Priapulus caudatus
Proteocephalus longicollis
Pyrosome
Rat lungworm
Red haplognathia
Salp
Sea nettle
Sea walnut
Seison nebaliae
Symbion pandora
Thimble jelly
Tropical brittle star

BELARUS

Asplanchna priodonta
Canine heartworm
Dog tapeworm
Freshwater sponge
Giant thorny-headed worm

Human blood fluke
Lancet fluke
Mermis nigrescens
Moniliformis moniliformis
Oerstedia dorsalis
Paragordius varius
Proteocephalus longicollis
Rat lungworm

BELGIUM

Asplanchna priodonta
Bucket-tailed loriciferan
Canine heartworm
Convolutriloba longifissura
Dactylogyrus vastator
Dog tapeworm
Fasciola hepatica
Freshwater sponge
Giant thorny-headed worm
Human blood fluke
Lancet fluke
Lepidodermella squamata
Limnognathia maerski
Moniliformis moniliformis
Nightlight jellyfish
Oerstedia dorsalis
Oikopleura labradoriensis
Paragordius varius
Pea urchin
Polystoma integerrimum
Priapulus caudatus
Proteocephalus longicollis
Pyrosome
Rat lungworm
Red haplognathia
Salp
Sand star
Sea nettle
Sea walnut
Seison nebaliae
Symbion pandora
Thimble jelly

BELIZE

Asplanchna priodonta

Botryllus schlosseri
Bucket-tailed loriciferan
Canine heartworm
Convolutriloba longifissura
Dactylogyrus vastator
Dog tapeworm
Fasciola hepatica
Freshwater sponge
Giant thorny-headed worm
Human blood fluke
Lancet fluke
Lepidodermella squamata
Limnognathia maerski
Moniliformis moniliformis
Nightlight jellyfish
Oerstedia dorsalis
Oikopleura labradoriensis
Paragordius varius
Pea urchin
Polystoma integerrimum
Priapulus caudatus
Proteocephalus longicollis
Pyrosome
Rat lungworm
Red haplognathia
Salp
Sea nettle
Sea walnut
Seison nebaliae
Symbion pandora
Thimble jelly
Tropical brittle star

BENIN

Asplanchna priodonta
Botryllus schlosseri
Bucket-tailed loriciferan
Canine heartworm
Convolutriloba longifissura
Dactylogyrus vastator
Dog tapeworm
Fasciola hepatica
Freshwater sponge
Giant thorny-headed worm
Human blood fluke
Lancet fluke

Lepidodermella squamata
Limnognathia maerski
Nightlight jellyfish
Oerstedia dorsalis
Oikopleura labradoriensis
Paragordius varius
Pea urchin
Polystoma integerrimum
Priapulus caudatus
Proteocephalus longicollis
Pyrosome
Rat lungworm
Red haplognathia
Salp
Sea nettle
Sea walnut
Seison nebaliae
Symbion pandora
Thimble jelly
Tropical brittle star

BHUTAN

Asplanchna priodonta
Canine heartworm
Dog tapeworm
Freshwater sponge
Giant thorny-headed worm
Human blood fluke
Lancet fluke
Oerstedia dorsalis
Paragordius varius
Polystoma integerrimum
Proteocephalus longicollis
Rat lungworm

BOLIVIA

Asplanchna priodonta
Canine heartworm
Convolutriloba longifissura
Dog tapeworm
Freshwater sponge
Giant thorny-headed worm
Human blood fluke
Lancet fluke
Moniliformis moniliformis

Oerstedia dorsalis
Oikopleura labradoriensis
Paragordius varius
Polystoma integerrimum
Proteocephalus longicollis
Rat lungworm

BOSNIA AND HERZEGOVINA

Asplanchna priodonta
Broad fish tapeworm
Bucket-tailed loriciferan
Canine heartworm
Convolutriloba longifissura
Dactylogyrus vastator
Dog tapeworm
Fasciola hepatica
Freshwater sponge
Giant thorny-headed worm
Human blood fluke
Lancet fluke
Lepidodermella squamata
Limnognathia maerski
Mermis nigrescens
Moniliformis moniliformis
Nightlight jellyfish
Oerstedia dorsalis
Oikopleura labradoriensis
Paragordius varius
Pea urchin
Polystoma integerrimum
Priapulus caudatus
Proteocephalus longicollis
Pyrosome
Rat lungworm
Red haplognathia
Salp
Seison nebaliae
Symbion pandora
Thimble jelly

BOTSWANA

Asplanchna priodonta
Canine heartworm
Dog tapeworm

Freshwater sponge
Giant thorny-headed worm
Human blood fluke
Lancet fluke
Moniliformis moniliformis
Oerstedia dorsalis
Paragordius varius
Polystoma integerrimum
Proteocephalus longicollis
Rat lungworm

BRAZIL

Asplanchna priodonta
Botryllus schlosseri
Bucket-tailed loriciferan
Canine heartworm
Convolutriloba longifissura
Dactylogyrus vastator
Dog tapeworm
Fasciola hepatica
Freshwater sponge
Giant thorny-headed worm
Human blood fluke
Lancet fluke
Lepidodermella squamata
Limnognathia maerski
Moniliformis moniliformis
Nightlight jellyfish
Oerstedia dorsalis
Oikopleura labradoriensis
Orange sea lily
Paragordius varius
Pea urchin
Polystoma integerrimum
Priapulus caudatus
Proteocephalus longicollis
Pyrosome
Rat lungworm
Red haplognathia
Salp
Sea nettle
Sea walnut
Seison nebaliae
Six keyhole sand dollar
Symbion pandora

Thimble jelly
Tropical brittle star

BRUNEI

Asplanchna priodonta
Blue starfish
Bucket-tailed loriciferan
Canine heartworm
Convolutriloba longifissura
Crown-of-thorns
Dactylogyrus vastator
Distichopora violacea
Dog tapeworm
Eukrohnia fowleri
Fasciola hepatica
Fire coral
Freshwater sponge
Giant thorny-headed worm
Human blood fluke
Lancet fluke
Lepidodermella squamata
Limnognathia maerski
Long-spined sea urchin
Nightlight jellyfish
Oerstedia dorsalis
Oikopleura labradoriensis
Paragordius varius
Pea urchin
Polystoma integerrimum
Portuguese man of war
Priapulus caudatus
Proteocephalus longicollis
Pterosagitta draco
Pyrosome
Rat lungworm
Red haplognathia
Salp
Sea apple
Sea nettle
Sea walnut
Seison nebaliae
Symbion pandora
Thimble jelly

BULGARIA

Asplanchna priodonta

Broad fish tapeworm
Bucket-tailed loriciferan
Canine heartworm
Convolutriloba longifissura
Dactylogyrus vastator
Dog tapeworm
Fasciola hepatica
Freshwater sponge
Giant thorny-headed worm
Human blood fluke
Lancet fluke
Lepidodermella squamata
Limnognathia maerski
Mermis nigrescens
Moniliformis moniliformis
Oerstedia dorsalis
Paragordius varius
Polystoma integerrimum
Priapulus caudatus
Proteocephalus longicollis
Pyrosome
Rat lungworm
Red haplognathia
Salp
Seison nebaliae
Symbion pandora

BURKINA FASO

Asplanchna priodonta
Canine heartworm
Dog tapeworm
Freshwater sponge
Giant thorny-headed worm
Human blood fluke
Lancet fluke
Moniliformis moniliformis
Oerstedia dorsalis
Paragordius varius
Polystoma integerrimum
Proteocephalus longicollis
Rat lungworm

BURUNDI

Asplanchna priodonta
Canine heartworm

Dog tapeworm
Freshwater sponge
Giant thorny-headed worm
Human blood fluke
Lancet fluke
Moniliformis moniliformis
Oerstedia dorsalis
Paragordius varius
Polystoma integerrimum
Proteocephalus longicollis
Rat lungworm

CAMBODIA

Asplanchna priodonta
Blue starfish
Canine heartworm
Convolutriloba longifissura
Crown-of-thorns
Dactylogyrus vastator
Distichopora violacea
Dog tapeworm
Eukrohnia fowleri
Fasciola hepatica
Fire coral
Freshwater sponge
Giant thorny-headed worm
Human blood fluke
Lancet fluke
Lepidodermella squamata
Limnognathia maerski
Long-spined sea urchin
Moniliformis moniliformis
Nightlight jellyfish
Oerstedia dorsalis
Oikopleura labradoriensis
Paragordius varius
Pea urchin
Polystoma integerrimum
Portuguese man of war
Priapulus caudatus
Proteocephalus longicollis
Pterosagitta draco
Pyrosome
Rat lungworm
Red haplognathia
Salp

Sea apple
Sea nettle
Sea walnut
Seison nebaliae
Symbion pandora
Thimble jelly
Tropical brittle star
Tuxedo pincushion urchin

CAMEROON
Asplanchna priodonta
Botryllus schlosseri
Bucket-tailed loriciferan
Canine heartworm
Convolutriloba longifissura
Dactylogyrus vastator
Dog tapeworm
Fasciola hepatica
Freshwater sponge
Giant thorny-headed worm
Human blood fluke
Lancet fluke
Lepidodermella squamata
Limnognathia maerski
Moniliformis moniliformis
Nightlight jellyfish
Oerstedia dorsalis
Paragordius varius
Pea urchin
Polystoma integerrimum
Priapulus caudatus
Proteocephalus longicollis
Pyrosome
Rat lungworm
Red haplognathia
Salp
Sea nettle
Sea walnut
Seison nebaliae
Symbion pandora
Thimble jelly
Tropical brittle star

CANADA
Asplanchna priodonta

Blue starfish
Botryllus schlosseri
Broad fish tapeworm
Bucket-tailed loriciferan
Canine heartworm
Convolutriloba longifissura
Crown-of-thorns
Dactylogyrus vastator
Distichopora violacea
Dog tapeworm
Eukrohnia fowleri
Fasciola hepatica
Fire coral
Freshwater planarian
Freshwater sponge
Giant green anemone
Giant thorny-headed worm
Human blood fluke
Lancet fluke
Lepidodermella squamata
Limnognathia maerski
Long-spined sea urchin
Mermis nigrescens
Moniliformis moniliformis
Northern Pacific sea star
Notoplana acticola
Oerstedia dorsalis
Oikopleura labradoriensis
Paragordius varius
Pea urchin
Polystoma integerrimum
Portuguese man of war
Priapulus caudatus
Proteocephalus longicollis
Pterosagitta draco
Pyrosome
Rat lungworm
Red haplognathia
Salp
Sea apple
Sea nettle
Sea walnut
Seison nebaliae
Symbion pandora
Thimble jelly
Western sand dollar

CAPE VERDE
Asplanchna priodonta
Botryllus schlosseri
Bucket-tailed loriciferan
Canine heartworm
Convolutriloba longifissura
Dactylogyrus vastator
Dog tapeworm
Fasciola hepatica
Freshwater sponge
Giant thorny-headed worm
Human blood fluke
Lancet fluke
Lepidodermella squamata
Limnognathia maerski
Moniliformis moniliformis
Oerstedia dorsalis
Oikopleura labradoriensis
Paragordius varius
Pea urchin
Polystoma integerrimum
Priapulus caudatus
Proteocephalus longicollis
Pyrosome
Rat lungworm
Red haplognathia
Salp
Sea nettle
Sea walnut
Seison nebaliae
Symbion pandora
Thimble jelly

CENTRAL AFRICAN REPUBLIC
Asplanchna priodonta
Canine heartworm
Dog tapeworm
Freshwater sponge
Giant thorny-headed worm
Human blood fluke
Lancet fluke
Moniliformis moniliformis
Oerstedia dorsalis
Paragordius varius
Polystoma integerrimum

Proteocephalus longicollis
Rat lungworm

CHAD
Asplanchna priodonta
Canine heartworm
Dog tapeworm
Freshwater sponge
Giant thorny-headed worm
Human blood fluke
Lancet fluke
Moniliformis moniliformis
Oerstedia dorsalis
Paragordius varius
Polystoma integerrimum
Proteocephalus longicollis
Rat lungworm

CHILE
Asplanchna priodonta
Blue starfish
Bucket-tailed loriciferan
Canine heartworm
Convolutriloba longifissura
Crown-of-thorns
Dactylogyrus vastator
Didemnum studeri
Distichopora violacea
Dog tapeworm
Eukrohnia fowleri
Fasciola hepatica
Fire coral
Freshwater sponge
Giant thorny-headed worm
Human blood fluke
Lancet fluke
Lepidodermella squamata
Limnognathia maerski
Long-spined sea urchin
Moniliformis moniliformis
Nightlight jellyfish
Oerstedia dorsalis
Oikopleura labradoriensis
Paragordius varius
Pea urchin

Polystoma integerrimum
Portuguese man of war
Priapulus caudatus
Proteocephalus longicollis
Pterosagitta draco
Pyrosome
Rat lungworm
Red haplognathia
Salp
Sea apple
Sea nettle
Sea walnut
Seison nebaliae
Symbion pandora
Thimble jelly
Tropical brittle star

CHINA
Asplanchna priodonta
Bucket-tailed loriciferan
Canine heartworm
Convolutriloba longifissura
Dactylogyrus vastator
Dog tapeworm
Fasciola hepatica
Freshwater sponge
Giant thorny-headed worm
Human blood fluke
Lancet fluke
Lepidodermella squamata
Limnognathia maerski
Moniliformis moniliformis
Nightlight jellyfish
Oerstedia dorsalis
Oikopleura labradoriensis
Paragordius varius
Pea urchin
Polystoma integerrimum
Priapulus caudatus
Proteocephalus longicollis
Pyrosome
Rat lungworm
Red haplognathia
Salp
Sea nettle
Sea walnut

Seison nebaliae
Symbion pandora
Thimble jelly
Tropical brittle star
Tuxedo pincushion urchin

COLOMBIA
Asplanchna priodonta
Blue starfish
Botryllus schlosseri
Bucket-tailed loriciferan
Canine heartworm
Convolutriloba longifissura
Crown-of-thorns
Dactylogyrus vastator
Distichopora violacea
Dog tapeworm
Eukrohnia fowleri
Fasciola hepatica
Fire coral
Freshwater sponge
Giant thorny-headed worm
Human blood fluke
Lancet fluke
Lepidodermella squamata
Limnognathia maerski
Long-spined sea urchin
Moniliformis moniliformis
Nightlight jellyfish
Oerstedia dorsalis
Oikopleura labradoriensis
Orange sea lily
Paragordius varius
Pea urchin
Polystoma integerrimum
Portuguese man of war
Priapulus caudatus
Proteocephalus longicollis
Pterosagitta draco
Pyrosome
Rat lungworm
Red haplognathia
Salp
Sea apple
Sea nettle
Sea walnut

Seison nebaliae
Six keyhole sand dollar
Symbion pandora
Thimble jelly
Tropical brittle star
Tuxedo pincushion urchin

COMOROS
Asplanchna priodonta
Blue starfish
Bucket-tailed loriciferan
Canine heartworm
Convolutriloba longifissura
Crown-of-thorns
Dactylogyrus vastator
Distichopora violacea
Dog tapeworm
Eukrohnia fowleri
Fasciola hepatica
Fire coral
Freshwater sponge
Giant thorny-headed worm
Human blood fluke
Lancet fluke
Lepidodermella squamata
Limnognathia maerski
Long-spined sea urchin
Moniliformis moniliformis
Nightlight jellyfish
Oerstedia dorsalis
Oikopleura labradoriensis
Paragordius varius
Pea urchin
Polystoma integerrimum
Portuguese man of war
Priapulus caudatus
Proteocephalus longicollis
Pterosagitta draco
Pyrosome
Rat lungworm
Red haplognathia
Salp
Sea apple
Sea nettle
Sea walnut
Seison nebaliae

Symbion pandora
Thimble jelly

COSTA RICA
Asplanchna priodonta
Botryllus schlosseri
Bucket-tailed loriciferan
Canine heartworm
Convolutriloba longifissura
Dactylogyrus vastator
Dog tapeworm
Fasciola hepatica
Freshwater sponge
Giant thorny-headed worm
Human blood fluke
Lancet fluke
Lepidodermella squamata
Limnognathia maerski
Moniliformis moniliformis
Nightlight jellyfish
Oerstedia dorsalis
Oikopleura labradoriensis
Paragordius varius
Pea urchin
Polystoma integerrimum
Priapulus caudatus
Proteocephalus longicollis
Pyrosome
Rat lungworm
Red haplognathia
Salp
Sea nettle
Sea walnut
Seison nebaliae
Symbion pandora
Thimble jelly
Tropical brittle star

CROATIA
Asplanchna priodonta
Broad fish tapeworm
Canine heartworm
Dog tapeworm
Freshwater sponge

Giant thorny-headed worm
Human blood fluke
Lancet fluke
Mermis nigrescens
Moniliformis moniliformis
Oerstedia dorsalis
Paragordius varius
Polystoma integerrimum
Proteocephalus longicollis
Rat lungworm

CUBA
Asplanchna priodonta
Botryllus schlosseri
Bucket-tailed loriciferan
Canine heartworm
Convolutriloba longifissura
Dactylogyrus vastator
Dog tapeworm
Fasciola hepatica
Freshwater sponge
Giant thorny-headed worm
Human blood fluke
Lancet fluke
Lepidodermella squamata
Limnognathia maerski
Moniliformis moniliformis
Oerstedia dorsalis
Oikopleura labradoriensis
Paragordius varius
Pea urchin
Polystoma integerrimum
Priapulus caudatus
Proteocephalus longicollis
Pyrosome
Rat lungworm
Red haplognathia
Salp
Sea nettle
Sea walnut
Seison nebaliae
Symbion pandora
Thimble jelly
Velcro sea star
West Atlantic stalked crinoid

CYPRUS

Asplanchna priodonta
Bucket-tailed loriciferan
Canine heartworm
Convolutriloba longifissura
Dactylogyrus vastator
Dog tapeworm
Fasciola hepatica
Freshwater sponge
Giant thorny-headed worm
Human blood fluke
Lancet fluke
Lepidodermella squamata
Limnognathia maerski
Moniliformis moniliformis
Oerstedia dorsalis
Oikopleura labradoriensis
Paragordius varius
Pea urchin
Polystoma integerrimum
Priapulus caudatus
Proteocephalus longicollis
Pyrosome
Rat lungworm
Red haplognathia
Salp
Sea nettle
Sea walnut
Seison nebaliae
Symbion pandora
Thimble jelly
Tropical brittle star

CZECH REPUBLIC

Asplanchna priodonta
Broad fish tapeworm
Canine heartworm
Dog tapeworm
Freshwater sponge
Giant thorny-headed worm
Human blood fluke
Lancet fluke
Mermis nigrescens
Moniliformis moniliformis
Oerstedia dorsalis
Paragordius varius

Polystoma integerrimum
Proteocephalus longicollis
Rat lungworm

DEMOCRATIC REPUBLIC OF THE CONGO

Asplanchna priodonta
Canine heartworm
Dog tapeworm
Freshwater sponge
Giant thorny-headed worm
Human blood fluke
Lancet fluke
Moniliformis moniliformis
Oerstedia dorsalis
Paragordius varius
Polystoma integerrimum
Proteocephalus longicollis
Rat lungworm

DENMARK

Asplanchna priodonta
Botryllus schlosseri
Broad fish tapeworm
Bucket-tailed loriciferan
Canine heartworm
Convolutriloba longifissura
Dactylogyrus vastator
Dog tapeworm
Fasciola hepatica
Freshwater sponge
Giant thorny-headed worm
Human blood fluke
Lancet fluke
Lepidodermella squamata
Limnognathia maerski
Marine colonial entoproct
Mermis nigrescens
Moniliformis moniliformis
Nightlight jellyfish
Oerstedia dorsalis
Oikopleura labradoriensis
Paragordius varius
Pea urchin

Polystoma integerrimum
Priapulus caudatus
Proteocephalus longicollis
Pyrosome
Rat lungworm
Red haplognathia
Salp
Sand star
Sea nettle
Sea walnut
Seison nebaliae
Symbion pandora
Thimble jelly

DJIBOUTI

Asplanchna priodonta
Blue starfish
Bucket-tailed loriciferan
Canine heartworm
Convolutriloba longifissura
Crown-of-thorns
Dactylogyrus vastator
Distichopora violacea
Dog tapeworm
Eukrohnia fowleri
Fasciola hepatica
Fire coral
Freshwater sponge
Giant thorny-headed worm
Human blood fluke
Lancet fluke
Lepidodermella squamata
Limnognathia maerski
Long-spined sea urchin
Moniliformis moniliformis
Nightlight jellyfish
Oerstedia dorsalis
Oikopleura labradoriensis
Paragordius varius
Pea urchin
Polystoma integerrimum
Portuguese man of war
Priapulus caudatus
Proteocephalus longicollis
Pterosagitta draco
Pyrosome

Rat lungworm
Red haplognathia
Salp
Sea apple
Sea nettle
Sea walnut
Seison nebaliae
Symbion pandora
Thimble jelly
Tropical brittle star

DOMINICA
Asplanchna priodonta
Botryllus schlosseri
Bucket-tailed loriciferan
Canine heartworm
Convolutriloba longifissura
Dactylogyrus vastator
Dog tapeworm
Fasciola hepatica
Freshwater sponge
Giant thorny-headed worm
Human blood fluke
Lancet fluke
Lepidodermella squamata
Limnognathia maerski
Moniliformis moniliformis
Nightlight jellyfish
Oerstedia dorsalis
Oikopleura labradoriensis
Paragordius varius
Pea urchin
Polystoma integerrimum
Priapulus caudatus
Proteocephalus longicollis
Pyrosome
Rat lungworm
Red haplognathia
Salp
Sea nettle
Sea walnut
Seison nebaliae
Symbion pandora
Thimble jelly
Tropical brittle star

DOMINICAN REPUBLIC
Asplanchna priodonta
Botryllus schlosseri
Bucket-tailed loriciferan
Canine heartworm
Convolutriloba longifissura
Dactylogyrus vastator
Dog tapeworm
Fasciola hepatica
Freshwater sponge
Giant thorny-headed worm
Human blood fluke
Lancet fluke
Lepidodermella squamata
Limnognathia maerski
Moniliformis moniliformis
Nightlight jellyfish
Oerstedia dorsalis
Oikopleura labradoriensis
Orange sea lily
Paragordius varius
Pea urchin
Polystoma integerrimum
Priapulus caudatus
Proteocephalus longicollis
Pyrosome
Rat lungworm
Red haplognathia
Salp
Sea nettle
Sea walnut
Seison nebaliae
Symbion pandora
Thimble jelly
Tropical brittle star
Velcro sea star

ECUADOR
Asplanchna priodonta
Blue starfish
Bucket-tailed loriciferan
Canine heartworm
Convolutriloba longifissura
Crown-of-thorns
Dactylogyrus vastator

Distichopora violacea
Dog tapeworm
Eukrohnia fowleri
Fasciola hepatica
Fire coral
Freshwater sponge
Giant thorny-headed worm
Human blood fluke
Lancet fluke
Lepidodermella squamata
Limnognathia maerski
Long-spined sea urchin
Moniliformis moniliformis
Nightlight jellyfish
Oerstedia dorsalis
Oikopleura labradoriensis
Paragordius varius
Pea urchin
Polystoma integerrimum
Portuguese man of war
Priapulus caudatus
Proteocephalus longicollis
Pterosagitta draco
Pyrosome
Rat lungworm
Red haplognathia
Salp
Sea apple
Sea nettle
Sea walnut
Seison nebaliae
Symbion pandora
Thimble jelly
Tropical brittle star

EGYPT
Asplanchna priodonta
Bucket-tailed loriciferan
Canine heartworm
Convolutriloba longifissura
Dactylogyrus vastator
Dog tapeworm
Fasciola hepatica
Freshwater sponge
Giant thorny-headed worm

Human blood fluke
Lancet fluke
Lepidodermella squamata
Limnognathia maerski
Moniliformis moniliformis
Nightlight jellyfish
Oerstedia dorsalis
Oikopleura labradoriensis
Paragordius varius
Pea urchin
Polystoma integerrimum
Priapulus caudatus
Proteocephalus longicollis
Pyrosome
Rat lungworm
Red haplognathia
Salp
Sea nettle
Sea walnut
Seison nebaliae
Symbion pandora
Thimble jelly
Tropical brittle star

EL SALVADOR

Asplanchna priodonta
Bucket-tailed loriciferan
Canine heartworm
Convolutriloba longifissura
Dactylogyrus vastator
Dog tapeworm
Fasciola hepatica
Freshwater sponge
Giant thorny-headed worm
Human blood fluke
Lancet fluke
Lepidodermella squamata
Limnognathia maerski
Moniliformis moniliformis
Nightlight jellyfish
Oerstedia dorsalis
Oikopleura labradoriensis
Paragordius varius
Pea urchin
Polystoma integerrimum
Priapulus caudatus

Proteocephalus longicollis
Pyrosome
Rat lungworm
Red haplognathia
Salp
Sea nettle
Sea walnut
Seison nebaliae
Symbion pandora
Thimble jelly
Tropical brittle star

EQUATORIAL GUINEA

Asplanchna priodonta
Botryllus schlosseri
Bucket-tailed loriciferan
Canine heartworm
Convolutriloba longifissura
Dactylogyrus vastator
Dog tapeworm
Fasciola hepatica
Freshwater sponge
Giant thorny-headed worm
Human blood fluke
Lancet fluke
Lepidodermella squamata
Limnognathia maerski
Moniliformis moniliformis
Nightlight jellyfish
Oerstedia dorsalis
Oikopleura labradoriensis
Paragordius varius
Pea urchin
Polystoma integerrimum
Priapulus caudatus
Proteocephalus longicollis
Pyrosome
Rat lungworm
Red haplognathia
Salp
Sea nettle
Sea walnut
Seison nebaliae
Symbion pandora
Thimble jelly
Tropical brittle star

ERITREA

Asplanchna priodonta
Bucket-tailed loriciferan
Canine heartworm
Convolutriloba longifissura
Dactylogyrus vastator
Dog tapeworm
Fasciola hepatica
Freshwater sponge
Giant thorny-headed worm
Human blood fluke
Lancet fluke
Lepidodermella squamata
Limnognathia maerski
Moniliformis moniliformis
Nightlight jellyfish
Oerstedia dorsalis
Oikopleura labradoriensis
Paragordius varius
Pea urchin
Polystoma integerrimum
Priapulus caudatus
Proteocephalus longicollis
Pyrosome
Rat lungworm
Red haplognathia
Salp
Sea nettle
Sea walnut
Seison nebaliae
Symbion pandora
Thimble jelly
Tropical brittle star

ESTONIA

Asplanchna priodonta
Bucket-tailed loriciferan
Canine heartworm
Convolutriloba longifissura
Dactylogyrus vastator
Dog tapeworm
Fasciola hepatica
Freshwater sponge
Giant thorny-headed worm
Human blood fluke
Lancet fluke

Lepidodermella squamata
Limnognathia maerski
Mermis nigrescens
Moniliformis moniliformis
Nightlight jellyfish
Oerstedia dorsalis
Oikopleura labradoriensis
Paragordius varius
Pea urchin
Polystoma integerrimum
Priapulus caudatus
Proteocephalus longicollis
Pyrosome
Rat lungworm
Red haplognathia
Salp
Sea nettle
Sea walnut
Seison nebaliae
Symbion pandora
Thimble jelly
Tropical brittle star

ETHIOPIA
Asplanchna priodonta
Canine heartworm
Dactylogyrus vastator
Dog tapeworm
Freshwater sponge
Giant thorny-headed worm
Human blood fluke
Lancet fluke
Moniliformis moniliformis
Oerstedia dorsalis
Paragordius varius
Polystoma integerrimum
Proteocephalus longicollis
Rat lungworm

FIJI
Asplanchna priodonta
Blue starfish
Bucket-tailed loriciferan
Canine heartworm
Convolutriloba longifissura

Crown-of-thorns
Dactylogyrus vastator
Distichopora violacea
Dog tapeworm
Eukrohnia fowleri
Fasciola hepatica
Fire coral
Freshwater sponge
Giant thorny-headed worm
Human blood fluke
Lancet fluke
Lepidodermella squamata
Limnognathia maerski
Long-spined sea urchin
Moniliformis moniliformis
Nightlight jellyfish
Oerstedia dorsalis
Oikopleura labradoriensis
Paragordius varius
Pea urchin
Polystoma integerrimum
Portuguese man of war
Priapulus caudatus
Proteocephalus longicollis
Pterosagitta draco
Pyrosome
Rat lungworm
Red haplognathia
Salp
Sea apple
Sea nettle
Sea walnut
Seison nebaliae
Symbion pandora
Thimble jelly
Tropical brittle star
Tuxedo pincushion urchin

FINLAND
Asplanchna priodonta
Broad fish tapeworm
Bucket-tailed loriciferan
Canine heartworm
Convolutriloba longifissura
Dactylogyrus vastator
Dog tapeworm

Fasciola hepatica
Freshwater sponge
Giant thorny-headed worm
Human blood fluke
Lancet fluke
Lepidodermella squamata
Limnognathia maerski
Marine colonial entoproct
Mermis nigrescens
Moniliformis moniliformis
Nightlight jellyfish
Oerstedia dorsalis
Oikopleura labradoriensis
Paragordius varius
Pea urchin
Polystoma integerrimum
Priapulus caudatus
Proteocephalus longicollis
Pyrosome
Rat lungworm
Red haplognathia
Salp
Sea nettle
Sea walnut
Seison nebaliae
Symbion pandora
Thimble jelly

FRANCE
Asplanchna priodonta
Botryllus schlosseri
Bucket-tailed loriciferan
Canine heartworm
Convolutriloba longifissura
Dactylogyrus vastator
Dog tapeworm
Fasciola hepatica
Freshwater sponge
Giant thorny-headed worm
Human blood fluke
Lancet fluke
Lepidodermella squamata
Limnognathia maerski
Mermis nigrescens
Moniliformis moniliformis
Nightlight jellyfish

Oerstedia dorsalis
Oikopleura labradoriensis
Paragordius varius
Pea urchin
Polystoma integerrimum
Priapulus caudatus
Proteocephalus longicollis
Pyrosome
Rat lungworm
Red haplognathia
Rhopalura ophiocomae
Salp
Sand star
Sea nettle
Sea walnut
Seison nebaliae
Symbion pandora
Thimble jelly

FRENCH GUIANA
Asplanchna priodonta
Botryllus schlosseri
Bucket-tailed loriciferan
Canine heartworm
Convolutriloba longifissura
Dactylogyrus vastator
Dog tapeworm
Fasciola hepatica
Freshwater sponge
Giant thorny-headed worm
Human blood fluke
Lancet fluke
Lepidodermella squamata
Limnognathia maerski
Moniliformis moniliformis
Nightlight jellyfish
Oerstedia dorsalis
Oikopleura labradoriensis
Orange sea lily
Paragordius varius
Pea urchin
Polystoma integerrimum
Priapulus caudatus
Proteocephalus longicollis
Pyrosome
Rat lungworm

Red haplognathia
Salp
Sea nettle
Sea walnut
Seison nebaliae
Six keyhole sand dollar
Symbion pandora
Thimble jelly

GABON
Asplanchna priodonta
Botryllus schlosseri
Bucket-tailed loriciferan
Canine heartworm
Convolutriloba longifissura
Dactylogyrus vastator
Dog tapeworm
Fasciola hepatica
Freshwater sponge
Giant thorny-headed worm
Human blood fluke
Lancet fluke
Lepidodermella squamata
Limnognathia maerski
Moniliformis moniliformis
Oerstedia dorsalis
Oikopleura labradoriensis
Paragordius varius
Pea urchin
Polystoma integerrimum
Priapulus caudatus
Proteocephalus longicollis
Pyrosome
Rat lungworm
Red haplognathia
Salp
Sea nettle
Sea walnut
Seison nebaliae
Symbion pandora
Thimble jelly

GAMBIA
Asplanchna priodonta
Botryllus schlosseri

Bucket-tailed loriciferan
Canine heartworm
Convolutriloba longifissura
Dactylogyrus vastator
Dog tapeworm
Fasciola hepatica
Freshwater sponge
Giant thorny-headed worm
Human blood fluke
Lancet fluke
Lepidodermella squamata
Limnognathia maerski
Moniliformis moniliformis
Nightlight jellyfish
Oerstedia dorsalis
Oikopleura labradoriensis
Paragordius varius
Pea urchin
Polystoma integerrimum
Priapulus caudatus
Proteocephalus longicollis
Pyrosome
Rat lungworm
Red haplognathia
Salp
Seison nebaliae
Symbion pandora
Thimble jelly

GEORGIA
Asplanchna priodonta
Bucket-tailed loriciferan
Canine heartworm
Convolutriloba longifissura
Dactylogyrus vastator
Dog tapeworm
Fasciola hepatica
Freshwater sponge
Giant thorny-headed worm
Human blood fluke
Lancet fluke
Lepidodermella squamata
Limnognathia maerski
Moniliformis moniliformis
Oerstedia dorsalis

Paragordius varius
Pea urchin
Polystoma integerrimum
Priapulus caudatus
Proteocephalus longicollis
Pyrosome
Rat lungworm
Red haplognathia
Salp
Sea nettle
Sea walnut
Seison nebaliae
Symbion pandora

GERMANY

Asplanchna priodonta
Bucket-tailed loriciferan
Canine heartworm
Convolutriloba longifissura
Dactylogyrus vastator
Dog tapeworm
Fasciola hepatica
Freshwater sponge
Giant thorny-headed worm
Human blood fluke
Lancet fluke
Lepidodermella squamata
Limnognathia maerski
Mermis nigrescens
Moniliformis moniliformis
Nightlight jellyfish
Oerstedia dorsalis
Oikopleura labradoriensis
Paragordius varius
Pea urchin
Polystoma integerrimum
Priapulus caudatus
Proteocephalus longicollis
Pyrosome
Rat lungworm
Red haplognathia
Salp
Sand star
Sea nettle
Sea walnut
Seison nebaliae

Symbion pandora
Thimble jelly

GHANA

Asplanchna priodonta
Botryllus schlosseri
Bucket-tailed loriciferan
Canine heartworm
Convolutriloba longifissura
Dactylogyrus vastator
Dog tapeworm
Fasciola hepatica
Freshwater sponge
Giant thorny-headed worm
Human blood fluke
Lancet fluke
Lepidodermella squamata
Limnognathia maerski
Moniliformis moniliformis
Nightlight jellyfish
Oerstedia dorsalis
Oikopleura labradoriensis
Paragordius varius
Pea urchin
Polystoma integerrimum
Priapulus caudatus
Proteocephalus longicollis
Pyrosome
Rat lungworm
Red haplognathia
Salp
Sea nettle
Sea walnut
Seison nebaliae
Symbion pandora
Thimble jelly
Tropical brittle star

GREECE

Asplanchna priodonta
Bucket-tailed loriciferan
Canine heartworm
Convolutriloba longifissura
Dactylogyrus vastator
Dog tapeworm

Fasciola hepatica
Freshwater sponge
Giant thorny-headed worm
Human blood fluke
Lancet fluke
Lepidodermella squamata
Limnognathia maerski
Mermis nigrescens
Moniliformis moniliformis
Nightlight jellyfish
Oerstedia dorsalis
Oikopleura labradoriensis
Paragordius varius
Pea urchin
Polystoma integerrimum
Priapulus caudatus
Proteocephalus longicollis
Pyrosome
Rat lungworm
Red haplognathia
Salp
Sea nettle
Sea walnut
Seison nebaliae
Symbion pandora
Thimble jelly
Tropical brittle star

GRENADA

Asplanchna priodonta
Botryllus schlosseri
Bucket-tailed loriciferan
Canine heartworm
Convolutriloba longifissura
Dactylogyrus vastator
Fasciola hepatica
Freshwater sponge
Giant thorny-headed worm
Human blood fluke
Lancet fluke
Lepidodermella squamata
Limnognathia maerski
Moniliformis moniliformis
Nightlight jellyfish
Oerstedia dorsalis
Oikopleura labradoriensis

Paragordius varius
Polystoma integerrimum
Priapulus caudatus
Proteocephalus longicollis
Pyrosome
Rat lungworm
Red haplognathia
Salp
Sea nettle
Sea walnut
Seison nebaliae
Symbion pandora
Thimble jelly
Tropical brittle star

GUATEMALA

Asplanchna priodonta
Botryllus schlosseri
Bucket-tailed loriciferan
Canine heartworm
Convolutriloba longifissura
Dactylogyrus vastator
Dog tapeworm
Fasciola hepatica
Freshwater sponge
Giant thorny-headed worm
Human blood fluke
Lancet fluke
Lepidodermella squamata
Limnognathia maerski
Moniliformis moniliformis
Nightlight jellyfish
Oerstedia dorsalis
Oikopleura labradoriensis
Paragordius varius
Pea urchin
Polystoma integerrimum
Priapulus caudatus
Proteocephalus longicollis
Pyrosome
Rat lungworm
Red haplognathia
Salp
Sea nettle
Sea walnut
Seison nebaliae

Symbion pandora
Thimble jelly
Tropical brittle star

GUINEA

Asplanchna priodonta
Botryllus schlosseri
Bucket-tailed loriciferan
Canine heartworm
Convolutriloba longifissura
Dactylogyrus vastator
Dog tapeworm
Fasciola hepatica
Freshwater sponge
Giant thorny-headed worm
Human blood fluke
Lancet fluke
Lepidodermella squamata
Limnognathia maerski
Moniliformis moniliformis
Nightlight jellyfish
Oerstedia dorsalis
Oikopleura labradoriensis
Paragordius varius
Pea urchin
Polystoma integerrimum
Priapulus caudatus
Proteocephalus longicollis
Pyrosome
Rat lungworm
Red haplognathia
Salp
Sea nettle
Sea walnut
Seison nebaliae
Symbion pandora
Thimble jelly
Tropical brittle star

GUINEA-BISSAU

Asplanchna priodonta
Botryllus schlosseri
Bucket-tailed loriciferan
Canine heartworm
Convolutriloba longifissura

Dactylogyrus vastator
Dog tapeworm
Fasciola hepatica
Freshwater sponge
Giant thorny-headed worm
Human blood fluke
Lancet fluke
Lepidodermella squamata
Limnognathia maerski
Moniliformis moniliformis
Nightlight jellyfish
Oerstedia dorsalis
Oikopleura labradoriensis
Paragordius varius
Pea urchin
Polystoma integerrimum
Priapulus caudatus
Proteocephalus longicollis
Pyrosome
Rat lungworm
Red haplognathia
Salp
Sea nettle
Sea walnut
Seison nebaliae
Symbion pandora
Thimble jelly

GUYANA

Asplanchna priodonta
Botryllus schlosseri
Bucket-tailed loriciferan
Canine heartworm
Convolutriloba longifissura
Dactylogyrus vastator
Dog tapeworm
Fasciola hepatica
Freshwater sponge
Giant thorny-headed worm
Human blood fluke
Lancet fluke
Lepidodermella squamata
Limnognathia maerski
Moniliformis moniliformis
Nightlight jellyfish
Oerstedia dorsalis

Oikopleura labradoriensis
Orange sea lily
Paragordius varius
Pea urchin
Polystoma integerrimum
Priapulus caudatus
Proteocephalus longicollis
Pyrosome
Rat lungworm
Red haplognathia
Salp
Sea nettle
Sea walnut
Seison nebaliae
Six keyhole sand dollar
Symbion pandora
Thimble jelly
Tropical brittle star

HAITI

Asplanchna priodonta
Botryllus schlosseri
Bucket-tailed loriciferan
Canine heartworm
Convolutriloba longifissura
Dactylogyrus vastator
Dog tapeworm
Fasciola hepatica
Freshwater sponge
Giant thorny-headed worm
Human blood fluke
Lancet fluke
Lepidodermella squamata
Limnognathia maerski
Moniliformis moniliformis
Nightlight jellyfish
Oerstedia dorsalis
Oikopleura labradoriensis
Orange sea lily
Paragordius varius
Pea urchin
Polystoma integerrimum
Priapulus caudatus
Proteocephalus longicollis
Pyrosome
Rat lungworm

Red haplognathia
Salp
Sea nettle
Sea walnut
Seison nebaliae
Symbion pandora
Thimble jelly
Velcro sea star

HONDURAS

Asplanchna priodonta
Botryllus schlosseri
Bucket-tailed loriciferan
Canine heartworm
Convolutriloba longifissura
Dactylogyrus vastator
Dog tapeworm
Fasciola hepatica
Freshwater sponge
Giant thorny-headed worm
Human blood fluke
Lancet fluke
Lepidodermella squamata
Limnognathia maerski
Moniliformis moniliformis
Nightlight jellyfish
Oerstedia dorsalis
Oikopleura labradoriensis
Paragordius varius
Pea urchin
Polystoma integerrimum
Priapulus caudatus
Proteocephalus longicollis
Pyrosome
Rat lungworm
Red haplognathia
Salp
Sea nettle
Sea walnut
Seison nebaliae
Symbion pandora
Thimble jelly
Tropical brittle star

HUNGARY

Asplanchna priodonta

Canine heartworm
Dog tapeworm
Freshwater sponge
Giant thorny-headed worm
Human blood fluke
Lancet fluke
Mermis nigrescens
Moniliformis moniliformis
Oerstedia dorsalis
Paragordius varius
Polystoma integerrimum
Proteocephalus longicollis
Rat lungworm

ICELAND

Canine heartworm
Convolutriloba longifissura
Dog tapeworm
Human blood fluke
Lancet fluke
Mermis nigrescens
Nightlight jellyfish
Oikopleura labradoriensis
Rat lungworm
Red haplognathia
Thimble jelly

INDIA

Asplanchna priodonta
Blue starfish
Bucket-tailed loriciferan
Canine heartworm
Convolutriloba longifissura
Crown-of-thorns
Dactylogyrus vastator
Distichopora violacea
Dog tapeworm
Eukrohnia fowleri
Fasciola hepatica
Fire coral
Freshwater sponge
Giant thorny-headed worm
Human blood fluke
Lancet fluke
Lepidodermella squamata

Limnognathia maerski
Long-spined sea urchin
Moniliformis moniliformis
Nightlight jellyfish
Oerstedia dorsalis
Oikopleura labradoriensis
Paragordius varius
Pea urchin
Polystoma integerrimum
Portuguese man of war
Priapulus caudatus
Proteocephalus longicollis
Pterosagitta draco
Pyrosome
Rat lungworm
Red haplognathia
Salp
Sea apple
Sea nettle
Sea walnut
Seison nebaliae
Symbion pandora
Thimble jelly
Tropical brittle star
Tuxedo pincushion urchin

INDIAN OCEAN

Asplanchna priodonta
Blue starfish
Bucket-tailed loriciferan
Canine heartworm
Crown-of-thorns
Dactylogyrus vastator
Deep water reef coral
Distichopora violacea
Dog tapeworm
Eukrohnia fowleri
Fasciola hepatica
Fire coral
Freshwater sponge
Hawaiian acorn worm
Human blood fluke
Lancet fluke
Lepidodermella squamata
Limnognathia maerski
Long-spined sea urchin

Nightlight jellyfish
Oerstedia dorsalis
Oikopleura labradoriensis
Paragordius varius
Pea urchin
Polystoma integerrimum
Portuguese man of war
Priapulus caudatus
Proteocephalus longicollis
Pterosagitta draco
Pyrosome
Rat lungworm
Red haplognathia
Salp
Sea apple
Sea nettle
Sea pig
Sea walnut
Seison nebaliae
Symbion pandora
Thimble jelly
Tropical brittle star
Tuxedo pincushion urchin

INDONESIA

Asplanchna priodonta
Blue starfish
Bucket-tailed loriciferan
Canine heartworm
Convolutriloba longifissura
Crown-of-thorns
Dactylogyrus vastator
Distichopora violacea
Dog tapeworm
Eukrohnia fowleri
Fasciola hepatica
Fire coral
Freshwater sponge
Giant thorny-headed worm
Human blood fluke
Lancet fluke
Lepidodermella squamata
Limnognathia maerski
Long-spined sea urchin
Moniliformis moniliformis
Nightlight jellyfish

Oerstedia dorsalis
Oikopleura labradoriensis
Paragordius varius
Pea urchin
Polystoma integerrimum
Portuguese man of war
Priapulus caudatus
Proteocephalus longicollis
Pterosagitta draco
Pyrosome
Rat lungworm
Red haplognathia
Salp
Sea apple
Sea nettle
Sea walnut
Seison nebaliae
Symbion pandora
Thimble jelly
Tropical brittle star
Tuxedo pincushion urchin

IRAN

Asplanchna priodonta
Bucket-tailed loriciferan
Canine heartworm
Convolutriloba longifissura
Dactylogyrus vastator
Dog tapeworm
Fasciola hepatica
Freshwater sponge
Human blood fluke
Lancet fluke
Lepidodermella squamata
Limnognathia maerski
Nightlight jellyfish
Oerstedia dorsalis
Oikopleura labradoriensis
Paragordius varius
Pea urchin
Polystoma integerrimum
Priapulus caudatus
Proteocephalus longicollis
Pyrosome
Rat lungworm
Red haplognathia

Salp
Sea nettle
Sea walnut
Seison nebaliae
Symbion pandora
Thimble jelly
Tropical brittle star

IRAQ
Asplanchna priodonta
Bucket-tailed loriciferan
Canine heartworm
Convolutriloba longifissura
Dactylogyrus vastator
Dog tapeworm
Fasciola hepatica
Freshwater sponge
Human blood fluke
Lancet fluke
Lepidodermella squamata
Limnognathia maerski
Nightlight jellyfish
Oerstedia dorsalis
Oikopleura labradoriensis
Paragordius varius
Pea urchin
Polystoma integerrimum
Priapulus caudatus
Proteocephalus longicollis
Pyrosome
Rat lungworm
Red haplognathia
Salp
Sea walnut
Seison nebaliae
Symbion pandora
Thimble jelly
Tropical brittle star

IRELAND
Asplanchna priodonta
Botryllus schlosseri
Broad fish tapeworm
Bucket-tailed loriciferan
Canine heartworm
Convolutriloba longifissura

Dactylogyrus vastator
Dog tapeworm
Fasciola hepatica
Freshwater sponge
Giant thorny-headed worm
Human blood fluke
Lancet fluke
Lepidodermella squamata
Limnognathia maerski
Mermis nigrescens
Moniliformis moniliformis
Nightlight jellyfish
Oerstedia dorsalis
Oikopleura labradoriensis
Paragordius varius
Pea urchin
Polystoma integerrimum
Priapulus caudatus
Proteocephalus longicollis
Pyrosome
Rat lungworm
Red haplognathia
Salp
Sand star
Sea nettle
Sea walnut
Seison nebaliae
Symbion pandora
Thimble jelly
Tropical brittle star

ISRAEL
Asplanchna priodonta
Bucket-tailed loriciferan
Canine heartworm
Convolutriloba longifissura
Dactylogyrus vastator
Dog tapeworm
Fasciola hepatica
Freshwater sponge
Giant thorny-headed worm
Human blood fluke
Lancet fluke
Lepidodermella squamata
Limnognathia maerski
Nightlight jellyfish

Oerstedia dorsalis
Oikopleura labradoriensis
Paragordius varius
Pea urchin
Polystoma integerrimum
Priapulus caudatus
Proteocephalus longicollis
Pyrosome
Rat lungworm
Red haplognathia
Salp
Sea nettle
Sea walnut
Seison nebaliae
Symbion pandora
Thimble jelly
Tropical brittle star

ITALY
Asplanchna priodonta
Bucket-tailed loriciferan
Canine heartworm
Convolutriloba longifissura
Dactylogyrus vastator
Dog tapeworm
Fasciola hepatica
Freshwater sponge
Giant thorny-headed worm
Human blood fluke
Lancet fluke
Lepidodermella squamata
Limnognathia maerski
Mermis nigrescens
Moniliformis moniliformis
Nightlight jellyfish
Oerstedia dorsalis
Oikopleura labradoriensis
Paragordius varius
Pea urchin
Polystoma integerrimum
Priapulus caudatus
Proteocephalus longicollis
Pyrosome
Rat lungworm
Red haplognathia
Rhopalura ophiocomae

Salp
Sea nettle
Sea walnut
Seison nebaliae
Symbion pandora
Thimble jelly
Tropical brittle star

IVORY COAST
Asplanchna priodonta
Botryllus schlosseri
Bucket-tailed loriciferan
Canine heartworm
Convolutriloba longifissura
Dactylogyrus vastator
Dog tapeworm
Fasciola hepatica
Freshwater sponge
Giant thorny-headed worm
Human blood fluke
Lancet fluke
Lepidodermella squamata
Limnognathia maerski
Moniliformis moniliformis
Nightlight jellyfish
Oerstedia dorsalis
Oikopleura labradoriensis
Paragordius varius
Pea urchin
Polystoma integerrimum
Priapulus caudatus
Proteocephalus longicollis
Pyrosome
Rat lungworm
Red haplognathia
Salp
Sea nettle
Sea walnut
Seison nebaliae
Symbion pandora
Thimble jelly
Tropical brittle star

JAMAICA
Asplanchna priodonta
Botryllus schlosseri

Bucket-tailed loriciferan
Canine heartworm
Convolutriloba longifissura
Dactylogyrus vastator
Dog tapeworm
Fasciola hepatica
Freshwater sponge
Giant thorny-headed worm
Human blood fluke
Lancet fluke
Lepidodermella squamata
Limnognathia maerski
Moniliformis moniliformis
Nightlight jellyfish
Oerstedia dorsalis
Oikopleura labradoriensis
Paragordius varius
Pea urchin
Polystoma integerrimum
Priapulus caudatus
Proteocephalus longicollis
Pyrosome
Rat lungworm
Red haplognathia
Salp
Sea nettle
Sea walnut
Seison nebaliae
Symbion pandora
Thimble jelly
Tropical brittle star

JAPAN
Asplanchna priodonta
Blue starfish
Broad fish tapeworm
Bucket-tailed loriciferan
Canine heartworm
Convolutriloba longifissura
Crown-of-thorns
Dactylogyrus vastator
Distichopora violacea
Dog tapeworm
Echinoderes sensibilis
Eukrohnia fowleri
Fasciola hepatica

Fire coral
Freshwater sponge
Giant thorny-headed worm
Hawaiian acorn worm
Human blood fluke
Lancet fluke
Lepidodermella squamata
Limnognathia maerski
Long-spined sea urchin
Moniliformis moniliformis
Nightlight jellyfish
Northern Pacific sea star
Oerstedia dorsalis
Oikopleura labradoriensis
Paragordius varius
Pea urchin
Polystoma integerrimum
Portuguese man of war
Priapulus caudatus
Proteocephalus longicollis
Pterosagitta draco
Pyrosome
Rat lungworm
Red haplognathia
Salp
Sea apple
Sea nettle
Sea walnut
Seison nebaliae
Symbion pandora
Thimble jelly
Tropical brittle star
Tuxedo pincushion urchin

JORDAN
Asplanchna priodonta
Bucket-tailed loriciferan
Canine heartworm
Convolutriloba longifissura
Dactylogyrus vastator
Dog tapeworm
Fasciola hepatica
Freshwater sponge
Human blood fluke
Lancet fluke
Lepidodermella squamata

Limnognathia maerski
Nightlight jellyfish
Oerstedia dorsalis
Oikopleura labradoriensis
Paragordius varius
Pea urchin
Polystoma integerrimum
Priapulus caudatus
Proteocephalus longicollis
Pyrosome
Rat lungworm
Red haplognathia
Salp
Sea nettle
Sea walnut
Seison nebaliae
Symbion pandora
Thimble jelly
Tropical brittle star

KAZAKHSTAN
Asplanchna priodonta
Canine heartworm
Convolutriloba longifissura
Dog tapeworm
Freshwater sponge
Giant thorny-headed worm
Human blood fluke
Lancet fluke
Moniliformis moniliformis
Oerstedia dorsalis
Oikopleura labradoriensis
Paragordius varius
Polystoma integerrimum
Proteocephalus longicollis
Rat lungworm

KENYA
Asplanchna priodonta
Blue starfish
Bucket-tailed loriciferan
Canine heartworm
Convolutriloba longifissura
Crown-of-thorns
Dactylogyrus vastator

Distichopora violacea
Dog tapeworm
Eukrohnia fowleri
Fasciola hepatica
Fire coral
Freshwater sponge
Human blood fluke
Lancet fluke
Lepidodermella squamata
Limnognathia maerski
Long-spined sea urchin
Moniliformis moniliformis
Nightlight jellyfish
Oerstedia dorsalis
Oikopleura labradoriensis
Paragordius varius
Pea urchin
Polystoma integerrimum
Portuguese man of war
Priapulus caudatus
Proteocephalus longicollis
Pterosagitta draco
Pyrosome
Rat lungworm
Red haplognathia
Salp
Sea apple
Sea nettle
Sea walnut
Seison nebaliae
Symbion pandora
Thimble jelly
Tropical brittle star

KIRIBATI
Asplanchna priodonta
Blue starfish
Bucket-tailed loriciferan
Canine heartworm
Convolutriloba longifissura
Crown-of-thorns
Dactylogyrus vastator
Distichopora violacea
Dog tapeworm
Eukrohnia fowleri
Fasciola hepatica

Fire coral
Freshwater sponge
Giant thorny-headed worm
Human blood fluke
Lancet fluke
Lepidodermella squamata
Limnognathia maerski
Long-spined sea urchin
Moniliformis moniliformis
Nightlight jellyfish
Oerstedia dorsalis
Oikopleura labradoriensis
Paragordius varius
Pea urchin
Polystoma integerrimum
Portuguese man of war
Priapulus caudatus
Proteocephalus longicollis
Pterosagitta draco
Pyrosome
Rat lungworm
Red haplognathia
Salp
Sea apple
Sea nettle
Sea walnut
Seison nebaliae
Symbion pandora
Thimble jelly
Tropical brittle star

KUWAIT
Asplanchna priodonta
Bucket-tailed loriciferan
Canine heartworm
Convolutriloba longifissura
Dactylogyrus vastator
Dog tapeworm
Fasciola hepatica
Freshwater sponge
Human blood fluke
Lancet fluke
Lepidodermella squamata
Limnognathia maerski
Nightlight jellyfish
Oerstedia dorsalis

Oikopleura labradoriensis
Paragordius varius
Pea urchin
Polystoma integerrimum
Priapulus caudatus
Proteocephalus longicollis
Pyrosome
Rat lungworm
Red haplognathia
Salp
Sea nettle
Sea walnut
Seison nebaliae
Symbion pandora
Thimble jelly
Tropical brittle star

KYRGYZSTAN
Asplanchna priodonta
Canine heartworm
Dog tapeworm
Freshwater sponge
Giant thorny-headed worm
Human blood fluke
Lancet fluke
Moniliformis moniliformis
Oerstedia dorsalis
Paragordius varius
Polystoma integerrimum
Proteocephalus longicollis
Rat lungworm

LAOS
Asplanchna priodonta
Blue starfish
Bucket-tailed loriciferan
Canine heartworm
Convolutriloba longifissura
Crown-of-thorns
Dactylogyrus vastator
Distichopora violacea
Dog tapeworm
Eukrohnia fowleri
Fasciola hepatica
Fire coral

Freshwater sponge
Giant thorny-headed worm
Human blood fluke
Lancet fluke
Lepidodermella squamata
Limnognathia maerski
Long-spined sea urchin
Moniliformis moniliformis
Nightlight jellyfish
Oerstedia dorsalis
Oikopleura labradoriensis
Paragordius varius
Pea urchin
Polystoma integerrimum
Portuguese man of war
Priapulus caudatus
Proteocephalus longicollis
Pterosagitta draco
Pyrosome
Rat lungworm
Red haplognathia
Salp
Sea apple
Sea nettle
Sea walnut
Seison nebaliae
Symbion pandora
Thimble jelly
Tropical brittle star
Tuxedo pincushion urchin

LATVIA
Asplanchna priodonta
Broad fish tapeworm
Bucket-tailed loriciferan
Canine heartworm
Convolutriloba longifissura
Dactylogyrus vastator
Dog tapeworm
Fasciola hepatica
Freshwater sponge
Giant thorny-headed worm
Human blood fluke
Lancet fluke
Lepidodermella squamata
Limnognathia maerski

Mermis nigrescens
Moniliformis moniliformis
Nightlight jellyfish
Oerstedia dorsalis
Paragordius varius
Pea urchin
Polystoma integerrimum
Priapulus caudatus
Proteocephalus longicollis
Pyrosome
Rat lungworm
Red haplognathia
Salp
Sea nettle
Sea walnut
Seison nebaliae
Symbion pandora
Thimble jelly

LEBANON
Asplanchna priodonta
Bucket-tailed loriciferan
Canine heartworm
Convolutriloba longifissura
Dactylogyrus vastator
Dog tapeworm
Fasciola hepatica
Freshwater sponge
Giant thorny-headed worm
Human blood fluke
Lancet fluke
Lepidodermella squamata
Limnognathia maerski
Moniliformis moniliformis
Nightlight jellyfish
Oerstedia dorsalis
Oikopleura labradoriensis
Paragordius varius
Pea urchin
Polystoma integerrimum
Priapulus caudatus
Proteocephalus longicollis
Pyrosome
Rat lungworm
Red haplognathia
Salp

Sea nettle
Sea walnut
Seison nebaliae
Symbion pandora
Thimble jelly

LESOTHO
Asplanchna priodonta
Canine heartworm
Demoscolex squamosus
Dog tapeworm
Freshwater sponge
Giant thorny-headed worm
Human blood fluke
Lancet fluke
Moniliformis moniliformis
Oerstedia dorsalis
Paragordius varius
Polystoma integerrimum
Proteocephalus longicollis
Rat lungworm

LESSER ANTILLES
Asplanchna priodonta
Bucket-tailed loriciferan
Canine heartworm
Dactylogyrus vastator
Dog tapeworm
Fasciola hepatica
Freshwater sponge
Giant thorny-headed worm
Human blood fluke
Lancet fluke
Lepidodermella squamata
Limnognathia maerski
Nightlight jellyfish
Oerstedia dorsalis
Oikopleura labradoriensis
Paragordius varius
Pea urchin
Polystoma integerrimum
Priapulus caudatus
Proteocephalus longicollis
Pyrosome
Rat lungworm
Red haplognathia

Salp
Sea nettle
Sea walnut
Seison nebaliae
Symbion pandora
Thimble jelly
Tropical brittle star

LIBERIA
Asplanchna priodonta
Botryllus schlosseri
Bucket-tailed loriciferan
Canine heartworm
Convolutriloba longifissura
Dactylogyrus vastator
Dog tapeworm
Fasciola hepatica
Freshwater sponge
Giant thorny-headed worm
Human blood fluke
Lancet fluke
Lepidodermella squamata
Limnognathia maerski
Moniliformis moniliformis
Nightlight jellyfish
Oerstedia dorsalis
Oikopleura labradoriensis
Paragordius varius
Pea urchin
Polystoma integerrimum
Priapulus caudatus
Proteocephalus longicollis
Pyrosome
Rat lungworm
Red haplognathia
Salp
Sea nettle
Sea walnut
Seison nebaliae
Symbion pandora
Thimble jelly
Tropical brittle star

LIBYA
Asplanchna priodonta

Bucket-tailed loriciferan
Canine heartworm
Convolutriloba longifissura
Dactylogyrus vastator
Dog tapeworm
Fasciola hepatica
Freshwater sponge
Human blood fluke
Lancet fluke
Lepidodermella squamata
Limnognathia maerski
Nightlight jellyfish
Oerstedia dorsalis
Oikopleura labradoriensis
Paragordius varius
Pea urchin
Polystoma integerrimum
Priapulus caudatus
Proteocephalus longicollis
Pyrosome
Rat lungworm
Red haplognathia
Salp
Sea nettle
Sea walnut
Seison nebaliae
Symbion pandora
Thimble jelly
Tropical brittle star

LIECHTENSTEIN
Asplanchna priodonta
Canine heartworm
Dog tapeworm
Freshwater sponge
Giant thorny-headed worm
Human blood fluke
Lancet fluke
Mermis nigrescens
Moniliformis moniliformis
Oerstedia dorsalis
Paragordius varius
Polystoma integerrimum
Proteocephalus longicollis
Rat lungworm

LITHUANIA

Asplanchna priodonta
Broad fish tapeworm
Bucket-tailed loriciferan
Canine heartworm
Convolutriloba longifissura
Dactylogyrus vastator
Dog tapeworm
Fasciola hepatica
Freshwater sponge
Giant thorny-headed worm
Human blood fluke
Lancet fluke
Lepidodermella squamata
Limnognathia maerski
Mermis nigrescens
Moniliformis moniliformis
Nightlight jellyfish
Oerstedia dorsalis
Oikopleura labradoriensis
Paragordius varius
Pea urchin
Polystoma integerrimum
Priapulus caudatus
Proteocephalus longicollis
Pyrosome
Rat lungworm
Red haplognathia
Salp
Sea nettle
Sea walnut
Seison nebaliae
Symbion pandora

LUXEMBOURG

Asplanchna priodonta
Canine heartworm
Dog tapeworm
Freshwater sponge
Giant thorny-headed worm
Human blood fluke
Lancet fluke
Mermis nigrescens
Moniliformis moniliformis
Oerstedia dorsalis
Paragordius varius

Polystoma integerrimum
Proteocephalus longicollis
Rat lungworm

MACEDONIA

Asplanchna priodonta
Bucket-tailed loriciferan
Canine heartworm
Convolutriloba longifissura
Dactylogyrus vastator
Dog tapeworm
Fasciola hepatica
Freshwater sponge
Giant thorny-headed worm
Human blood fluke
Lancet fluke
Lepidodermella squamata
Limnognathia maerski
Mermis nigrescens
Moniliformis moniliformis
Nightlight jellyfish
Oerstedia dorsalis
Paragordius varius
Pea urchin
Polystoma integerrimum
Priapulus caudatus
Proteocephalus longicollis
Pyrosome
Rat lungworm
Red haplognathia
Salp
Sea nettle
Sea walnut
Seison nebaliae
Symbion pandora
Thimble jelly

MADAGASCAR

Asplanchna priodonta
Blue starfish
Bucket-tailed loriciferan
Canine heartworm
Convolutriloba longifissura
Crown-of-thorns
Dactylogyrus vastator

Distichopora violacea
Dog tapeworm
Eukrohnia fowleri
Fasciola hepatica
Fire coral
Freshwater sponge
Giant thorny-headed worm
Human blood fluke
Lancet fluke
Lepidodermella squamata
Limnognathia maerski
Long-spined sea urchin
Moniliformis moniliformis
Nightlight jellyfish
Oerstedia dorsalis
Oikopleura labradoriensis
Paragordius varius
Pea urchin
Polystoma integerrimum
Portuguese man of war
Priapulus caudatus
Proteocephalus longicollis
Pterosagitta draco
Pyrosome
Rat lungworm
Red haplognathia
Salp
Sea apple
Sea nettle
Sea walnut
Seison nebaliae
Symbion pandora
Thimble jelly
Tropical brittle star

MALAWI

Asplanchna priodonta
Canine heartworm
Dog tapeworm
Freshwater sponge
Giant thorny-headed worm
Human blood fluke
Lancet fluke
Moniliformis moniliformis
Oerstedia dorsalis
Paragordius varius

Polystoma integerrimum
Proteocephalus longicollis
Rat lungworm

MALAYSIA

Asplanchna priodonta
Blue starfish
Bucket-tailed loriciferan
Canine heartworm
Convolutriloba longifissura
Crown-of-thorns
Dactylogyrus vastator
Distichopora violacea
Dog tapeworm
Eukrohnia fowleri
Fasciola hepatica
Fire coral
Freshwater sponge
Giant thorny-headed worm
Human blood fluke
Lancet fluke
Lepidodermella squamata
Limnognathia maerski
Long-spined sea urchin
Moniliformis moniliformis
Nightlight jellyfish
Oerstedia dorsalis
Oikopleura labradoriensis
Paragordius varius
Pea urchin
Polystoma integerrimum
Portuguese man of war
Priapulus caudatus
Proteocephalus longicollis
Pterosagitta draco
Pyrosome
Rat lungworm
Red haplognathia
Salp
Sea apple
Sea nettle
Sea walnut
Seison nebaliae
Symbion pandora
Thimble jelly
Tropical brittle star

MALDIVES

Asplanchna priodonta
Bucket-tailed loriciferan
Canine heartworm
Convolutriloba longifissura
Dactylogyrus vastator
Dog tapeworm
Fasciola hepatica
Freshwater sponge
Giant thorny-headed worm
Hawaiian acorn worm
Human blood fluke
Lancet fluke
Lepidodermella squamata
Limnognathia maerski
Moniliformis moniliformis
Nightlight jellyfish
Oerstedia dorsalis
Oikopleura labradoriensis
Paragordius varius
Pea urchin
Polystoma integerrimum
Priapulus caudatus
Proteocephalus longicollis
Pyrosome
Rat lungworm
Red haplognathia
Salp
Sea nettle
Sea walnut
Seison nebaliae
Symbion pandora
Thimble jelly
Tropical brittle star

MALI

Asplanchna priodonta
Canine heartworm
Dog tapeworm
Freshwater sponge
Giant thorny-headed worm
Human blood fluke
Lancet fluke
Moniliformis moniliformis
Oerstedia dorsalis
Paragordius varius

Polystoma integerrimum
Proteocephalus longicollis
Rat lungworm

MALTA

Asplanchna priodonta
Bucket-tailed loriciferan
Canine heartworm
Convolutriloba longifissura
Dactylogyrus vastator
Dog tapeworm
Fasciola hepatica
Freshwater sponge
Giant thorny-headed worm
Human blood fluke
Lancet fluke
Lepidodermella squamata
Limnognathia maerski
Mermis nigrescens
Moniliformis moniliformis
Nightlight jellyfish
Oerstedia dorsalis
Oikopleura labradoriensis
Paragordius varius
Pea urchin
Polystoma integerrimum
Priapulus caudatus
Proteocephalus longicollis
Pyrosome
Rat lungworm
Red haplognathia
Salp
Sea nettle
Sea walnut
Seison nebaliae
Symbion pandora
Thimble jelly

MARIANA ISLANDS

Asplanchna priodonta
Bucket-tailed loriciferan
Canine heartworm
Convolutriloba longifissura
Dactylogyrus vastator
Dog tapeworm

Fasciola hepatica
Freshwater sponge
Giant thorny-headed worm
Human blood fluke
Lancet fluke
Lepidodermella squamata
Limnognathia maerski
Moniliformis moniliformis
Nightlight jellyfish
Oerstedia dorsalis
Oikopleura labradoriensis
Paragordius varius
Pea urchin
Polystoma integerrimum
Priapulus caudatus
Proteocephalus longicollis
Pyrosome
Rat lungworm
Red haplognathia
Salp
Sea nettle
Sea walnut
Seison nebaliae
Symbion pandora
Thimble jelly
Tropical brittle star

MARSHALL ISLANDS
Asplanchna priodonta
Blue starfish
Bucket-tailed loriciferan
Canine heartworm
Convolutriloba longifissura
Crown-of-thorns
Dactylogyrus vastator
Distichopora violacea
Dog tapeworm
Eukrohnia fowleri
Fasciola hepatica
Fire coral
Freshwater sponge
Giant thorny-headed worm
Human blood fluke
Lancet fluke
Lepidodermella squamata
Limnognathia maerski

Long-spined sea urchin
Moniliformis moniliformis
Nightlight jellyfish
Oerstedia dorsalis
Oikopleura labradoriensis
Paragordius varius
Pea urchin
Polystoma integerrimum
Portuguese man of war
Priapulus caudatus
Proteocephalus longicollis
Pterosagitta draco
Pyrosome
Rat lungworm
Red haplognathia
Salp
Sea apple
Sea nettle
Sea walnut
Seison nebaliae
Symbion pandora
Thimble jelly
Tropical brittle star

MAURITANIA
Asplanchna priodonta
Botryllus schlosseri
Bucket-tailed loriciferan
Canine heartworm
Convolutriloba longifissura
Dactylogyrus vastator
Dog tapeworm
Fasciola hepatica
Freshwater sponge
Giant thorny-headed worm
Human blood fluke
Lancet fluke
Lepidodermella squamata
Limnognathia maerski
Moniliformis moniliformis
Nightlight jellyfish
Oerstedia dorsalis
Oikopleura labradoriensis
Paragordius varius
Pea urchin
Polystoma integerrimum

Priapulus caudatus
Proteocephalus longicollis
Pyrosome
Rat lungworm
Red haplognathia
Salp
Sea nettle
Sea walnut
Seison nebaliae
Symbion pandora
Thimble jelly
Tropical brittle star

MAURITIUS
Asplanchna priodonta
Blue starfish
Bucket-tailed loriciferan
Canine heartworm
Convolutriloba longifissura
Crown-of-thorns
Dactylogyrus vastator
Distichopora violacea
Dog tapeworm
Eukrohnia fowleri
Fasciola hepatica
Fire coral
Freshwater sponge
Giant thorny-headed worm
Hawaiian acorn worm
Human blood fluke
Lancet fluke
Lepidodermella squamata
Limnognathia maerski
Long-spined sea urchin
Moniliformis moniliformis
Nightlight jellyfish
Oerstedia dorsalis
Oikopleura labradoriensis
Paragordius varius
Pea urchin
Polystoma integerrimum
Portuguese man of war
Priapulus caudatus
Proteocephalus longicollis
Pterosagitta draco
Pyrosome

Rat lungworm
Red haplognathia
Salp
Sea apple
Sea nettle
Sea walnut
Seison nebaliae
Symbion pandora
Thimble jelly
Tropical brittle star

MEDITERRANEAN SEA

Asplanchna priodonta
Bird's nest sponge
Bucket-tailed loriciferan
Canine heartworm
Dactylogyrus vastator
Dog tapeworm
Fasciola hepatica
Freshwater sponge
Human blood fluke
Lancet fluke
Lepidodermella squamata
Limnognathia maerski
Nightlight jellyfish
Oerstedia dorsalis
Oikopleura labradoriensis
Paragordius varius
Pea urchin
Polystoma integerrimum
Portuguese man of war
Priapulus caudatus
Proteocephalus longicollis
Pyrosome
Rat lungworm
Red coral
Red haplognathia
Salp
Sea nettle
Sea pig
Sea walnut
Seison nebaliae
Symbion pandora
Thimble jelly
Tropical brittle star
Venus's girdle

MEXICO

Asplanchna priodonta
Blue starfish
Botryllus schlosseri
Bucket-tailed loriciferan
Canine heartworm
Convolutriloba longifissura
Crown-of-thorns
Dactylogyrus vastator
Distichopora violacea
Dog tapeworm
Eukrohnia fowleri
Fasciola hepatica
Fire coral
Florida lancelet
Freshwater planarian
Freshwater sponge
Giant green anemone
Giant thorny-headed worm
Human blood fluke
Lancet fluke
Lepidodermella squamata
Limnognathia maerski
Long-spined sea urchin
Mermis nigrescens
Moniliformis moniliformis
Nightlight jellyfish
Northern Pacific sea star
Notoplana acticola
Oerstedia dorsalis
Oikopleura labradoriensis
Paragordius varius
Pea urchin
Polystoma integerrimum
Portuguese man of war
Priapulus caudatus
Proteocephalus longicollis
Pterosagitta draco
Pyrosome
Rat lungworm
Red haplognathia
Salp
Sea apple
Sea nettle
Sea walnut
Seison nebaliae

Six keyhole sand dollar
Symbion pandora
Thimble jelly
Tropical brittle star
Western sand dollar

MICRONESIA

Asplanchna priodonta
Blue starfish
Bucket-tailed loriciferan
Canine heartworm
Convolutriloba longifissura
Crown-of-thorns
Dactylogyrus vastator
Distichopora violacea
Dog tapeworm
Eukrohnia fowleri
Fasciola hepatica
Fire coral
Freshwater sponge
Giant thorny-headed worm
Human blood fluke
Lancet fluke
Lepidodermella squamata
Limnognathia maerski
Long-spined sea urchin
Moniliformis moniliformis
Nightlight jellyfish
Oerstedia dorsalis
Oikopleura labradoriensis
Paragordius varius
Pea urchin
Polystoma integerrimum
Portuguese man of war
Priapulus caudatus
Proteocephalus longicollis
Pterosagitta draco
Pyrosome
Rat lungworm
Red haplognathia
Salp
Sea apple
Sea nettle
Sea walnut
Seison nebaliae
Symbion pandora

Thimble jelly
Tropical brittle star
Tuxedo pincushion urchin

MOLDOVA
Asplanchna priodonta
Bucket-tailed loriciferan
Canine heartworm
Convolutriloba longifissura
Dactylogyrus vastator
Dog tapeworm
Fasciola hepatica
Freshwater sponge
Giant thorny-headed worm
Human blood fluke
Lancet fluke
Lepidodermella squamata
Limnognathia maerski
Mermis nigrescens
Moniliformis moniliformis
Nightlight jellyfish
Oerstedia dorsalis
Oikopleura labradoriensis
Paragordius varius
Pea urchin
Polystoma integerrimum
Priapulus caudatus
Proteocephalus longicollis
Pyrosome
Rat lungworm
Red haplognathia
Salp
Sea nettle
Sea walnut
Seison nebaliae
Symbion pandora
Thimble jelly

MONACO
Asplanchna priodonta
Bucket-tailed loriciferan
Canine heartworm
Convolutriloba longifissura
Dactylogyrus vastator
Dog tapeworm

Fasciola hepatica
Freshwater sponge
Giant thorny-headed worm
Human blood fluke
Lancet fluke
Lepidodermella squamata
Limnognathia maerski
Mermis nigrescens
Moniliformis moniliformis
Nightlight jellyfish
Oerstedia dorsalis
Oikopleura labradoriensis
Paragordius varius
Pea urchin
Polystoma integerrimum
Priapulus caudatus
Proteocephalus longicollis
Pyrosome
Rat lungworm
Red haplognathia
Sea nettle
Sea walnut
Seison nebaliae
Symbion pandora
Thimble jelly

MONGOLIA
Asplanchna priodonta
Canine heartworm
Convolutriloba longifissura
Dog tapeworm
Freshwater sponge
Giant thorny-headed worm
Human blood fluke
Lancet fluke
Moniliformis moniliformis
Oerstedia dorsalis
Oikopleura labradoriensis
Paragordius varius
Polystoma integerrimum
Proteocephalus longicollis
Rat lungworm

MOROCCO
Asplanchna priodonta
Botryllus schlosseri

Bucket-tailed loriciferan
Canine heartworm
Convolutriloba longifissura
Dactylogyrus vastator
Dog tapeworm
Fasciola hepatica
Freshwater sponge
Human blood fluke
Lancet fluke
Lepidodermella squamata
Limnognathia maerski
Nightlight jellyfish
Oerstedia dorsalis
Oikopleura labradoriensis
Paragordius varius
Pea urchin
Polystoma integerrimum
Priapulus caudatus
Proteocephalus longicollis
Pyrosome
Rat lungworm
Red haplognathia
Salp
Sand star
Sea nettle
Sea walnut
Seison nebaliae
Symbion pandora
Thimble jelly

MOZAMBIQUE
Asplanchna priodonta
Blue starfish
Bucket-tailed loriciferan
Canine heartworm
Convolutriloba longifissura
Crown-of-thorns
Dactylogyrus vastator
Demoscolex squamosus
Distichopora violacea
Dog tapeworm
Eukrohnia fowleri
Fasciola hepatica
Fire coral
Freshwater sponge
Giant thorny-headed worm

Human blood fluke
Lancet fluke
Lepidodermella squamata
Limnognathia maerski
Long-spined sea urchin
Moniliformis moniliformis
Nightlight jellyfish
Oerstedia dorsalis
Oikopleura labradoriensis
Paragordius varius
Pea urchin
Polystoma integerrimum
Portuguese man of war
Priapulus caudatus
Proteocephalus longicollis
Pterosagitta draco
Pyrosome
Rat lungworm
Red haplognathia
Salp
Sea apple
Sea nettle
Sea walnut
Seison nebaliae
Symbion pandora
Thimble jelly
Tropical brittle star

MYANMAR

Asplanchna priodonta
Blue starfish
Bucket-tailed loriciferan
Canine heartworm
Convolutriloba longifissura
Crown-of-thorns
Dactylogyrus vastator
Distichopora violacea
Dog tapeworm
Eukrohnia fowleri
Fasciola hepatica
Fire coral
Freshwater sponge
Giant thorny-headed worm
Human blood fluke
Lancet fluke
Lepidodermella squamata

Limnognathia maerski
Long-spined sea urchin
Moniliformis moniliformis
Nightlight jellyfish
Oerstedia dorsalis
Oikopleura labradoriensis
Paragordius varius
Pea urchin
Polystoma integerrimum
Portuguese man of war
Priapulus caudatus
Proteocephalus longicollis
Pterosagitta draco
Pyrosome
Rat lungworm
Red haplognathia
Salp
Sea apple
Sea nettle
Sea walnut
Seison nebaliae
Symbion pandora
Thimble jelly
Tropical brittle star
Tuxedo pincushion urchin

NAMIBIA

Asplanchna priodonta
Botryllus schlosseri
Bucket-tailed loriciferan
Canine heartworm
Convolutriloba longifissura
Dactylogyrus vastator
Dog tapeworm
Fasciola hepatica
Freshwater sponge
Giant thorny-headed worm
Human blood fluke
Lancet fluke
Lepidodermella squamata
Limnognathia maerski
Moniliformis moniliformis
Nightlight jellyfish
Oerstedia dorsalis
Oikopleura labradoriensis
Paragordius varius

Pea urchin
Polystoma integerrimum
Priapulus caudatus
Proteocephalus longicollis
Pyrosome
Rat lungworm
Red haplognathia
Salp
Sea nettle
Sea walnut
Seison nebaliae
Symbion pandora
Thimble jelly
Tropical brittle star

NAURU

Asplanchna priodonta
Blue starfish
Bucket-tailed loriciferan
Canine heartworm
Convolutriloba longifissura
Crown-of-thorns
Dactylogyrus vastator
Distichopora violacea
Dog tapeworm
Eukrohnia fowleri
Fasciola hepatica
Fire coral
Freshwater sponge
Giant thorny-headed worm
Human blood fluke
Lancet fluke
Lepidodermella squamata
Limnognathia maerski
Long-spined sea urchin
Moniliformis moniliformis
Nightlight jellyfish
Oerstedia dorsalis
Oikopleura labradoriensis
Paragordius varius
Pea urchin
Polystoma integerrimum
Portuguese man of war
Priapulus caudatus
Proteocephalus longicollis
Pterosagitta draco

Pyrosome
Rat lungworm
Red haplognathia
Salp
Sea apple
Sea nettle
Sea walnut
Seison nebaliae
Symbion pandora
Thimble jelly
Tropical brittle star
Tuxedo pincushion urchin

NEPAL
Asplanchna priodonta
Canine heartworm
Dog tapeworm
Freshwater sponge
Giant thorny-headed worm
Human blood fluke
Lancet fluke
Moniliformis moniliformis
Oerstedia dorsalis
Paragordius varius
Polystoma integerrimum
Proteocephalus longicollis
Rat lungworm

NETHERLANDS
Asplanchna priodonta
Botryllus schlosseri
Broad fish tapeworm
Bucket-tailed loriciferan
Canine heartworm
Convolutriloba longifissura
Dactylogyrus vastator
Dog tapeworm
Fasciola hepatica
Freshwater sponge
Giant thorny-headed worm
Human blood fluke
Lancet fluke
Lepidodermella squamata
Limnognathia maerski
Marine colonial entoproct

Mermis nigrescens
Moniliformis moniliformis
Nightlight jellyfish
Oerstedia dorsalis
Oikopleura labradoriensis
Paragordius varius
Pea urchin
Polystoma integerrimum
Priapulus caudatus
Proteocephalus longicollis
Pyrosome
Rat lungworm
Red haplognathia
Salp
Sand star
Sea nettle
Sea walnut
Seison nebaliae
Symbion pandora
Thimble jelly
Tropical brittle star

NEW ZEALAND
Asplanchna priodonta
Black coral
Blue starfish
Bucket-tailed loriciferan
Candy cane sea cucumber
Canine heartworm
Convolutriloba longifissura
Crown-of-thorns
Dactylogyrus vastator
Deep water reef coral
Distichopora violacea
Dog tapeworm
Eukrohnia fowleri
Fasciola hepatica
Fire coral
Freshwater sponge
Giant thorny-headed worm
Human blood fluke
Lancet fluke
Lepidodermella squamata
Limnognathia maerski
Long-spined sea urchin
Medusiform sea daisy

Moniliformis moniliformis
Nightlight jellyfish
Oerstedia dorsalis
Oikopleura labradoriensis
Paragordius varius
Pea urchin
Polystoma integerrimum
Portuguese man of war
Priapulus caudatus
Proteocephalus longicollis
Pterosagitta draco
Pyrosome
Rat lungworm
Red haplognathia
Salp
Sea apple
Sea nettle
Sea walnut
Seison nebaliae
Symbion pandora
Thimble jelly
Tropical brittle star

NICARAGUA
Asplanchna priodonta
Botryllus schlosseri
Bucket-tailed loriciferan
Canine heartworm
Convolutriloba longifissura
Dactylogyrus vastator
Dog tapeworm
Fasciola hepatica
Freshwater sponge
Giant thorny-headed worm
Human blood fluke
Lancet fluke
Lepidodermella squamata
Limnognathia maerski
Moniliformis moniliformis
Nightlight jellyfish
Oerstedia dorsalis
Oikopleura labradoriensis
Paragordius varius
Pea urchin
Polystoma integerrimum
Priapulus caudatus

Proteocephalus longicollis
Pyrosome
Rat lungworm
Red haplognathia
Salp
Sea nettle
Sea walnut
Seison nebaliae
Symbion pandora
Thimble jelly
Tropical brittle star

NIGER

Asplanchna priodonta
Botryllus schlosseri
Canine heartworm
Dog tapeworm
Freshwater sponge
Giant thorny-headed worm
Human blood fluke
Lancet fluke
Moniliformis moniliformis
Oerstedia dorsalis
Paragordius varius
Polystoma integerrimum
Proteocephalus longicollis
Rat lungworm

NIGERIA

Asplanchna priodonta
Bucket-tailed loriciferan
Canine heartworm
Convolutriloba longifissura
Dactylogyrus vastator
Dog tapeworm
Fasciola hepatica
Freshwater sponge
Giant thorny-headed worm
Human blood fluke
Lancet fluke
Lepidodermella squamata
Limnognathia maerski
Moniliformis moniliformis
Nightlight jellyfish
Oerstedia dorsalis

Oikopleura labradoriensis
Paragordius varius
Pea urchin
Polystoma integerrimum
Priapulus caudatus
Proteocephalus longicollis
Pyrosome
Rat lungworm
Red haplognathia
Salp
Sea nettle
Sea walnut
Seison nebaliae
Symbion pandora
Thimble jelly
Tropical brittle star

NORTH KOREA

Asplanchna priodonta
Blue starfish
Bucket-tailed loriciferan
Canine heartworm
Convolutriloba longifissura
Crown-of-thorns
Dactylogyrus vastator
Distichopora violacea
Dog tapeworm
Eukrohnia fowleri
Fasciola hepatica
Fire coral
Freshwater sponge
Giant thorny-headed worm
Human blood fluke
Lancet fluke
Lepidodermella squamata
Limnognathia maerski
Long-spined sea urchin
Moniliformis moniliformis
Nightlight jellyfish
Oerstedia dorsalis
Oikopleura labradoriensis
Paragordius varius
Pea urchin
Polystoma integerrimum
Portuguese man of war
Priapulus caudatus

Proteocephalus longicollis
Pterosagitta draco
Pyrosome
Rat lungworm
Red haplognathia
Salp
Sea apple
Sea nettle
Sea walnut
Seison nebaliae
Symbion pandora
Thimble jelly

NORWAY

Asplanchna priodonta
Botryllus schlosseri
Broad fish tapeworm
Bucket-tailed loriciferan
Canine heartworm
Convolutriloba longifissura
Dactylogyrus vastator
Dog tapeworm
Fasciola hepatica
Freshwater sponge
Giant thorny-headed worm
Human blood fluke
Lancet fluke
Lepidodermella squamata
Limnognathia maerski
Marine colonial entoproct
Mermis nigrescens
Moniliformis moniliformis
Nightlight jellyfish
Oerstedia dorsalis
Oikopleura labradoriensis
Paragordius varius
Pea urchin
Polystoma integerrimum
Priapulus caudatus
Proteocephalus longicollis
Pyrosome
Rat lungworm
Red haplognathia
Salp
Sand star

Sea nettle
Sea walnut
Seison nebaliae
Symbion pandora
Thimble jelly

OMAN

Asplanchna priodonta
Blue starfish
Bucket-tailed loriciferan
Canine heartworm
Convolutriloba longifissura
Crown-of-thorns
Dactylogyrus vastator
Distichopora violacea
Dog tapeworm
Eukrohnia fowleri
Fasciola hepatica
Fire coral
Freshwater sponge
Human blood fluke
Lancet fluke
Lepidodermella squamata
Limnognathia maerski
Long-spined sea urchin
Nightlight jellyfish
Oerstedia dorsalis
Oikopleura labradoriensis
Paragordius varius
Pea urchin
Polystoma integerrimum
Portuguese man of war
Priapulus caudatus
Proteocephalus longicollis
Pterosagitta draco
Pyrosome
Rat lungworm
Red haplognathia
Salp
Sea apple
Sea nettle
Sea walnut
Seison nebaliae
Symbion pandora
Thimble jelly

PACIFIC OCEAN

Acquorea victoria
Aglantha digitale
Asplanchna priodonta
Black coral
Blue starfish
Bucket-tailed loriciferan
Candy cane sea cucumber
Canine heartworm
Crown-of-thorns
Dactylogyrus vastator
Deep water reef coral
Dicyemodeca deca
Didemnum studeri
Distaplia cylindrica
Distichopora violacea
Dog tapeworm
Eukrohnia fowleri
Fasciola hepatica
Fire coral
Freshwater sponge
Frilled anemone
Giant green anemone
Hawaiian acorn worm
Human blood fluke
Lancet fluke
Lepidodermella squamata
Limnognathia maerski
Long-spined sea urchin
Nightlight jellyfish
Northern Pacific sea star
Oerstedia dorsalis
Oikopleura labradoriensis
Paragordius varius
Pea urchin
Polystoma integerrimum
Portuguese man of war
Priapulus caudatus
Proteocephalus longicollis
Pterosagitta draco
Pyrosome
Rat lungworm
Red haplognathia
Salp
Sea apple
Sea nettle

Sea pig
Sea walnut
Seison nebaliae
Spaghetti worm
Symbion pandora
Thimble jelly
Tropical brittle star
Tuxedo pincushion urchin
Venus's girdle

PAKISTAN

Asplanchna priodonta
Blue starfish
Bucket-tailed loriciferan
Canine heartworm
Convolutriloba longifissura
Crown-of-thorns
Dactylogyrus vastator
Distichopora violacea
Dog tapeworm
Eukrohnia fowleri
Fasciola hepatica
Fire coral
Freshwater sponge
Giant thorny-headed worm
Human blood fluke
Lancet fluke
Lepidodermella squamata
Limnognathia maerski
Long-spined sea urchin
Moniliformis moniliformis
Nightlight jellyfish
Oerstedia dorsalis
Oikopleura labradoriensis
Paragordius varius
Pea urchin
Polystoma integerrimum
Portuguese man of war
Priapulus caudatus
Proteocephalus longicollis
Pterosagitta draco
Pyrosome
Rat lungworm
Red haplognathia
Salp
Sea apple

Sea nettle
Sea walnut
Seison nebaliae
Symbion pandora
Thimble jelly
Tropical brittle star
Tuxedo pincushion urchin

PALAU
Asplanchna priodonta
Blue starfish
Bucket-tailed loriciferan
Canine heartworm
Convolutriloba longifissura
Crown-of-thorns
Dactylogyrus vastator
Distichopora violacea
Dog tapeworm
Eukrohnia fowleri
Fasciola hepatica
Fire coral
Freshwater sponge
Giant thorny-headed worm
Human blood fluke
Lancet fluke
Lepidodermella squamata
Limnognathia maerski
Long-spined sea urchin
Moniliformis moniliformis
Nightlight jellyfish
Oerstedia dorsalis
Oikopleura labradoriensis
Paragordius varius
Pea urchin
Polystoma integerrimum
Portuguese man of war
Priapulus caudatus
Proteocephalus longicollis
Pterosagitta draco
Pyrosome
Rat lungworm
Red haplognathia
Salp
Sea apple
Sea nettle
Sea walnut

Seison nebaliae
Symbion pandora
Thimble jelly
Tropical brittle star

PANAMA
Asplanchna priodonta
Botryllus schlosseri
Bucket-tailed loriciferan
Canine heartworm
Convolutriloba longifissura
Dactylogyrus vastator
Dog tapeworm
Fasciola hepatica
Freshwater sponge
Giant thorny-headed worm
Human blood fluke
Lancet fluke
Lepidodermella squamata
Limnognathia maerski
Moniliformis moniliformis
Nightlight jellyfish
Oerstedia dorsalis
Oikopleura labradoriensis
Paragordius varius
Pea urchin
Polystoma integerrimum
Priapulus caudatus
Proteocephalus longicollis
Pyrosome
Rat lungworm
Red haplognathia
Salp
Sea nettle
Sea walnut
Seison nebaliae
Symbion pandora
Thimble jelly

PAPUA NEW GUINEA
Asplanchna priodonta
Blue starfish
Bucket-tailed loriciferan
Canine heartworm
Convolutriloba longifissura

Crown-of-thorns
Dactylogyrus vastator
Distichopora violacea
Dog tapeworm
Eukrohnia fowleri
Fasciola hepatica
Fire coral
Freshwater sponge
Giant thorny-headed worm
Human blood fluke
Lancet fluke
Lepidodermella squamata
Limnognathia maerski
Long-spined sea urchin
Moniliformis moniliformis
Nightlight jellyfish
Oerstedia dorsalis
Oikopleura labradoriensis
Paragordius varius
Pea urchin
Polystoma integerrimum
Portuguese man of war
Priapulus caudatus
Proteocephalus longicollis
Pterosagitta draco
Pyrosome
Rat lungworm
Red haplognathia
Salp
Sea apple
Sea nettle
Sea walnut
Sea wasp
Seison nebaliae
Symbion pandora
Thimble jelly
Tropical brittle star

PARAGUAY
Asplanchna priodonta
Bucket-tailed loriciferan
Canine heartworm
Dactylogyrus vastator
Dog tapeworm
Fasciola hepatica
Freshwater sponge

Giant thorny-headed worm
Human blood fluke
Lancet fluke
Lepidodermella squamata
Limnognathia maerski
Moniliformis moniliformis
Nightlight jellyfish
Oerstedia dorsalis
Paragordius varius
Pea urchin
Polystoma integerrimum
Priapulus caudatus
Proteocephalus longicollis
Pyrosome
Rat lungworm
Red haplognathia
Salp
Sea nettle
Sea walnut
Seison nebaliae
Symbion pandora
Thimble jelly
Tropical brittle star
Tuxedo pincushion urchin

PERU

Asplanchna priodonta
Blue starfish
Bucket-tailed loriciferan
Canine heartworm
Convolutriloba longifissura
Crown-of-thorns
Dactylogyrus vastator
Distichopora violacea
Dog tapeworm
Eukrohnia fowleri
Fasciola hepatica
Fire coral
Freshwater sponge
Giant thorny-headed worm
Human blood fluke
Lancet fluke
Lepidodermella squamata
Limnognathia maerski
Long-spined sea urchin
Moniliformis moniliformis

Nightlight jellyfish
Oerstedia dorsalis
Oikopleura labradoriensis
Paragordius varius
Pea urchin
Polystoma integerrimum
Portuguese man of war
Priapulus caudatus
Proteocephalus longicollis
Pterosagitta draco
Pyrosome
Rat lungworm
Red haplognathia
Salp
Sea apple
Sea nettle
Sea walnut
Seison nebaliae
Symbion pandora
Thimble jelly
Tropical brittle star

PHILIPPINES

Asplanchna priodonta
Blue starfish
Bucket-tailed loriciferan
Canine heartworm
Convolutriloba longifissura
Crown-of-thorns
Dactylogyrus vastator
Distichopora violacea
Dog tapeworm
Eukrohnia fowleri
Fasciola hepatica
Fire coral
Freshwater sponge
Giant thorny-headed worm
Human blood fluke
Lancet fluke
Lepidodermella squamata
Limnognathia maerski
Long-spined sea urchin
Moniliformis moniliformis
Nightlight jellyfish
Oerstedia dorsalis
Oikopleura labradoriensis

Paragordius varius
Pea urchin
Polystoma integerrimum
Portuguese man of war
Priapulus caudatus
Proteocephalus longicollis
Pterosagitta draco
Pyrosome
Rat lungworm
Red haplognathia
Salp
Sea apple
Sea nettle
Sea walnut
Sea wasp
Seison nebaliae
Symbion pandora
Thimble jelly
Tropical brittle star
Tuxedo pincushion urchin

POLAND

Asplanchna priodonta
Broad fish tapeworm
Bucket-tailed loriciferan
Canine heartworm
Convolutriloba longifissura
Dactylogyrus vastator
Dog tapeworm
Fasciola hepatica
Freshwater sponge
Giant thorny-headed worm
Human blood fluke
Lancet fluke
Lepidodermella squamata
Limnognathia maerski
Mermis nigrescens
Moniliformis moniliformis
Nightlight jellyfish
Oerstedia dorsalis
Paragordius varius
Pea urchin
Polystoma integerrimum
Priapulus caudatus
Proteocephalus longicollis
Pyrosome

Rat lungworm
Red haplognathia
Salp
Sea nettle
Sea walnut
Seison nebaliae
Symbion pandora
Thimble jelly

PORTUGAL

Asplanchna priodonta
Botryllus schlosseri
Bucket-tailed loriciferan
Canine heartworm
Convolutriloba longifissura
Dactylogyrus vastator
Dog tapeworm
Fasciola hepatica
Freshwater sponge
Giant thorny-headed worm
Human blood fluke
Lancet fluke
Lepidodermella squamata
Limnognathia maerski
Mermis nigrescens
Moniliformis moniliformis
Nightlight jellyfish
Oerstedia dorsalis
Oikopleura labradoriensis
Paragordius varius
Pea urchin
Polystoma integerrimum
Priapulus caudatus
Proteocephalus longicollis
Pyrosome
Rat lungworm
Red coral
Red haplognathia
Salp
Sand star
Sea nettle
Sea walnut
Seison nebaliae
Symbion pandora
Thimble jelly

PUERTO RICO

Asplanchna priodonta
Botryllus schlosseri
Bucket-tailed loriciferan
Canine heartworm
Convolutriloba longifissura
Dactylogyrus vastator
Dog tapeworm
Fasciola hepatica
Freshwater sponge
Giant thorny-headed worm
Human blood fluke
Lancet fluke
Lepidodermella squamata
Limnognathia maerski
Moniliformis moniliformis
Nightlight jellyfish
Oerstedia dorsalis
Oikopleura labradoriensis
Orange sea lily
Paragordius varius
Pea urchin
Polystoma integerrimum
Priapulus caudatus
Proteocephalus longicollis
Pyrosome
Rat lungworm
Red haplognathia
Salp
Sea nettle
Sea walnut
Seison nebaliae
Symbion pandora
Thimble jelly
Tropical brittle star
Velcro sea star

QATAR

Asplanchna priodonta
Bucket-tailed loriciferan
Canine heartworm
Convolutriloba longifissura
Dactylogyrus vastator
Dog tapeworm
Fasciola hepatica
Freshwater sponge

Human blood fluke
Lancet fluke
Lepidodermella squamata
Limnognathia maerski
Nightlight jellyfish
Oerstedia dorsalis
Oikopleura labradoriensis
Paragordius varius
Pea urchin
Polystoma integerrimum
Priapulus caudatus
Proteocephalus longicollis
Pyrosome
Rat lungworm
Red haplognathia
Salp
Sea nettle
Sea walnut
Seison nebaliae
Symbion pandora
Thimble jelly

REPUBLIC OF THE CONGO

Asplanchna priodonta
Botryllus schlosseri
Bucket-tailed loriciferan
Canine heartworm
Convolutriloba longifissura
Dactylogyrus vastator
Dog tapeworm
Fasciola hepatica
Freshwater sponge
Giant thorny-headed worm
Human blood fluke
Lancet fluke
Lepidodermella squamata
Limnognathia maerski
Moniliformis moniliformis
Nightlight jellyfish
Oerstedia dorsalis
Oikopleura labradoriensis
Paragordius varius
Pea urchin
Polystoma integerrimum
Priapulus caudatus

Proteocephalus longicollis
Pyrosome
Rat lungworm
Red haplognathia
Salp
Sea nettle
Sea walnut
Seison nebaliae
Symbion pandora
Thimble jelly

ROMANIA

Asplanchna priodonta
Broad fish tapeworm
Bucket-tailed loriciferan
Canine heartworm
Convolutriloba longifissura
Dactylogyrus vastator
Dog tapeworm
Fasciola hepatica
Freshwater sponge
Giant thorny-headed worm
Human blood fluke
Lancet fluke
Lepidodermella squamata
Limnognathia maerski
Mermis nigrescens
Moniliformis moniliformis
Nightlight jellyfish
Oerstedia dorsalis
Oikopleura labradoriensis
Paragordius varius
Pea urchin
Polystoma integerrimum
Priapulus caudatus
Proteocephalus longicollis
Pyrosome
Rat lungworm
Red haplognathia
Salp
Sea nettle
Sea walnut
Seison nebaliae
Symbion pandora
Thimble jelly

RUSSIA

Asplanchna priodonta
Broad fish tapeworm
Bucket-tailed loriciferan
Canine heartworm
Convolutriloba longifissura
Dactylogyrus vastator
Dog tapeworm
Fasciola hepatica
Freshwater sponge
Giant thorny-headed worm
Human blood fluke
Lancet fluke
Lepidodermella squamata
Limnognathia maerski
Mermis nigrescens
Moniliformis moniliformis
Nightlight jellyfish
Oerstedia dorsalis
Oikopleura labradoriensis
Paragordius varius
Pea urchin
Polystoma integerrimum
Priapulus caudatus
Proteocephalus longicollis
Pyrosome
Rat lungworm
Red haplognathia
Salp
Sea nettle
Sea walnut
Seison nebaliae
Symbion pandora
Thimble jelly

RWANDA

Asplanchna priodonta
Canine heartworm
Dog tapeworm
Freshwater sponge
Giant thorny-headed worm
Human blood fluke
Lancet fluke
Moniliformis moniliformis
Oerstedia dorsalis
Paragordius varius

Polystoma integerrimum
Proteocephalus longicollis
Rat lungworm

ST. KITTS-NEVIS

Asplanchna priodonta
Botryllus schlosseri
Bucket-tailed loriciferan
Canine heartworm
Convolutriloba longifissura
Dactylogyrus vastator
Dog tapeworm
Fasciola hepatica
Freshwater sponge
Giant thorny-headed worm
Human blood fluke
Lancet fluke
Lepidodermella squamata
Limnognathia maerski
Moniliformis moniliformis
Nightlight jellyfish
Oerstedia dorsalis
Oikopleura labradoriensis
Paragordius varius
Pea urchin
Polystoma integerrimum
Priapulus caudatus
Proteocephalus longicollis
Pyrosome
Rat lungworm
Red haplognathia
Salp
Sea nettle
Sea walnut
Seison nebaliae
Symbion pandora
Thimble jelly
Tropical brittle star

ST. LUCIA

Asplanchna priodonta
Botryllus schlosseri
Bucket-tailed loriciferan
Canine heartworm
Convolutriloba longifissura

Dactylogyrus vastator
Dog tapeworm
Fasciola hepatica
Freshwater sponge
Giant thorny-headed worm
Human blood fluke
Lancet fluke
Lepidodermella squamata
Limnognathia maerski
Moniliformis moniliformis
Nightlight jellyfish
Oerstedia dorsalis
Oikopleura labradoriensis
Paragordius varius
Pea urchin
Polystoma integerrimum
Priapulus caudatus
Proteocephalus longicollis
Pyrosome
Rat lungworm
Red haplognathia
Salp
Sea nettle
Sea walnut
Seison nebaliae
Symbion pandora
Thimble jelly
Tropical brittle star

ST. VINCENT/ GRENADINES
Botryllus schlosseri
Convolutriloba longifissura
Giant thorny-headed worm
Moniliformis moniliformis
Oikopleura labradoriensis

SAMOA
Asplanchna priodonta
Blue starfish
Bucket-tailed loriciferan
Canine heartworm
Convolutriloba longifissura
Crown-of-thorns
Dactylogyrus vastator

Distichopora violacea
Dog tapeworm
Eukrohnia fowleri
Fasciola hepatica
Fire coral
Freshwater sponge
Giant thorny-headed worm
Human blood fluke
Lancet fluke
Lepidodermella squamata
Limnognathia maerski
Long-spined sea urchin
Moniliformis moniliformis
Nightlight jellyfish
Oerstedia dorsalis
Oikopleura labradoriensis
Paragordius varius
Pea urchin
Polystoma integerrimum
Portuguese man of war
Priapulus caudatus
Proteocephalus longicollis
Pterosagitta draco
Pyrosome
Rat lungworm
Red haplognathia
Salp
Sea apple
Sea nettle
Sea walnut
Seison nebaliae
Symbion pandora
Thimble jelly
Tropical brittle star

SAN MARINO
Asplanchna priodonta
Canine heartworm
Convolutriloba longifissura
Dog tapeworm
Freshwater sponge
Giant thorny-headed worm
Human blood fluke
Lancet fluke
Mermis nigrescens
Moniliformis moniliformis

Oerstedia dorsalis
Paragordius varius
Polystoma integerrimum
Proteocephalus longicollis
Rat lungworm

SÃO TOMÉ AND PRÍNCIPE
Asplanchna priodonta
Botryllus schlosseri
Bucket-tailed loriciferan
Canine heartworm
Convolutriloba longifissura
Dactylogyrus vastator
Dog tapeworm
Fasciola hepatica
Freshwater sponge
Human blood fluke
Lancet fluke
Lepidodermella squamata
Limnognathia maerski
Nightlight jellyfish
Oerstedia dorsalis
Oikopleura labradoriensis
Paragordius varius
Pea urchin
Polystoma integerrimum
Priapulus caudatus
Proteocephalus longicollis
Pyrosome
Rat lungworm
Red haplognathia
Salp
Sea nettle
Sea walnut
Seison nebaliae
Symbion pandora
Thimble jelly
Tropical brittle star

SAUDI ARABIA
Asplanchna priodonta
Bucket-tailed loriciferan
Canine heartworm
Convolutriloba longifissura

Dactylogyrus vastator
Dog tapeworm
Fasciola hepatica
Freshwater sponge
Human blood fluke
Lancet fluke
Lepidodermella squamata
Limnognathia maerski
Nightlight jellyfish
Oerstedia dorsalis
Oikopleura labradoriensis
Paragordius varius
Pea urchin
Polystoma integerrimum
Priapulus caudatus
Proteocephalus longicollis
Pyrosome
Rat lungworm
Red haplognathia
Salp
Sea nettle
Sea walnut
Seison nebaliae
Symbion pandora
Thimble jelly

SENEGAL

Asplanchna priodonta
Botryllus schlosseri
Bucket-tailed loriciferan
Canine heartworm
Convolutriloba longifissura
Dactylogyrus vastator
Dog tapeworm
Fasciola hepatica
Freshwater sponge
Giant thorny-headed worm
Human blood fluke
Lancet fluke
Lepidodermella squamata
Limnognathia maerski
Moniliformis moniliformis
Nightlight jellyfish
Oerstedia dorsalis
Oikopleura labradoriensis
Paragordius varius

Pea urchin
Polystoma integerrimum
Priapulus caudatus
Proteocephalus longicollis
Pyrosome
Rat lungworm
Red haplognathia
Salp
Sea nettle
Sea walnut
Seison nebaliae
Symbion pandora
Thimble jelly
Tropical brittle star

SERBIA AND MONTENEGRO

Asplanchna priodonta
Broad fish tapeworm
Bucket-tailed loriciferan
Canine heartworm
Dactylogyrus vastator
Dog tapeworm
Fasciola hepatica
Freshwater sponge
Giant thorny-headed worm
Human blood fluke
Lancet fluke
Lepidodermella squamata
Limnognathia maerski
Mermis nigrescens
Moniliformis moniliformis
Nightlight jellyfish
Oerstedia dorsalis
Oikopleura labradoriensis
Paragordius varius
Pea urchin
Polystoma integerrimum
Priapulus caudatus
Proteocephalus longicollis
Pyrosome
Rat lungworm
Red haplognathia
Salp
Sea nettle
Sea walnut

Seison nebaliae
Symbion pandora
Thimble jelly

SEYCHELLES

Asplanchna priodonta
Blue starfish
Bucket-tailed loriciferan
Canine heartworm
Convolutriloba longifissura
Crown-of-thorns
Dactylogyrus vastator
Distichopora violacea
Dog tapeworm
Eukrohnia fowleri
Fasciola hepatica
Fire coral
Freshwater sponge
Giant thorny-headed worm
Human blood fluke
Lancet fluke
Lepidodermella squamata
Limnognathia maerski
Long-spined sea urchin
Moniliformis moniliformis
Nightlight jellyfish
Oerstedia dorsalis
Oikopleura labradoriensis
Paragordius varius
Pea urchin
Polystoma integerrimum
Portuguese man of war
Priapulus caudatus
Proteocephalus longicollis
Pterosagitta draco
Pyrosome
Rat lungworm
Red haplognathia
Salp
Sea apple
Sea nettle
Sea walnut
Seison nebaliae
Symbion pandora
Thimble jelly
Tropical brittle star

SIERRA LEONE

Asplanchna priodonta
Botryllus schlosseri
Bucket-tailed loriciferan
Canine heartworm
Convolutriloba longifissura
Dactylogyrus vastator
Dog tapeworm
Fasciola hepatica
Freshwater sponge
Giant thorny-headed worm
Human blood fluke
Lancet fluke
Lepidodermella squamata
Limnognathia maerski
Moniliformis moniliformis
Nightlight jellyfish
Oerstedia dorsalis
Oikopleura labradoriensis
Paragordius varius
Pea urchin
Polystoma integerrimum
Priapulus caudatus
Proteocephalus longicollis
Pyrosome
Rat lungworm
Red haplognathia
Salp
Sea nettle
Sea walnut
Seison nebaliae
Symbion pandora
Thimble jelly

SINGAPORE

Asplanchna priodonta
Blue starfish
Bucket-tailed loriciferan
Candy cane sea cucumber
Canine heartworm
Convolutriloba longifissura
Crown-of-thorns
Dactylogyrus vastator
Distichopora violacea
Dog tapeworm
Eukrohnia fowleri

Fasciola hepatica
Fire coral
Freshwater sponge
Giant thorny-headed worm
Human blood fluke
Lancet fluke
Lepidodermella squamata
Limnognathia maerski
Long-spined sea urchin
Moniliformis moniliformis
Nightlight jellyfish
Oerstedia dorsalis
Oikopleura labradoriensis
Paragordius varius
Pea urchin
Polystoma integerrimum
Portuguese man of war
Priapulus caudatus
Proteocephalus longicollis
Pterosagitta draco
Pyrosome
Rat lungworm
Red haplognathia
Salp
Sea apple
Sea nettle
Sea walnut
Seison nebaliae
Symbion pandora
Thimble jelly
Tropical brittle star

SLOVAKIA

Asplanchna priodonta
Broad fish tapeworm
Canine heartworm
Dog tapeworm
Freshwater sponge
Giant thorny-headed worm
Human blood fluke
Lancet fluke
Mermis nigrescens
Moniliformis moniliformis
Oerstedia dorsalis
Paragordius varius
Polystoma integerrimum

Proteocephalus longicollis
Rat lungworm

SLOVENIA

Asplanchna priodonta
Broad fish tapeworm
Canine heartworm
Convolutriloba longifissura
Dog tapeworm
Freshwater sponge
Giant thorny-headed worm
Human blood fluke
Lancet fluke
Mermis nigrescens
Moniliformis moniliformis
Oerstedia dorsalis
Paragordius varius
Polystoma integerrimum
Proteocephalus longicollis
Rat lungworm

SOLOMON ISLANDS

Asplanchna priodonta
Blue starfish
Bucket-tailed loriciferan
Canine heartworm
Convolutriloba longifissura
Crown-of-thorns
Dactylogyrus vastator
Distichopora violacea
Dog tapeworm
Eukrohnia fowleri
Fasciola hepatica
Fire coral
Freshwater sponge
Giant thorny-headed worm
Human blood fluke
Lancet fluke
Lepidodermella squamata
Limnognathia maerski
Long-spined sea urchin
Moniliformis moniliformis
Nightlight jellyfish
Oerstedia dorsalis
Oikopleura labradoriensis

Paragordius varius
Pea urchin
Polystoma integerrimum
Portuguese man of war
Priapulus caudatus
Proteocephalus longicollis
Pterosagitta draco
Pyrosome
Rat lungworm
Red haplognathia
Salp
Sea apple
Sea nettle
Sea walnut
Seison nebaliae
Symbion pandora
Thimble jelly
Tropical brittle star

SOMALIA

Asplanchna priodonta
Blue starfish
Bucket-tailed loriciferan
Canine heartworm
Convolutriloba longifissura
Crown-of-thorns
Dactylogyrus vastator
Distichopora violacea
Dog tapeworm
Eukrohnia fowleri
Fasciola hepatica
Fire coral
Freshwater sponge
Giant thorny-headed worm
Human blood fluke
Lancet fluke
Lepidodermella squamata
Limnognathia maerski
Long-spined sea urchin
Moniliformis moniliformis
Nightlight jellyfish
Oerstedia dorsalis
Oikopleura labradoriensis
Paragordius varius
Pea urchin
Polystoma integerrimum

Portuguese man of war
Priapulus caudatus
Proteocephalus longicollis
Pterosagitta draco
Pyrosome
Rat lungworm
Red haplognathia
Salp
Sea apple
Sea nettle
Sea walnut
Seison nebaliae
Symbion pandora
Thimble jelly

SOUTH AFRICA

Asplanchna priodonta
Blue starfish
Botryllus schlosseri
Bucket-tailed loriciferan
Canine heartworm
Convolutriloba longifissura
Crown-of-thorns
Dactylogyrus vastator
Demoscolex squamosus
Distichopora violacea
Dog tapeworm
Eukrohnia fowleri
Fasciola hepatica
Fire coral
Freshwater sponge
Giant thorny-headed worm
Human blood fluke
Lancet fluke
Lepidodermella squamata
Limnognathia maerski
Long-spined sea urchin
Moniliformis moniliformis
Nightlight jellyfish
Oerstedia dorsalis
Oikopleura labradoriensis
Paragordius varius
Pea urchin
Polystoma integerrimum
Portuguese man of war
Priapulus caudatus

Proteocephalus longicollis
Pterosagitta draco
Pyrosome
Rat lungworm
Red haplognathia
Salp
Sea apple
Sea nettle
Sea walnut
Seison nebaliae
Symbion pandora
Thimble jelly

SOUTH KOREA

Asplanchna priodonta
Blue starfish
Bucket-tailed loriciferan
Canine heartworm
Convolutriloba longifissura
Crown-of-thorns
Dactylogyrus vastator
Distichopora violacea
Dog tapeworm
Eukrohnia fowleri
Fasciola hepatica
Fire coral
Freshwater sponge
Frilled anemone
Giant thorny-headed worm
Human blood fluke
Lancet fluke
Lepidodermella squamata
Limnognathia maerski
Long-spined sea urchin
Moniliformis moniliformis
Nightlight jellyfish
Northern Pacific sea star
Oerstedia dorsalis
Oikopleura labradoriensis
Paragordius varius
Pea urchin
Polystoma integerrimum
Portuguese man of war
Priapulus caudatus
Proteocephalus longicollis
Pterosagitta draco

Pyrosome
Rat lungworm
Red haplognathia
Salp
Sea apple
Sea nettle
Sea walnut
Seison nebaliae
Symbion pandora
Thimble jelly

SPAIN
Asplanchna priodonta
Botryllus schlosseri
Bucket-tailed loriciferan
Canine heartworm
Convolutriloba longifissura
Dactylogyrus vastator
Dog tapeworm
Fasciola hepatica
Freshwater sponge
Frilled anemone
Giant thorny-headed worm
Human blood fluke
Lancet fluke
Lepidodermella squamata
Limnognathia maerski
Mermis nigrescens
Moniliformis moniliformis
Nightlight jellyfish
Oerstedia dorsalis
Oikopleura labradoriensis
Paragordius varius
Pea urchin
Polystoma integerrimum
Priapulus caudatus
Proteocephalus longicollis
Pyrosome
Rat lungworm
Red coral
Red haplognathia
Salp
Sand star
Sea nettle
Sea walnut
Seison nebaliae

Symbion pandora
Thimble jelly

SRI LANKA
Asplanchna priodonta
Blue starfish
Bucket-tailed loriciferan
Canine heartworm
Convolutriloba longifissura
Crown-of-thorns
Dactylogyrus vastator
Distichopora violacea
Dog tapeworm
Eukrohnia fowleri
Fasciola hepatica
Fire coral
Freshwater sponge
Giant thorny-headed worm
Human blood fluke
Lancet fluke
Lepidodermella squamata
Limnognathia maerski
Long-spined sea urchin
Moniliformis moniliformis
Nightlight jellyfish
Oerstedia dorsalis
Oikopleura labradoriensis
Paragordius varius
Pea urchin
Polystoma integerrimum
Portuguese man of war
Priapulus caudatus
Proteocephalus longicollis
Pterosagitta draco
Pyrosome
Rat lungworm
Red haplognathia
Salp
Sea apple
Sea nettle
Sea walnut
Seison nebaliae
Symbion pandora
Thimble jelly
Tuxedo pincushion urchin

SUDAN
Asplanchna priodonta
Canine heartworm
Dog tapeworm
Freshwater sponge
Human blood fluke
Lancet fluke
Oerstedia dorsalis
Paragordius varius
Polystoma integerrimum
Proteocephalus longicollis
Rat lungworm

SURINAME
Asplanchna priodonta
Botryllus schlosseri
Bucket-tailed loriciferan
Canine heartworm
Convolutriloba longifissura
Dactylogyrus vastator
Dog tapeworm
Fasciola hepatica
Freshwater sponge
Giant thorny-headed worm
Human blood fluke
Lancet fluke
Lepidodermella squamata
Limnognathia maerski
Moniliformis moniliformis
Nightlight jellyfish
Oerstedia dorsalis
Oikopleura labradoriensis
Orange sea lily
Paragordius varius
Pea urchin
Polystoma integerrimum
Priapulus caudatus
Proteocephalus longicollis
Pyrosome
Rat lungworm
Red haplognathia
Salp
Sea nettle
Sea walnut
Seison nebaliae
Symbion pandora

Thimble jelly
Tropical brittle star

SWAZILAND
Asplanchna priodonta
Canine heartworm
Demoscolex squamosus
Dog tapeworm
Freshwater sponge
Giant thorny-headed worm
Human blood fluke
Lancet fluke
Moniliformis moniliformis
Oerstedia dorsalis
Paragordius varius
Polystoma integerrimum
Proteocephalus longicollis
Rat lungworm

SWEDEN
Asplanchna priodonta
Botryllus schlosseri
Broad fish tapeworm
Bucket-tailed loriciferan
Canine heartworm
Convolutriloba longifissura
Dactylogyrus vastator
Dog tapeworm
Fasciola hepatica
Freshwater sponge
Giant thorny-headed worm
Human blood fluke
Lancet fluke
Lepidodermella squamata
Limnognathia maerski
Mermis nigrescens
Moniliformis moniliformis
Nightlight jellyfish
Oerstedia dorsalis
Oikopleura labradoriensis
Paragordius varius
Pea urchin
Polystoma integerrimum
Priapulus caudatus
Proteocephalus longicollis

Pyrosome
Rat lungworm
Red haplognathia
Salp
Sand star
Sea nettle
Sea walnut
Seison nebaliae
Symbion pandora
Thimble jelly

SWITZERLAND
Asplanchna priodonta
Canine heartworm
Dog tapeworm
Freshwater sponge
Giant thorny-headed worm
Human blood fluke
Lancet fluke
Mermis nigrescens
Moniliformis moniliformis
Oerstedia dorsalis
Paragordius varius
Polystoma integerrimum
Proteocephalus longicollis
Rat lungworm

SYRIA
Asplanchna priodonta
Bucket-tailed loriciferan
Canine heartworm
Convolutriloba longifissura
Dactylogyrus vastator
Dog tapeworm
Fasciola hepatica
Freshwater sponge
Human blood fluke
Lancet fluke
Lepidodermella squamata
Limnognathia maerski
Nightlight jellyfish
Oerstedia dorsalis
Oikopleura labradoriensis
Paragordius varius
Pea urchin

Polystoma integerrimum
Priapulus caudatus
Proteocephalus longicollis
Pyrosome
Rat lungworm
Red haplognathia
Salp
Sea nettle
Sea walnut
Seison nebaliae
Symbion pandora
Thimble jelly

TAIWAN
Asplanchna priodonta
Bucket-tailed loriciferan
Canine heartworm
Convolutriloba longifissura
Dactylogyrus vastator
Dog tapeworm
Fasciola hepatica
Freshwater sponge
Giant thorny-headed worm
Human blood fluke
Lancet fluke
Lepidodermella squamata
Limnognathia maerski
Moniliformis moniliformis
Nightlight jellyfish
Oerstedia dorsalis
Oikopleura labradoriensis
Paragordius varius
Pea urchin
Polystoma integerrimum
Priapulus caudatus
Proteocephalus longicollis
Pyrosome
Rat lungworm
Red haplognathia
Salp
Sea nettle
Sea walnut
Seison nebaliae
Symbion pandora
Thimble jelly
Tuxedo pincushion urchin

TAJIKISTAN

Asplanchna priodonta
Canine heartworm
Dog tapeworm
Freshwater sponge
Giant thorny-headed worm
Human blood fluke
Lancet fluke
Moniliformis moniliformis
Oerstedia dorsalis
Paragordius varius
Polystoma integerrimum
Proteocephalus longicollis
Rat lungworm

TANZANIA

Asplanchna priodonta
Blue starfish
Bucket-tailed loriciferan
Canine heartworm
Convolutriloba longifissura
Crown-of-thorns
Dactylogyrus vastator
Distichopora violacea
Dog tapeworm
Eukrohnia fowleri
Fasciola hepatica
Fire coral
Freshwater sponge
Giant thorny-headed worm
Human blood fluke
Lancet fluke
Lepidodermella squamata
Limnognathia maerski
Long-spined sea urchin
Moniliformis moniliformis
Nightlight jellyfish
Oerstedia dorsalis
Oikopleura labradoriensis
Paragordius varius
Pea urchin
Polystoma integerrimum
Portuguese man of war
Priapulus caudatus
Proteocephalus longicollis
Pterosagitta draco

Pyrosome
Rat lungworm
Red haplognathia
Salp
Sea apple
Sea nettle
Sea walnut
Seison nebaliae
Symbion pandora
Thimble jelly
Tropical brittle star

THAILAND

Asplanchna priodonta
Blue starfish
Bucket-tailed loriciferan
Canine heartworm
Convolutriloba longifissura
Crown-of-thorns
Dactylogyrus vastator
Distichopora violacea
Dog tapeworm
Eukrohnia fowleri
Fasciola hepatica
Fire coral
Freshwater sponge
Giant thorny-headed worm
Human blood fluke
Lancet fluke
Lepidodermella squamata
Limnognathia maerski
Long-spined sea urchin
Moniliformis moniliformis
Nightlight jellyfish
Oerstedia dorsalis
Oikopleura labradoriensis
Paragordius varius
Pea urchin
Polystoma integerrimum
Portuguese man of war
Priapulus caudatus
Proteocephalus longicollis
Pterosagitta draco
Pyrosome
Rat lungworm

Red haplognathia
Salp
Sea apple
Sea nettle
Sea walnut
Seison nebaliae
Symbion pandora
Thimble jelly
Tropical brittle star
Tuxedo pincushion urchin

TIMOR-LESTE

Asplanchna priodonta
Bucket-tailed loriciferan
Canine heartworm
Convolutriloba longifissura
Dactylogyrus vastator
Dog tapeworm
Fasciola hepatica
Freshwater sponge
Giant thorny-headed worm
Human blood fluke
Lancet fluke
Lepidodermella squamata
Limnognathia maerski
Moniliformis moniliformis
Nightlight jellyfish
Oerstedia dorsalis
Oikopleura labradoriensis
Paragordius varius
Pea urchin
Polystoma integerrimum
Priapulus caudatus
Proteocephalus longicollis
Pyrosome
Rat lungworm
Red haplognathia
Salp
Sea nettle
Sea walnut
Seison nebaliae
Symbion pandora
Thimble jelly
Tropical brittle star
Tuxedo pincushion urchin

TOGO

Asplanchna priodonta
Botryllus schlosseri
Bucket-tailed loriciferan
Canine heartworm
Convolutriloba longifissura
Dactylogyrus vastator
Dog tapeworm
Fasciola hepatica
Freshwater sponge
Giant thorny-headed worm
Human blood fluke
Lancet fluke
Lepidodermella squamata
Limnognathia maerski
Moniliformis moniliformis
Nightlight jellyfish
Oerstedia dorsalis
Oikopleura labradoriensis
Paragordius varius
Pea urchin
Polystoma integerrimum
Priapulus caudatus
Proteocephalus longicollis
Pyrosome
Rat lungworm
Red haplognathia
Salp
Sea nettle
Sea walnut
Seison nebaliae
Symbion pandora
Thimble jelly
Tropical brittle star
Tuxedo pincushion urchin

TONGA

Asplanchna priodonta
Blue starfish
Bucket-tailed loriciferan
Canine heartworm
Convolutriloba longifissura
Crown-of-thorns
Dactylogyrus vastator
Distichopora violacea
Dog tapeworm

Eukrohnia fowleri
Fasciola hepatica
Fire coral
Freshwater sponge
Giant thorny-headed worm
Human blood fluke
Lancet fluke
Lepidodermella squamata
Limnognathia maerski
Long-spined sea urchin
Moniliformis moniliformis
Nightlight jellyfish
Oerstedia dorsalis
Oikopleura labradoriensis
Paragordius varius
Pea urchin
Polystoma integerrimum
Portuguese man of war
Priapulus caudatus
Proteocephalus longicollis
Pterosagitta draco
Pyrosome
Rat lungworm
Red haplognathia
Salp
Sea apple
Sea nettle
Sea walnut
Seison nebaliae
Symbion pandora
Thimble jelly
Tropical brittle star
Tuxedo pincushion urchin

TRINIDAD AND TOBAGO

Asplanchna priodonta
Botryllus schlosseri
Bucket-tailed loriciferan
Canine heartworm
Convolutriloba longifissura
Dactylogyrus vastator
Dog tapeworm
Fasciola hepatica
Freshwater sponge
Giant thorny-headed worm
Human blood fluke

Lancet fluke
Lepidodermella squamata
Limnognathia maerski
Moniliformis moniliformis
Nightlight jellyfish
Oerstedia dorsalis
Oikopleura labradoriensis
Paragordius varius
Pea urchin
Polystoma integerrimum
Priapulus caudatus
Proteocephalus longicollis
Pyrosome
Rat lungworm
Red haplognathia
Salp
Sea nettle
Sea walnut
Seison nebaliae
Symbion pandora
Thimble jelly

TUNISIA

Asplanchna priodonta
Bucket-tailed loriciferan
Canine heartworm
Convolutriloba longifissura
Dactylogyrus vastator
Dog tapeworm
Fasciola hepatica
Freshwater sponge
Giant thorny-headed worm
Human blood fluke
Lancet fluke
Lepidodermella squamata
Limnognathia maerski
Moniliformis moniliformis
Nightlight jellyfish
Oerstedia dorsalis
Oikopleura labradoriensis
Paragordius varius
Pea urchin
Polystoma integerrimum
Priapulus caudatus
Proteocephalus longicollis
Pyrosome

Rat lungworm
Red haplognathia
Salp
Sea nettle
Sea walnut
Seison nebaliae
Symbion pandora
Thimble jelly

TURKEY

Asplanchna priodonta
Bucket-tailed loriciferan
Canine heartworm
Convolutriloba longifissura
Dactylogyrus vastator
Dog tapeworm
Fasciola hepatica
Freshwater sponge
Giant thorny-headed worm
Human blood fluke
Lancet fluke
Lepidodermella squamata
Limnognathia maerski
Mermis nigrescens
Moniliformis moniliformis
Nightlight jellyfish
Oerstedia dorsalis
Oikopleura labradoriensis
Paragordius varius
Pea urchin
Polystoma integerrimum
Priapulus caudatus
Proteocephalus longicollis
Pyrosome
Rat lungworm
Red haplognathia
Salp
Sea nettle
Sea walnut
Seison nebaliae
Symbion pandora
Thimble jelly

TURKMENISTAN

Asplanchna priodonta

Bucket-tailed loriciferan
Canine heartworm
Convolutriloba longifissura
Dactylogyrus vastator
Dog tapeworm
Fasciola hepatica
Freshwater sponge
Giant thorny-headed worm
Human blood fluke
Lancet fluke
Lepidodermella squamata
Limnognathia maerski
Moniliformis moniliformis
Nightlight jellyfish
Oerstedia dorsalis
Paragordius varius
Pea urchin
Polystoma integerrimum
Priapulus caudatus
Proteocephalus longicollis
Pyrosome
Rat lungworm
Red haplognathia
Salp
Sea nettle
Sea walnut
Seison nebaliae
Symbion pandora
Thimble jelly

TUVALU

Moniliformis moniliformis
Asplanchna priodonta
Blue starfish
Bucket-tailed loriciferan
Canine heartworm
Convolutriloba longifissura
Crown-of-thorns
Dactylogyrus vastator
Distichopora violacea
Dog tapeworm
Eukrohnia fowleri
Fasciola hepatica
Fire coral
Freshwater sponge
Giant thorny-headed worm

Human blood fluke
Lancet fluke
Lepidodermella squamata
Limnognathia maerski
Long-spined sea urchin
Nightlight jellyfish
Oerstedia dorsalis
Oikopleura labradoriensis
Paragordius varius
Pea urchin
Polystoma integerrimum
Portuguese man of war
Priapulus caudatus
Proteocephalus longicollis
Pterosagitta draco
Pyrosome
Rat lungworm
Red haplognathia
Salp
Sea apple
Sea nettle
Sea walnut
Seison nebaliae
Symbion pandora
Thimble jelly
Tropical brittle star

UGANDA

Asplanchna priodonta
Canine heartworm
Dog tapeworm
Freshwater sponge
Giant thorny-headed worm
Human blood fluke
Lancet fluke
Moniliformis moniliformis
Oerstedia dorsalis
Paragordius varius
Polystoma integerrimum
Proteocephalus longicollis
Rat lungworm

UKRAINE

Asplanchna priodonta
Canine heartworm

Convolutriloba longifissura
Dog tapeworm
Freshwater sponge
Giant thorny-headed worm
Human blood fluke
Lancet fluke
Mermis nigrescens
Moniliformis moniliformis
Oerstedia dorsalis
Paragordius varius
Polystoma integerrimum
Proteocephalus longicollis
Rat lungworm

UNITED ARAB EMIRATES

Asplanchna priodonta
Blue starfish
Bucket-tailed loriciferan
Canine heartworm
Convolutriloba longifissura
Crown-of-thorns
Dactylogyrus vastator
Distichopora violacea
Dog tapeworm
Eukrohnia fowleri
Fasciola hepatica
Fire coral
Freshwater sponge
Human blood fluke
Lancet fluke
Lepidodermella squamata
Limnognathia maerski
Long-spined sea urchin
Nightlight jellyfish
Oerstedia dorsalis
Oikopleura labradoriensis
Paragordius varius
Pea urchin
Polystoma integerrimum
Portuguese man of war
Priapulus caudatus
Proteocephalus longicollis
Pterosagitta draco
Pyrosome
Rat lungworm

Red haplognathia
Salp
Sea apple
Sea nettle
Sea walnut
Seison nebaliae
Symbion pandora
Thimble jelly
Tropical brittle star

UNITED KINGDOM

Asplanchna priodonta
Botryllus schlosseri
Bucket-tailed loriciferan
Canine heartworm
Convolutriloba longifissura
Dactylogyrus vastator
Dog tapeworm
Fasciola hepatica
Freshwater sponge
Giant thorny-headed worm
Human blood fluke
Lancet fluke
Lepidodermella squamata
Limnognathia maerski
Mermis nigrescens
Moniliformis moniliformis
Nightlight jellyfish
Oerstedia dorsalis
Oikopleura labradoriensis
Paragordius varius
Pea urchin
Polystoma integerrimum
Priapulus caudatus
Proteocephalus longicollis
Pyrosome
Rat lungworm
Red haplognathia
Rhopalura ophiocomae
Salp
Sand star
Sea nettle
Sea walnut
Seison nebaliae
Symbion pandora
Thimble jelly

UNITED STATES

Asplanchna priodonta
Blue starfish
Botryllus schlosseri
Broad fish tapeworm
Bucket-tailed loriciferan
Canine heartworm
Convolutriloba longifissura
Crown-of-thorns
Dactylogyrus vastator
Distichopora violacea
Dog tapeworm
Eukrohnia fowleri
Fasciola hepatica
Fire coral
Florida lancelet
Freshwater planarian
Freshwater sponge
Frilled anemone
Giant green anemone
Giant thorny-headed worm
Human blood fluke
Lancet fluke
Lepidodermella squamata
Limnognathia maerski
Long-spined sea urchin
Mermis nigrescens
Moniliformis moniliformis
Nightlight jellyfish
Northern Pacific sea star
Notoplana acticola
Oerstedia dorsalis
Oikopleura labradoriensis
Orange sea lily
Oyster leech
Paragordius varius
Pea urchin
Polystoma integerrimum
Portuguese man of war
Priapulus caudatus
Proteocephalus longicollis
Pterosagitta draco
Pyrosome
Rat lungworm
Red haplognathia
Rhopalura ophiocomae

Salp
Sea apple
Sea nettle
Sea walnut
Seison nebaliae
Six keyhole sand dollar
Symbion pandora
Thimble jelly
Velcro sea star
West Atlantic stalked crinoid
Western sand dollar

UNKNOWN
Trichoplax adhaerens

URUGUAY
Asplanchna priodonta
Botryllus schlosseri
Bucket-tailed loriciferan
Canine heartworm
Convolutriloba longifissura
Dactylogyrus vastator
Dog tapeworm
Fasciola hepatica
Freshwater sponge
Giant thorny-headed worm
Human blood fluke
Lancet fluke
Lepidodermella squamata
Limnognathia maerski
Moniliformis moniliformis
Nightlight jellyfish
Oerstedia dorsalis
Oikopleura labradoriensis
Paragordius varius
Pea urchin
Polystoma integerrimum
Priapulus caudatus
Proteocephalus longicollis
Pyrosome
Rat lungworm
Red haplognathia
Salp
Sea nettle
Sea walnut

Seison nebaliae
Six keyhole sand dollar
Symbion pandora
Thimble jelly

UZBEKISTAN
Asplanchna priodonta
Canine heartworm
Dog tapeworm
Freshwater sponge
Giant thorny-headed worm
Human blood fluke
Lancet fluke
Moniliformis moniliformis
Oerstedia dorsalis
Polystoma integerrimum
Proteocephalus longicollis
Rat lungworm

VANUATU
Asplanchna priodonta
Blue starfish
Bucket-tailed loriciferan
Canine heartworm
Convolutriloba longifissura
Crown-of-thorns
Dactylogyrus vastator
Distichopora violacea
Dog tapeworm
Eukrohnia fowleri
Fasciola hepatica
Fire coral
Freshwater sponge
Giant thorny-headed worm
Human blood fluke
Lancet fluke
Lepidodermella squamata
Limnognathia maerski
Long-spined sea urchin
Moniliformis moniliformis
Nightlight jellyfish
Oerstedia dorsalis
Oikopleura labradoriensis
Paragordius varius
Pea urchin

Polystoma integerrimum
Portuguese man of war
Priapulus caudatus
Proteocephalus longicollis
Pterosagitta draco
Pyrosome
Rat lungworm
Red haplognathia
Salp
Sea apple
Sea nettle
Sea walnut
Seison nebaliae
Symbion pandora
Thimble jelly
Tropical brittle star

VATICAN CITY
Asplanchna priodonta
Canine heartworm
Dog tapeworm
Freshwater sponge
Giant thorny-headed worm
Human blood fluke
Lancet fluke
Mermis nigrescens
Moniliformis moniliformis
Oerstedia dorsalis
Polystoma integerrimum
Proteocephalus longicollis
Rat lungworm

VENEZUELA
Asplanchna priodonta
Botryllus schlosseri
Bucket-tailed loriciferan
Canine heartworm
Convolutriloba longifissura
Dactylogyrus vastator
Dog tapeworm
Fasciola hepatica
Freshwater sponge
Giant thorny-headed worm
Human blood fluke
Lancet fluke

Lepidodermella squamata
Limnognathia maerski
Moniliformis moniliformis
Nightlight jellyfish
Oerstedia dorsalis
Oikopleura labradoriensis
Orange sea lily
Paragordius varius
Pea urchin
Polystoma integerrimum
Priapulus caudatus
Proteocephalus longicollis
Pyrosome
Rat lungworm
Red haplognathia
Salp
Sea nettle
Sea walnut
Seison nebaliae
Six keyhole sand dollar
Symbion pandora
Thimble jelly

VIETNAM

Asplanchna priodonta
Blue starfish
Bucket-tailed loriciferan
Canine heartworm
Convolutriloba longifissura
Crown-of-thorns
Dactylogyrus vastator
Distichopora violacea
Dog tapeworm
Eukrohnia fowleri
Fasciola hepatica
Fire coral
Freshwater sponge
Giant thorny-headed worm
Human blood fluke
Lancet fluke
Lepidodermella squamata
Limnognathia maerski
Long-spined sea urchin
Moniliformis moniliformis
Nightlight jellyfish
Oerstedia dorsalis

Oikopleura labradoriensis
Paragordius varius
Pea urchin
Polystoma integerrimum
Portuguese man of war
Priapulus caudatus
Proteocephalus longicollis
Pterosagitta draco
Pyrosome
Rat lungworm
Red haplognathia
Salp
Sea apple
Sea nettle
Sea walnut
Sea wasp
Seison nebaliae
Symbion pandora
Thimble jelly
Tuxedo pincushion urchin

YEMEN

Asplanchna priodonta
Blue starfish
Bucket-tailed loriciferan
Canine heartworm
Convolutriloba longifissura
Crown-of-thorns
Dactylogyrus vastator
Distichopora violacea
Dog tapeworm
Eukrohnia fowleri
Fasciola hepatica
Fire coral
Freshwater sponge
Human blood fluke
Lancet fluke
Lepidodermella squamata
Limnognathia maerski
Long-spined sea urchin
Nightlight jellyfish
Oerstedia dorsalis
Oikopleura labradoriensis
Paragordius varius
Pea urchin
Polystoma integerrimum

Portuguese man of war
Priapulus caudatus
Proteocephalus longicollis
Pterosagitta draco
Pyrosome
Rat lungworm
Red haplognathia
Salp
Sea apple
Sea nettle
Sea walnut
Seison nebaliae
Symbion pandora
Thimble jelly
Tropical brittle star

ZAMBIA

Asplanchna priodonta
Canine heartworm
Dog tapeworm
Freshwater sponge
Giant thorny-headed worm
Human blood fluke
Lancet fluke
Moniliformis moniliformis
Oerstedia dorsalis
Polystoma integerrimum
Proteocephalus longicollis
Rat lungworm

ZIMBABWE

Asplanchna priodonta
Canine heartworm
Demoscolex squamosus
Dog tapeworm
Freshwater sponge
Giant thorny-headed worm
Human blood fluke
Lancet fluke
Moniliformis moniliformis
Oerstedia dorsalis
Polystoma integerrimum
Proteocephalus longicollis
Rat lungworm

Index

Italic type indicates volume number; **boldface** type indicates entries and their pages; (ill.) indicates illustrations.